P[illegible]ER!

Stoke City

-

10 Years in the Premier League

David Lee

Proverbial

FIRST PUBLISHED IN GREAT BRITAIN IN 2018 BY

Proverbial
www.impossibledreamers.co.uk
Stoke-on-Trent

A CIP catalogue record for this book is available from the British Library

ISBN 978-0-9929769-3-4

All characters and events in this publication are Premier League. No Championship, League One, or League Two elements were used in the making of this book…well, apart from Coventry; oh and Hartlepool, but the less said about them the better. And not to mention Swindon…or Bristol City. But apart from all of them (and Derby), it's all 10 years of Premier League.

ACKNOWLEDGEMENTS!

Where possible, permission for reproducing material has been sought, and we thank the many generous people & organisations who have allowed us to use this material. Sincere apologies to any organisation that we've missed or we were just unable to trace. Furthermore, we have striven to ensure that all is factual, & hope that you agree that we have been fair in our appraisal. Note: Some text has been lifted from previous DL books "Scrapbook" & "41 Shades". Special thanks to Martin Spinks, Keith Wales & Pete Smith at The Sentinel; Martin Smith & everyone at The Oatcake; + Steve Mifflin, Sue Bryan, Dave Harrison, Simon Lowe, Adam Cheshire, James Knowles, The Wizards Of Drivel, Hairy Potter, Marc Espley, & Martin Poole.

Special thanks to Shell and Dylan for the inspiration.

INTRODUCTION!

"You know, I think they might just do it this time!"

This was a phrase that was heard a lot in The Potteries during the 2007-08 season (even after losing 1-3 at home to lowly Coventry).

The "it" was promotion to the Premier League, which a lot of people – well, most people, let's be frank – didn't think Stoke City deserved. You couldn't get more unfashionable than a side from the North-West-Midlands managed by a lower-division luddite like Tony Pulis. Where was the European sophistication? Where was the critical post-modern business infrastructure? Where could you get a skinny-latte-macchiato??

But Stoke and The Britannia Stadium were different: a tough team to beat and a tough place to play. And they had a fan-base who remembered the bear-pit mentality of their old Victoria Ground days. They may had been away for 23 years from the top-flight, but now they were back, they intended to make an impact. And this time they'd got Rory Delap.

This book is to remind people of that impact before each monumental game fades from memory, misremembered or just merged together into some sort of blur. After all, those hammerings of Wenger's Arsenal need to be remembered individually.

It seems an age since 2008's final day 0-0 draw with Leicester. It was arguably Tony Pulis' happiest day (partly because it relegated his ex-boss and adversary Milan Mandaric). The game wasn't even a classic. In fact, Stoke's biggest hero that day was probably an ex-Port Vale player called Alan Lee, who scored Ipswich's only goal on 70 minutes to sink rivals Hull, and thus ensure certain promotion for Stoke.

But Stoke's team that extraordinary day was:

Carlo Nash;
Carl Dickinson, Ryan Shawcross, Leon Cort, Andy Wilkinson (Lewis Buxton 21);
Liam Lawrence (Danny Pugh 90), Rory Delap, Glenn Whelan, Richard Cresswell;
Ricardo Fuller, Mamady Sidibe (Shola Ameobi 90).

So, what happened to newly promoted Stoke City in the Premier League? Many didn't see them lasting very long. But amazingly they did. Here, game-by-game, is 10 year's worth. A full-tilt, bare-knuckle, roller-coaster ride.

2008-09 - The Saga Begins

16/08/08 Bolton (3) 3 Stoke (0) 1 – Stoke City's first ever Premier League game, and the question is, how prepared are Stoke? Well, Tony Pulis has spent £22million on the likes of Danny Higginbotham (£2.5m), Abdoulaye Faye (£2.2m) and goalkeeper Thomas Sorensen (free! yes, FREE!), which sounds impressive. But £13m of that also goes on Michael Tonge, Tom Soares, Andrew Davies, Ibrahim Sonko, Seyi Olofinjana and in particular striker Dave Kitson (a record £5.5m), which just seems to be making up the numbers. Revealingly, of all these new boys only three (Kitson, Olofinjana & Sorensen) feature in today's 18-man squad at the Reebok (Stoke's first match at this level since a 0-1 defeat to Coventry in front of only 10,740 fans at the Victoria Ground, where Stuart Pearce scored from the penalty spot). Appropriately, Kitson becomes the first Stoke player to touch the ball in the Premier League, but sadly Bolton go on to make The Potters look like a Championship side. This might explain why, just after the half-hour mark, Stoke experience 11 minutes of arse-elbow shenanigans, and by the time you can say "Carl Dickinson", Bolton snatch 3 goals. Substitute Ricardo Fuller spurns all of Rory Delap's long throws ("about 350," count The Sentinel) only to head home Stoke's first Premier League strike from an actual *cross,* which is very "old-school". One suspects it's going to be the first of a long line of very late Stoke goals.

23/08/08 Stoke (1) 3 Aston Villa (0) 2 – This is where Stoke City's Premier League adventure really begins. A truly awesome game! In the build-up, PaddyPower cockily proclaim they're paying out on bets for Stoke-to-go-down after only ONE game. It turns out only a precious few have bet on Stoke, but hell, it's cheaper than advertising (the stunt costs a mere £30k). It's also a poke in the eye for their Etruria-based rivals bet365, and rattles a few people behind the scenes at The Brit. But Paddy's stunt starts to unravel as a full house witness one of Stoke's greatest games ever, against Martin O'Neill's Top 4 wannabe Villa. A Lawrence penalty puts Stoke ahead on the half-hour. Then after a 2nd-half equaliser, Fuller leaves Laursen for dead in the 81st minute, and cracks in one of the Premier's goals of the season into the far corner. Three minutes later it's 2-2, but in the 4th and final minute of injury time, Sidibe gently brushes his head against a final Delap throw for the mental winner. AAAAAAAHHHHHHHHHHH!! But the most astonishing thing about this match is that The Sentinel (no doubt bracing themselves for greater games to come) only rate this match 8/10 for entertainment, yet over 4 years later all 27,500 are still shaking like a leaf! "I don't think I will ever forget this game," gush The Oatcake.

26/08/08 Cheltenham (0) 2 Stoke (0) 3 (Carling Cup) – 10 changes mean recalls for promotion-winning players such as Glenn Whelan, Ryan Shawcross, Wilko, Richard Cresswell and Lewis Buxton. But the eye-candy (?) is the strike-partnership of Jon "The Beast" Parkin & Vincent "not-really-ex-Juventus" Pericard. Now, of course Pericard is going to have a first-half goal disallowed (offside), so fans have to wait for a crazy 6 minutes just before the hour when Whelan curls a free-kick (1-0), Cresswell drills home (2-0), & Town pull one back (2-1). The Beast finishes it off from a Danny Pugh cross (3-1) on 78 minutes, but Town sweat City with a time-added consolation goal. Remember Dominic Matteo & Demar Phillips? Well, they come on as subs. Oh, and a guy called Ryan Shotton comes on for a 5 minute debut. Stoke are now in unknown territory; no, not the Premier League, but the 3rd round of the League Cup. Even Pulis has only been there ONCE in 16 years of management!

30/08/10 Middlesbrough (1) 2 Stoke (0) 1 – In the days when little Gareth Southgate was a manager (I wonder what happened to him?), Boro were gifted 3 points by Amdy Faye (red card), Olofinjana (penalty), Wilkinson (2nd goal) & Tuncay (2nd goal again). Alves scores from that Faye conceded freekick (he's sent off) on 37 minutes; dozy Downing's penalty hits the bar; then Wilkinson plays Tuncay (then a Boro player) onside for him to score the late winner. For the record, Hoyte kindly pokes home an own-goal equaliser from Lawrence's cross on 71 minutes. Otherwise, it's generally agreed that Stoke are the better team! No, really.

Premier League football cards were now being collected by literally...1 or 2 keen Stoke fans

14/09/08 Stoke (0) 2 Everton (1) 3 – Stoke have scored 7 goals in 4 games, yet they're 2nd from bottom? How's that? Well, a Sunday lunchtime SKY audience find out as Stoke come from 0-2 down (either side of half-time), to 2-2, only to let little Tim Cahill (5ft 9in) outsmart the giant Stoke defence and head home the winner on 77 minutes. There are so many giant defenders (Cort (6'3"), Sonko (6'3"), Higgs (6'1") and … Andy Griffin? (5'1") that Abdoulaye Faye (6'2") has to play in central midfield(!). Olofinjana's 54th minute volleyed goal is great, but Stoke's equaliser 9 minutes later is hilarious as a Delap missile so dumbfounds the Everton defence that Jagielka heads past his own keeper Tim Howard. Carlo Nash (now resting on Everton's bench) would have saved that. Next up: Liverpool and Chelsea. Grief! (Actually Griffin is 5'8".)

20/09/08 Liverpool 0 Stoke 0 – The start of the decline of Rafa Benitez can be traced to this game (well, sort of). One of their best starts to a Premier season I blighted as the likes of Gerrard, Torres, Carragher, Alonso & Robbie Keane (??) falter at the hands of Tony Pulis, as Stoke cling on for a heroic point. Afterall, isn't this the same side that has just beaten Manchester United and Marseille? But this is the game that Gerrard scores after just 90 seconds from a wide free-kick, but ref (Andre Marriner) weirdly gives Kuyt offside for some reason. Even Stoke fans are left scratching their heads.

23/09/08 Stoke (1) 2 Reading (1) 2 (City win 4-3 on penalties) (Carling Cup) – "Nine minutes gone, as Whelan floats in a corner from the left, and it's headed in!!! ...by Pericard! VINCENT PERICARD!! VINCENT PERICARD HAS SCORED!!! Oh My God! Everyone will remember where they were when Vincent Pericard scored for Stoke City!!!" Well, that's the story of this one. No, hang on, Reading equalise on half-time with a penalty, Sidibe makes it 2-1, and James Henry takes the game into extra-time & penalties. Henry misses his spot-kick, but so does Buxton in his last game for Stoke. So, who's the hero taking the winning penalty? IT'S VINCENT PERICARD! There, kids, that shows what can be achieved with good preparation. As Vince says after the game: "I cannot remember the last time I took a penalty. We didn't even practice penalties before the game." Oh, for goodness sake.

27/09/08 Stoke 0 Chelsea (1) 2 – Tabloid victim Wayne Bridge sits quietly on the bench, wondering what his missus is up to. Nothing whilst John Terry dominates on the pitch. His mates Lampard, Drogba, Ashley Cole & co sweep Stoke aside, as they struggle without injured Delap, replaced with no real enthusiasm by Pulis' favourite fall-guy Richard Cresswell. Bosingwa shoots wide (typically), but the shot (supposedly) gets a nick off Griffin to curve back in to beat Sorensen (well, that's Tom's story). Anelka comes off the bench to make it 2 when Cort makes it as easy as possible by chesting the ball right at him. Anelka goes on to have a superb season, Cort loses his place, but Ab Faye is starting to dominate at the back. What's really irritating is that fellow promoted clubs Hull and West Brom are 6th and 10th when Stoke are 18th! Less irritating would be if they both finish in the bottom 4, which of course they do.

After scoring the winner, Rory Delap felt compelled to tear the Spurs net apart

05/10/08 Portsmouth (1) 2 Stoke (0) 1 – Star-studded FA Cup winners Pompey fresh from UEFA Cup duties aren't as clever as manager Harry Redknapp thinks, as Delap's throw is flicked on by Kitson for Fuller to head home an equaliser early in the second half. Annoyingly, Jermain Defoe whips in the winner only 3 minutes later, his 6th of the season. The world's tallest header of the ball, Peter Crouch, scores the first with (obviously) an overhead kick, which really catches Pulis' eye; what he could do with a player like that! After the match, Redknapp corners Pulis, his old mate from Bournemouth days, and asks if Stoke can do their best to beat Spurs the following week as Harry reckons there's a job going there. Really? No, of course not. Although interestingly, Spurs are bottom of the league after being beaten 2-0 the previous week by…Portsmouth (Defoe & Crouch again). Stoke, one place above Spurs, are in no position to argue.

19/10/08 Stoke (1) 2 Spurs (1) 1 – As daft a game as you're likely to see anywhere. A sold-out Britannia Stadium is joined by SKY TV viewers who witness what Peter Coates just can't see: a gale force wind. When the mighty Gareth Bale is red-carded for tripping debutant Tom Soares in the box on 19 mins, Danny Higginbotham has FIVE attempts to put the ball on the penalty spot, but this wind stuff keeps blowing it off. Eventually, Higgs blasts it home, only for Darren Bent to equalise 6 minutes later. Offside, reckon The Sentinel's Martin Spinks & The Oatcake, or is that a deflection in the final pass? The second half is electric as Delap iconically ends up roaring with joy whilst gripping the netting as he celebrates sinking the winner on 53 mins. And that should be it, but that's just the starter. Clown goalkeeper Gomes knocks out his own defender Corluka, who is stretchered off. His replacement Michael Dawson barely lasts 10 minutes, as he unpleasantly clatters Sidibe and is also shown a straight red. Several minutes into injury time, Soares topples over (yes, again!), but this time Fuller's penalty hits both posts and zips straight to Delap who smacks it off the bar. In the 101th minute (no, I'm NOT making this up!), Fuller hits the bar again for good measure. Several days later the game is still going on, but eventually it does end, and sure enough Spurs manager Ramos (& assistant Gus Poyet) are given the chop after Spurs' worse start to a season since records began. Later (a lot later, as no one seems to notice at the time) this game supposedly becomes famous for Gomes supposedly crying like a baby, supposedly about all Delap's long-throws. In fact, he's just taken one in the goolies (as The Guardian diplomatically observe). Stoke have won the relegation 6 pointer (as it was billed) against the bottom club, and with Shawcross & Fuller now back in the team, the only way is up. Surely?

25/10/08 Man City (1) 3 Stoke 0 – Tony Pulis vs Mark Hughes, Part 1. Sparky Hughes takes over at Citeh, and is given a shed-load-of-money to buy Jo, Kompany, Wright-Phillips, & Zambaleta for £40m. He then caps it all with £32.5m for Robinho. For that money, Citeh should be top-of-the-league. But (as everyone has noticed) they're only 10th, and that's where they stay. Pulis would sneer at all this if he could, but Stoke ship another easy 3 goals in the North-West, just like against Bolton. Everyone flags the fact that it's Robinho that scores the hat-track (it could have been 6, reckon The Oatcake), but even a few months later Man City are wanting to off-load him. Ched Evans (yes, *that* Ched Evans) sets up Rob's first goal (& Ched is off-loaded soon after too). Stephen Ireland (who goes on to win Citeh's player of the season) almost makes it 4-0 late on. But for Stoke, it never rains but it pours, and those who went got considerably wet.

29/10/08 Stoke (0) 1 Sunderland 0 – Playing Sunderland always seems like a scouting exercise for Pulis, as he's pinched so many of their players. 17 minutes from time, Fuller out-jumps Dean Whitehead (then a Black Cat) to head home from ex-Cat Delap's long throw number 193 – hell, one of them had to work. Sunderland are still agog from their earth-shattering win against Newcastle (their first for 30 years) the previous Saturday. However, this turns out to be the first of 7 defeats in 8 games, resulting in Roy Keane resigning. We really are the kiss of death to these people.

01/11/08 Stoke (1) 2 Arsenal (0) 1 – What's the point of Match Of The Day or SKY Sport or YouTube or VHS tapes if Arsene Wenger doesn't watch them?? Surely he must have noticed Delap's throw-ins? Surely he must have noticed the sheer size of the Stoke team? Obviously not, as he turns out a side of relative midgets, who clearly haven't seen a long-throw in their lives. After only 11 minutes it's another amusing Delap-Fuller moment for 1-0. On 73, Olofinjana blunders in a second from another Delap throw. Then to make things laughable, baby Van Persie barges theatrically into keeper Sorensen, and is red-carded. Late on, Clichy's fluky free-kick ricochets into the net off several players. Incredibly, Wenger tries to hide his ineptitude in fielding such an unprepared side by bellyaching about Stoke's rough tactics (Adebayor limps off, Walcott dislocates shoulder), glossing over the fact that it was HIS player that got sent off. Duh!

08/11/08 Wigan 0 Stoke 0 – The most boring game of the season. ("A dog of a game" – The Oatcake.) The Sentinel's Martin Spinks is forced (probably at gun-point) to write ***1000 words*** about the match, before no doubt tearing his own arms off and running screaming from the room. The only thing worth saying is that Thomas Sorensen is man of the match. However, Simon Lowe writes that it's the last match on that night's Match Of The Day. Steve Mifflin writes that "It is shown last on Match Of The Day". Thankfully, Stephen Foster has a different tack: he quotes Wigan manager Steve Bruce saying "I think it will be the last game on Match Of The Day." Oh, for goodness sake, guys! Get a grip!

11/11/08 Stoke (1) 2 Rotherham 0 (Carling Cup) – Pulis may have seen the light over Shawcross, but he's still leaving Whelan languishing on the bench most days. But here he is made captain, and scores a decent free-kick goal on 20 minutes. The striking duo this evening is the magical pairing of Pericard and Kitson. Dave is impressive, but then this is a League Two side barely able to beat Port Vale. Kitson sets up Pugh for 2-0 on the hour. Everyone has nose-bleeds, as Pulis has never made the Quarter-Finals before and Stoke haven't been here since Pink Floyd released The Wall (which is NOT the story of Pulis' back-four).

15/11/08 Man Utd (2) 5 Stoke 0 – More shocking than the result is the fact that many Stoke fans never got to this game, their coaches being turned back by the police. They miss out on Stoke being demolished by Ronaldo, Tevez and Berbatov (Rooney, Ferdinand and Giggs are rested, thankfully). Sorensen is flummoxed by a brutal 4th minute free kick by Ronny Ronaldo, and it's downhill from there. Although United have 20 goal attempts to Stoke's rather paltry 2, it should be noted that the Potters survived at Anfield with only 2 attempts to Liverpool's 26! The attendance was 75,369. 12 months previously, Stoke were beating Scunthorpe 3-2 in the Championship in front of only 5,521. Makes you think.

22/11/08 Stoke (0) 1 West Brom 0 – Ha Ha Ha Ha Ha Ha Ha Ha Ha Ha Ha Ha Ha Ha Ha Ha Ha Ha Ha Ha Ha Ha Ha Ha Ha Ha Ha Ha Ha. Sorry, but it's always funny beating West Brom. With Fuller suspended *already*, and Kitson injured after only 11 minutes, it is left to Sidibe to head home from Higginbotham's cross in the EIGHTY-FOURTH MINUTE. God, how we sweated. Tony Mowbray's supposedly "attractive" football turns out – unsurprisingly – to be rubbish. Significantly, writer James Knowles puts the mockers on Stoke by observing: "Another 3 points against Hull will leave us half way to that magical 40-point mark, and a win against Derby will see us inches away from Wembley. It's an exciting time to be a Stokie!" Subsequently, Stoke don't win again till February is dawning, by which time they are sharing bottom place with … the Baggies.

30/11/08 Stoke (0) 1 Hull (1) 1 – Best remembered for substitute Dean Windass pretending to warm-up in front of Delap as he prepares for his long-throw, and hilariously getting booked for his troubles. It's a typical Hull stunt, but Fuller isn't distracted by their tricks, and drives home a 73rd minute equaliser from the spot after keeper Myhill catches him trying to go past. Hull had surprisingly taken the lead on the stroke of half-time, but their luck is running out. After a great start to the season, Hull have just reached the start of their meteoric plummet down the league from 3rd place to last game survival. Poor old Phil Brown, soon to be manager of Southend.

There was clear evidence that superhero Abdoulaye Faye lived in a little world of his own...

02/12/08 Stoke 0 Derby (0) 1 (Carling Cup Qtr Final) – It beggars belief that Stoke get beat by a side in the bottom-half of The Championship, but it's all blamed on ref Rob Styles, or "Mr Magoo" as The Sentinel depicts him. In the last minute of time-added, just as extra-time beckons, Styles decides that a cross hitting Griffin from behind has somehow hit his hand. Nobody else can see it, but Ellington strokes home the penalty in the 94th minute. More fool Pulis for picking a stronger than normal side, and playing the likes of Fuller instead of, er, Pericard.

06/12/08 Newcastle (2) 2 Stoke (0) 2 – Little baby-faced Michael Owen puts the toons two-up in 24 minutes against a Stoke side that hasn't scored away for over 6 hours of foota. But after an appalling first half, it's Stoke fans that turn things around...well, that and Fuller coming off the bench on the hour to set up Sidibe to slot home past a bewildered Shay Given for 1-2. Then in time-added, Newcastle manager Joe Kinnear is "sent-off" (or rather "sent-out") when Fuller wins a late free kick, from which Ab Faye equalises in the 91st minute against his former club. He seems quite pleased by this, but then Pulis knew it was going to happen: "I'd told him I fancied him to score against his old club. Mind you, I said something similar to the other 9 outfielders too!" Kinnear's heart problems probably start here. Spinks: "game of 2 halves"; Mifflin: "game of 2 halves"; Oatcake: "game of 2 halves"; Me: "game of Subbuteo then time for bed."

13/12/08 Stoke 0 Fulham 0 – Things are so desperate that even Vincent Pericard comes on as substitute in the Premier League, a sight no one thought they'd ever see. Unloved Richard Cresswell is already on for much maligned Sidibe (knee gives way after 8 minutes). With goal-shy Kitson out, we're running out of strikers fast. Event of the game: Higginbotham gets away with murder; well, handball in the area.

20/12/08 Blackburn (3) 3 Stoke 0 – People are starting to talk. They are saying "Stoke can't win away" and "Stoke are on a slide". Free coach travel to the game condemns 5000 Stoke fans to endure this debacle, a real low. It had disaster written all over it before the start when loser Paul Ince is sacked and Sam Allardyce becomes Rovers' manager. Pulis is bewildering, fielding Pericard up front, Am Faye in midfield, Cresswell on the left, a dilapidated Delap on the right (signs of shoulder strain), Simonsen in goal (late finger injury to Sorensen), Shawcross at right back, making way for Sonko in defence, who starts as he means to go on by "scything" Pederson for a ninth minute penalty. Allardyce thinks Xmas has come early, and it has; Rovers are 3 up in 27 minutes.

26/12/08 Stoke 0 Man Utd (0) 1 – Manchester United aren't at The Brit for their health or some free mince pies. They arrive on Boxing Day in 4th place, 7 points off leaders Liverpool. Points are desperate for both sides, and there is no resting for Rooney & Giggs this time. Rooney rams his elbow into Abdoulaye's face and lives! The ref doesn't even notice. Ronaldo then kicks out at Wilkinson after receiving one of Andy's assertive tackles, and Ronnie's lucky to walk away in one piece! The ref doesn't even notice. Ferguson is so rattled that he sends on striker Berbatov for a defender. Now Stoke are up against Ronaldo, Berbatov, Rooney, Tevez and Giggs! It's like the five forwards of apocalypse, in the old 2-3-5 formation that clubs used to play in Stan Matthews' days. Stoke hold their own till Wilkinson's 2nd yellow for toppling Ronaldo again, and Tevez stabs home from Berbatov on 83 minutes. There isn't really that much between these two clubs, except lucky United go on to be champions.

28/12/08 West Ham (0) 2 Stoke (1) 1 – The game everyone remembers for Ricardo Fuller slapping captain Andy Griffin and getting sent off by a rather stunned (or is it gleeful?) referee. Some say that Griffin is carrying an injury or is talking too much to the ref. Either way, Fuller should know better. Abdoulaye Faye heads Stoke an early lead, but the equaliser sparks the fisticuffs as Fuller feels Griffin is at fault. The Hammers grab an 88th minute winner, which doesn't half look offside. Griffin is never seen again (well, apart from a couple of substitute appearances), which proves you should never upset Ricardo. Although only 5 points divide the whole bottom half of the Premier League, this look grim for Stoke in 18th (of 20). Particularly as their next 4 games are Liverpool, Chelsea, Spurs & Man City. Maybe the FA Cup may provide the turning point.

03/01/09 Hartlepool (0) 2 Stoke 0 (FA Cup) – "The turning point, or perhaps the wake-up point, is the FA Cup exit at Hartlepool. Tony Pulis proudly fields most of his expensive signings from the previous August, some of whom have barely had a game all season. They included Andrew Davies (£2m from Southampton), Ibrahima Sonko (£2.25m Reading), Tom Soares (£1.25m Crystal Palace), Seyi Olofinjana (£3m Wolves), Michael Tonge (£2m Sheffield United) & luckless Dave Kitson (£5.5m Reading). With £16m worth of new signings on display (and, er, ex-Juventus player Vincent Pericard) Stoke lose pitifully by 2-0, revealing a real lack of quality in the Stoke squad. Worse, Kitson can't even score against a League One side; the striker that Tony had pinned his hopes on goes on to finish the season goalless." (from "Triffic – The Biography Of Tony Pulis")

"Hm," thought Tony Pulis, "maybe I should play all my new signings at Hartlepool. What could possibly go wrong...?"

10/01/09 Stoke 0 Liverpool 0 – After going out of the cup to Hartlepool, league leaders Liverpool turn up to annoy us. But it is Fearless Wilkinson at the back, and new boy Matty Etherington on the left wing that belittle the visitors. Sadly, Etherington only has Cresswell and Kitson up front to cross to (both miss certain goals), although Delap hits the bar and Shawcross has a goal disallowed. Steven Gerrard is in despair after hitting the bar and then the post late on. How sad. The Stoke fans chant that he'll soon be in prison anyway for his alleged role in a bar brawl, but to their understandable disappointment he is let off. The draw leaves Liverpool still 4 points clear of Chelsea, who are slaughtered by Man Utd the following day by 3-0. But the two 0-0 draws against Stoke prove VERY costly to Liverpool. Meanwhile, in The Sentinel Sue Bryan pines for the return of Mama Sidibe. Yes, things are getting desperate.

17/01/09 Chelsea (0) 2 Stoke (0) 1 – Thankfully after United and Liverpool, Stoke have an easy game at last: it's at Stamford Bridge. AND they have new signing James Beattie (£3m from Sheffield United) up front partnering (you'll never guess) Cresswell ("So often his team's ninth defender," sagely observes Martin Spinks). Despite John Terry wilting & retiring during the warm-up (!) the 1972-losing-League-Cup-finalists as they are affectionately called still have a teamful of odd-sounding players (minus Drogba) that pepper Sorensen's goal relentlessly. But on the hour, Shawcross lofts it forward, Beattie (looking like one of those professional footballers you see on the telly) takes it on the chest and lays off

Delap, and Rory…well, he fobs off Ashley Cole and pops it over Cech into the net for a 1-0 mental. Well, you know the rest. With only one league win in 5 (against WBA!), Chelsea look beat, until substitute Belletti heads home a lucky equaliser on 88 mins. A header? Where were all Stoke's giant defenders? Thousands of Blues fans have already left. They miss all this. It's the only consolation as with only seconds left Lampard scores a winner through a crowd of players as thick as the London Underground at rush hour. It's a shock, it's a blow, it's…it's…NOT FAIR!!!

27/01/09 Spurs (3) 3 Stoke (0) 1 – Hang on, a relegation 6-pointer away to a Harry Redknapp side with Jermain Defoe in? Haven't we played this fixture already this season? Yes, we have, but now Harry has unceremoniously ditched Pompey for Spurs. This is bad news as Pulis (8 league games without a win) has never got the better of Redknapp (6 league games without a win), and it never looked like happening here. 3 goals in 16 minutes (Lennon, Defoe, Dawson) demolish Stoke before the half-hour. Pulis takes off both Fayes, bringing on Fuller. Etherington feeds Beattie to score his first Stoke goal (if you exclude his own-goal for us last season against Sheffield Utd). Predictably, West Brom keep Stoke off the bottom on goal-difference, thanks mainly to Man Utd thrashing them 5-0 that same evening. Grim.

31/01/09 Stoke (1) 1 Man City 0 – Tony Pulis vs Mark Hughes, Part 2. Money can't buy you happiness. Joint bottom of the Premier, no win in 11 games, Stoke are at crisis point: backs-against-the-wall, it's death-or-glory in front of the early-game SKY cameras. Finally, Pulis is able to play Fuller up front alongside Beattie against Mark Hughes' £100m side. But on 38 mins, Delap is red-carded after blasting the ball at prone Wright-Phillips (whom the FA censures a few days later). This rouses the Brit crowd. Their roar, aka Stoke's 12th man (well, the 11th, in this case), is deafening, and in the FIFTH extra minute of the 1st half, Whelan feeds Etherington, who crosses for Beattie's extraordinary header into the corner of the net. Pulis then brings on THREE extra defenders (well, one is Cresswell), & Hughes is left fuming. Pivotal & awesome! A HUGE victory. Even Stephen Foster begins to warm to Tony Pulis...well, just a bit. But even this can't induce Martin Spinks to give it more than 8/10, using the immortal line that "Stoke's fate may not lie entirely in Delap of the Gods". Oh, Martin, *really*!

07/02/09 Sunderland (0) 2 Stoke 0 – Yes, it's a 4th red card in 7 league games. This time it's Matthew Etherington for kicking out at Danny Collins after being blocked. Yes, it's the same Danny Collins who goes on to win Player Of The Year, before joining Stoke a few months later. Kenwyne Jones leaps above Ab Faye to head home the first on 78 minutes, whilst ex-Vale David Healy makes it 2-0 in the dying seconds. Yes, it's the same Kenwyne Jones who a year later joins the rest of the growing ex-Sunderland clan/patriots at Stoke. City lose Wilkinson, Shawcross & Fuller to injury in the *first half hour*! And yes, this is the game that Danny Pugh gets away with punching the ball off the line in clear view of everyone but the ref. Yes, this is the game that witnesses the unlikeliest of Stoke songs: "There's only one Rob Styles."

21/02/09 Stoke (0) 2 Portsmouth (0) 2 - Crisis-hit Pompey arrive at the Brit for a 6-pointer without freshly-sacked Tony Adams. Stoke hail return of Liam Lawrence back from falling over his dog. Dire game till last 15 minutes, then 3 goals in 5 minutes: Pompey score, then Beattie wins a dubious handball penalty, and then a minute later he nods in a second. The Beattie-hating away fans are stopped in their tracks...until a heartbroken Shawcross stabs in an injury-time own-goal. The Oatcake blames Cresswell, which is a bit on the harsh side.

01/03/09 Aston Villa (1) 2 Stoke (0) 2 - Poor old Villa. They are currently in 4th place, a Champions League place, so Martin O'Neill controversially leaves 8 first-teamers at home for Thursday's UEFA Cup game against CSKA Moscow, in order to keep them fresh for Sunday's home game with Stoke. The plan backfires. Villa lose dismally in Russia, and the travelling fans are apoplectic! But surely it'll be worth it? Afterall, O'Neill's side is cruising after substitute John Carew makes it 2-0 on 79 minutes. But then Stoke scrap their ill-conceived 5-3-1-1 line-up – or is it 10-0-0, says Stephen Foster – and bring on Fuller & Whelan. Shawcross heads a supposed consolation on 87 mins. But then on 91, Whelan hits a stonker from outside the box to bring the house down. "80 minutes of pure rubbish," says Dave Harrison in The Sentinel. But worth it in the end, Dave?

04/03/09 Stoke (1) 2 Bolton 0 - Stoke's first ever Premier win by 2 clear goals. An unbeaten run is forming. Beattie is turning into the bargain of the season. He is put through by a Whelan header on 14 minutes, before Fuller comes on for Sidibe to finish Bolton off on 74. This mid-week game causes Stoke to jump from 19th to 15th. First game since October NOT to feature the much maligned Richard Cresswell. Just saying.

14/03/09 Everton (2) 3 Stoke (0) 1 - This was away game number 15 out of 19, and not a win in sight. In fact Stoke haven't won away in the top flight since 1984 when they beat Luton (now in the Conference)! Away fans getting exceedingly hacked off by Pulis' disrespect for them & away games in general. This Everton game goes the way of so many this season: Stoke 2 down (Jo on 18 minutes, Lescott on 24), then try & recover a point. Beattie gets nothing against his old club, but eventually Shawcross heads home a corner from Lawrence on 52 minutes, and almost scores an equaliser at 1-2. To cap it al Fellaini makes it 1-3 in time-added. Stoke sink back to 18th again. Will they EVER win an away game in the Premier? Not like this.

21/03/09 Stoke (0) 1 Middlesbrough 0 – Gareth Southgate's Middlesbrough arrive at the Brit in freefall (one win in 17 league games). Pulis, who describes this game as "massive" (not really sure what isn't a "massive" game these days), takes the opportunity to slyly look over the impressive Tuncay and Robert Huth, whom he thinks might be in the shop window soon (he ain't wrong). "Tuncay should play for us," says Stephen Foster, sagely. Huth though is outfoxed by his later-colleague Shawcross who heads in a Delap throw for an 84th minute winner. I bet Shawcross reminds him of this fact daily. I would. Stoke climb to 16th, but heartbroken Boro are nearly doomed in 19th. "A *massive* win," says Adam Cheshire. Oh, don't you start!

04/04/09 West Brom 0 Stoke (1) 2 - Ha ha ha ha ha ha... OK, you get the idea of that. We should have seen this one coming a mile away. As The Beastie Boys would put it: "No Win Till West Brom!". Stoke's 17th away game of 19 is obviously going to provide us with a long overdue away win, particularly as Albion are bottom of the league. It's also the first time this season that Tony Pulis has been able to field what turns out to be the dream-team of the season:

Sorensen;
Wilkinson-Shawcross-AbFaye-Higginbotham;
Lawrence-Delap-Whelan-Etherington;
Beattie-Fuller

Fuller starts this pointless exercise in only the 2nd minute when his "20-yard drive somehow squirms under Scott Carson's uncomfortable dive", as Martin Spinks puts it. Is this the same expensive yet uncomfortable Scott Carson who turned down Stoke for Albion, whilst Stoke got the excellent Sorensen on a FREE?! Well, yes it is. Not a day goes by without Stoke fans feeling sorry for him. Beattie poaches the second goal in the 2nd minute of the second half. Fans celebrate at the end like they've won the cup (hell, it's always funny when we beat the Baggies), and Stoke rise to 13th. Also, it's Stoke's ONLY League win in that awful yellow 2nd strip. If only all away games were like this. Hell, even Heineken couldn't make them any better.

11/04/09 Stoke (1) 1 Newcastle (0) 1 - The Toons are in so much trouble they have recruited TV pundit Alan Shearer to be their fourth manager this season. But United are shamed for selling Abdoulaye Faye, who shows why he is Stoke's Player Of The Year. He even heads home a Liam Lawrence corner (that should have been a goal kick! says Martin Spinks) on 33 mins. Stoke should (but fail) to score more against a side featuring ex-Stoke promotion player Shola Ameobi. But little Michael Owen and his team are dreadful...until joined by a tall, young, unknown stranger from the bench (replacing Ameobi, ironically) who heads a late equaliser. His name is Andy Carroll - whatever happened to him? Shearer & his fellow goons go mad, like they've won the cup. God-knows-why: a draw leaves them as good as doomed.

18/04/09 Stoke (0) 1 Blackburn 0 – Sam Allardyce's Blackburn are unfortunate to face a stoic Stoke side still more worried about relegation than is healthy, and determined to make themselves safe. A "dour stalemate" (Mifflin) is overturned by superstar Liam Lawrence, who even scores the dramatic winner on 75 minutes, his first goal since the opening Villa-thriller. He receives the ball from a Beattie flick, cuts inside his marker, before "drilling" (says Martin Spinks) the ball through England keeper Paul Robinson's outstretched fingertips. The joy & relief amongst fans is audible (ie. Bloody Loud). It's like Stoke've won the cup…again. Or beaten West Brom. But is it a "massive" win? Nope, it's "monumental", says James Knowles. Stoke are now 11th with 39 points, and Premier football is secured, surely, celebrated by new captain Ab Faye in dignified manner by "bouncing round the perimeter punching the air". That's my boy.

25/04/09 Fulham (1) 1 Stoke 0 - Dire. Martin Spinks generously gives it 6/10. He's struggling to say anything positive about the game, so he tells us that John Motson is commentating on Stoke for the first time! The only goal comes on 28 minutes from Nevland "sweeping" (Spinks) home against something I'd never thought I'd ever hear "Stoke's horribly stretched defences". Oh, Tony Pulis, hang your head in shame. (TP runs the London Marathon the following day for charity, so we'll let him off with a warning.) His cause is not helped by his wayward team selection, which includes the return of Richard Cresswell, who looks so out of his depth that even Stephen Foster is starting to feel sorry for him. In contrast, Roy Hodgson's team end up finishing 7th, qualifying for the Europa League, & ultimately only losing in the final after extra time to Atletico Madrid. Roy then moves to Anfield. Duh! Like that's a good idea.

02/05/09 Stoke 0 West Ham (1) 1 – Once upon a time - just like in the fairy tales - West Ham (under Zola) were in the top half of the Premier league, and did the double over Stoke. Hard to believe, but true. Diego Tristan scores the winner, as he did at Upton Park, this time from a 32nd minute free kick into the top corner. The ref disallows Fuller's goal, Lawrence's penalty, and is oblivious to West Ham's pushing and shoving. Typical. At the end, the West Ham fans celebrate like they've won the cup. What is going on?!

09/05/09 Hull (0) 1 Stoke (1) 2 - This game is massive, even monumental. Well, for Hull it is. For Stoke it's a chance to have a damn good laugh at their manager, the orange-tinged Phil Brown. Hull had been 3rd in the Prem, and then Brown decided to humiliate his team after a poor first half at Eastlands by berating them out on the pitch at half time. What may have seemed a good idea at the time led to a meteoric dive of biblical proportions down the league (only 2 wins in 26), & they are now favourites for the drop. To make things worse for them, Fuller blasts home as Hull fail to defend a corner, and in the 2nd half Fuller feeds Lawrence who hits a beaut from 25 yards. Hull pull one back in the dying seconds from a free kick, and then graze the post to just miss an equaliser, but what eventually saves them from relegation are the useless teams below them, namely The Toons, 'Boro & the Baggies. Which is a shame as Stoke fans so enjoy pumping out: "Your Oompa Loompa is taking you down!".

16/05/09 Stoke (0) 2 Wigan 0 – The ice-cream game: PaddyPower try to apologise to Stoke fans (for paying out on bets on Stoke to be relegated) by giving away free ice-creams. Stoke fans aren't in the forgiving mood, and generously tell Paddy where to shove his cones. The game itself is best remembered for Delap finally scoring direct from a throw-in – it had to happen eventually – but it's disallowed, and a goal-kick given. "Because of Rule 15", says Stephen Foster, (Can't score from a frow-in). Martin Spinks thinks it's not given because of a shove on the keeper. Second half goals from Fuller shaking off three defenders for a superb solo effort, and a Beattie header from Etherington's cross see off a sorry Wigan. Stoke fans sign off the season at home in great merriment.

24/05/09 Arsenal (4) 4 Stoke (1) 1 – Stoke's first visit to the Emirates Stadium, full of such comfy wide seats that Stoke fans *stand* for the whole game and do the conga. The architects must have wondered why they bothered. Simonsen and Dickinson are drafted in, but as the Stoke players are already on the beach, it's 0-3 by the 18th minute. Beattie taps in an own-goal, van Persie converts a penalty, and Diaby heads home unchallenged. It's a farce. Simonsen is knackered by now – hip injury – and is replaced by Sorensen, and the game turns. Well, sort of. Fuller is tripped by Denilson, and scores the subsequent penalty to make it 1-3, but then Delap's header aimed for Sorensen gifts the ball to van Persie who makes it 1-4 before half-time. It could have been more, with a full strength Arsenal side, but frankly as it's the last game of the season, people are just bothered whether it's Newcastle or Hull going down. Everyone seems to want it to be Newcastle, and sure enough Damien Duff dutifully puts through his own net at Villa, and they are back in the Championship. Stoke finish 12th with 45 points, and a goal difference of -17. How did that happen?

			Home					Away					Overall						
	Team	**Pl**	**W**	**D**	**L**	**F**	**A**	**W**	**D**	**L**	**F**	**A**	**W**	**D**	**L**	**F**	**A**	**Pts**	**GD**
1	Manchester United	38	16	2	1	43	13	12	4	3	25	11	28	6	4	68	24	90	44
2	Liverpool	38	12	7	0	41	13	13	4	2	36	14	25	11	2	77	27	86	50
3	Chelsea	38	11	6	2	33	12	14	2	3	35	12	25	8	5	68	24	83	44
4	Arsenal	38	11	5	3	31	16	9	7	3	37	21	20	12	6	68	37	72	31
5	Everton	38	8	6	5	31	20	9	6	4	24	17	17	12	9	55	37	63	18
6	Aston Villa	38	7	9	3	27	21	10	2	7	27	27	17	11	10	54	48	62	6
7	Fulham	38	11	3	5	28	16	3	8	8	11	18	14	11	13	39	34	53	5
8	Tottenham Hotspur	38	10	5	4	21	10	4	4	11	24	35	14	9	15	45	45	51	0
9	West Ham United	38	9	2	8	23	22	5	7	7	19	23	14	9	15	42	45	51	-3
10	Manchester City	38	13	0	6	40	18	2	5	12	18	32	15	5	18	58	50	50	8
11	Wigan Athletic	38	8	5	6	17	18	4	4	11	17	27	12	9	17	34	45	45	-11
12	**Stoke City**	38	10	5	4	22	15	2	4	13	16	40	12	9	17	38	55	45	-17
13	Bolton Wanderers	38	7	5	7	21	21	4	3	12	20	32	11	8	19	41	53	41	-12
14	Portsmouth	38	8	3	8	26	29	2	8	9	12	28	10	11	17	38	57	41	-19
15	Blackburn Rovers	38	6	7	6	22	23	4	4	11	18	37	10	11	17	40	60	41	-20
16	Sunderland	38	6	3	10	21	25	3	6	10	13	29	9	9	20	34	54	36	-20
17	Hull City	38	3	5	11	18	36	5	6	8	21	28	8	11	19	39	64	35	-25
18	Newcastle United	38	5	7	7	24	29	2	6	11	16	30	7	13	18	40	59	34	-19
19	Middlesbrough	38	5	9	5	17	20	2	2	15	11	37	7	11	20	28	57	32	-29
20	West Bromwich Albion	38	7	3	9	26	33	1	5	13	10	34	8	8	22	36	67	32	-31

2009-10 - London 2 Stoke 4

15/08/09 Stoke (2) 2 Burnley 0 – It's Stoke's 2nd season in the Premier League, and folk still reckon City won't survive long at this level. A good test is against newly promoted Burnley. Before casually ditching The Clarets for Bolton, Owen Coyle steered this Burnley side to a 1-0 play-off final win against Sheffield United. His first Premier game is at Stoke, who are at full strength, with new boy Dean Whitehead (£3m from Sunderland) in midfield. Burnley are lambs to the slaughter, as Lawrence's free kick is headed home by Shawcross on 19 minutes. 15 minutes later it's 2-0, an own-goal headed in from (you guessed it) a Delap throw-in. It's too easy. Even Kitson comes on and hits the bar. So, not that easy, I suppose.

19/08/09 Liverpool (2) 4 Stoke 0 - It comes to something when Liverpool want revenge on Stoke for costing them the premier league title. Yes, if The Reds had won those two 0-0 draws last season, they would have beaten Man Utd on goal difference. What a shame for them. No really. Oh, what do we care. Unfortunately, Tony Pulis decides this is an opportune moment to throw Richard Cresswell to the lions. This basically means recalling him to play wide on the left in a five man midfield, trying desperately to stop on-form Glen Johnson on the wing. No luck. Fernando Torres scores on 4 minutes, and Johnson makes it 2-0 before the break. It has to be said that Stoke battle on, and the two late goals (Kuyt & Ngog) flatter Liverpool in this mid-week clash. But that's it as far as poor old Cresswell is concerned; this is his last league game before his move to Sheffield Utd.

22/08/09 Birmingham 0 Stoke 0 - An eye-opener. Despite being at full strength (Beattie & Fuller up front, Whelan & Delap in midfield, etc), Stoke can't make a break-through. Well, actually, Beattie is injured after 10 minutes & replaced by ....Kitson . It just shows that Stoke's squad is lacking depth. If only we could sign somebody with, I don't know, say, a bit of flair...? Oh, Peter Reid arrives as new assistant manager (I don't think he counts).

26/08/09 Orient 0 Stoke (0) 1 (Carling Cup) - "Two minutes into extra time, and Stoke's corner is cleared, but it's loose on the edge of the area, and Kitson hits one…AND HE SCORES!! DAVE KITSON!! DAVE KITSON HAS SCORED!! Oh My God! Everyone will remember where they were when Dave Kitson scored for Stoke City!!!" Well, that's the story of this one. Actually, co-star tonight is keeper Steve Simonsen, who has to keep out shots from the likes of (get this) Andros Townsend (on loan from Spurs). Other starters for Stoke include Shotton, Cort, Sonko, Soares, and Tonge; with Davies, Moult (coming on for his debut), Lund, Wedderburn and Parton on the bench. Phew! Also, worth knowing for the 556 Stoke fans who braved the journey, that this is Stoke's ONLY victory in their black 2nd strip. If only they'd known this back then in August.

29/08/09 Stoke (1) 1 Sunderland 0 - Kitson scores again!!! Yes, after a whole year after his £5m arrival, Dave Kitson collects a deflection and wallops it home for his first League goal to deafening celebrations. It's like buses - two always come along at once. "If he were an athlete, the authorities would probably be demanding a gender test," observes Martin Spinks. Er, right. Strangely this game should have been about the £10m new arrivals, Robert Huth and Tuncay ("This is officially a very happy day," comments Stephen Foster on the day they signed), but they only manage to come on as late substitutes (so not so much a happy day). Spinks immediately sees a problem: "Where on earth do you play Tuncay?" I'm sure Pulis will work it out…

12/09/09 Stoke (1) 1 Chelsea (1) 2 - Chelsea come from behind to win 2-1 in injury time??! Haven't we done this one before as well?? Yes, but last season's daylight bloody robbery was at Stamford Bridge. This one unfolds in front of 27,440 disbelieving gob-smacked fans at The Brit. Astonishingly (actually, not that astonishingly) Tony Pulis plays FIVE across the back at home. So Huth starts his first game as a central defender alongside Faye & Shawcross, whilst Danny Collins (£3 from Sunderland) makes his debut on the left (Wilko, of course, is on the right). As Martin Spinks puts it: "Pulis sanctioned a gameplan which didn't so much park the bus in front of the goal, but wheeled in Leon's entire fleet of coaches, mini-buses & stretch-limos." Get through that, Drogba! On 45+3 minutes, he does just that, from a cool ball from Lampard. In fact, the first half goes on for 45+8 due to injuries to Beattie (off again after 10 minutes) & then Sorensen. But by then Stoke are 1-0 up, Whelan crosses for Ab Faye to easily head home on the half-hour. However, Malouda takes until 90+4 to poke home through all the buses. All together: "It's not FAIR!!!!...again!"

The montage of faces outside The Brit

19/09/09 Bolton (0) 1 Stoke (0) 1- One of the reasons why the 2009/2010 season is often quite forgettable. Can't remember this one at all, although it is an improvement on last season's horrendous opening game. Huth takes up what will become a regular position for him, right back, even though he's thought to be left footed. Kitson then scores again! Fuller heading on for Kitson to confidently sweep home, only for new boy Collins to give away a lousy late penalty. Optimistically, Pulis starts predicting 10-15 goals for Kitson! In fact he only ever scores ONE more goal for the club, in the return match against...Bolton.

22/09/09 Stoke (0) 4 Blackpool (1) 3 (Carling Cup) – Remember when I said that Andy Griffin was never seen again after slapping Ricardo Fuller? Well, I lied. He resurfaced briefly as captain & hero in this ding-dong game. With goals either side of half-time, Ian Holloway's promotion-chasing Blackpool are 2-0 up, and even Liam Lawrence has a penalty saved. "Tony, Tony, sort 'em out!" chant the crowd, so off go Diego Arismendi (a

£2.6m mistake from Uruguay) & Tom Soares, and on come Fuller & Etherington. Suddenly, it all goes bonkers for 7 minutes: Ethers sets up Higginbotham for 1-2, Ethers volleys for 2-2, Tuncay pulls back for Fuller for 3-2, but a minute later The Tangs make it 3-3 in the 80th minute! Griffin & Fuller are now brothers-in-arms, until Ricardo is injured, leaving Stoke with 10 men. So, it's Griffin who has to power forward in the SIXTH minute of time-added and hits a cracker to bring the house down. Sadly, this doesn't revive his career. Instead, Pulis notices one of Olly's new signings from Rangers who tries to lob Simonsen from his own half, with it just clearing Stoke's bar. Enter Charlie Adam, and his presence is clearly noted.

26/09/09 Stoke 0 Man Utd (0) 2 – So forgettable that even The Sentinel only rates it 5/10. After playing 5 at the back when Chelsea visit, Pulis plays 5 in midfield for United, although Etherington keeps popping up as an inside left to help lone striker...Dave Kitson. Thus, Stoke have only 3 attempts on goal (one on target). By the time Tuncay comes on United are cruising as super-sub and all-round-good-guy Ryan Giggs crosses for Berbatov to tap home on the hour. Giggs then does same for O'Shea's header for 2-0. All-round-good-guy? Even before the lurid stories about Giggs appeared, Stoke fans didn't like him much.

04/10/09 Everton (0) 1 Stoke (0) 1 - Sceptics need to be reminded that this isn't a bad result. It's another improvement on last season (a 1-3 defeat), & that Everton have just won 5 on the trot. But although a draw is always welcome at Goodison, this feels like a defeat. Fuller & Diao are recalled as Pulis plays a tougher 4-4-2 away from home, & it works. Huth gets his first goal from a second half corner, but Osman quickly equalises from long range. But really this game is only noteworthy for the curious names of the Everton players: Agard, Bilyaletdinov, Jo and...er...Rodwell. What?!

17/10/09 Stoke (1) 2 West Ham (1) 1 - The game that Huth smacked Matthew Upson in the mush, and got away with it! That's more like it! Upson had just blocked him in a penalty area jostle, so fair enough. Ok, so Huth later got a ban, but you gotta laugh. Might not have been so bad if Upson hadn't already had to leave the field with blood pouring from a wound after receiving a kick in the head from Shawcross. However, the game should be remembered for a sportingly fought home win. Former Hammer Etherington is tripped on 10 minutes, and Beattie puts in the penalty. Although Upson heads an equaliser from a corner soon after, his unfortunate day at The Brit is completed by Fuller leaving him for dead in the 69th minute. Fuller's shot is parried, leaving Beattie to tap home. After last week's silly names, this week it's silly hairdos. The Sentinel's Fashion editor, Martin Spinks: "Alessandro Diamanti's combination of short, back, and sides with periodic dreadlocks represented the worst hair day in the Potteries since someone mischievously slipped some Domestos into George Berry's bottle of shampoo back in 1986." More to the point, Stoke silence the sceptics by rising to 9th in the Premier League, the greatest league in the WORLD. And with no silly hair.

24/10/09 Spurs 0 Stoke (0) 1 - One of Stoke's greatest games of recent years; in fact one of Tony Pulis' greatest moments too. Whelan's cracking 86th minute strike gives Stoke only their second EVER win at White Hart Lane (their worst away venue, worse than Anfield, Old Trafford, Highbury…). Their only other win there was to Waddington's giants in 1975. Perhaps more importantly it is Pulis' first ever win over his old boss, Harry Redknapp. But it's not just a great result, it's a great game too. Spurs are on fire this season at the top, and pepper late-inclusion-coz-of-flu Steve Simonsen with headers from Crouch, and shots from

Kranjcar, Lennon and Robbie Keane. As Stoke rally, Harry throws on Jenas & Pavlyuchenko (Woodgate's comeback lasts only 13 minutes!), but has run out of subs when Lennon is tumbled by Whelan, and trundles off down the tunnel to Redknapp's dismay. Then Fuller goes on a meandering run (actually, more like an amble) down the right touchline...where the hell is he going? When he nears the corner flag he suddenly skips inside through several startled defenders (including a docile Wilson Palacios), slips it in to Whelan who curls the ball into the far corner. Oh wow!!! The otherwise brilliant Salif Diao almost gives away a late penalty, but the replay (after several looks) shows he got the ball before Kranjcar falls over him. This victory is mega! No really, it is! "A sensational win & a sensational performance," raves Adam Cheshire, and reckons it's "Simmo's best ever game." Simon Lowe & David Lee write that it was a "magnificent victory". And then on Match Of The Day, Alan Hansen gushes: "Sensational ... Absolutely magnificent ... One of the performances of the season." Yeah, well, we could have told you that. But despite sour Spurs fans whining that it was an "embarrassment to football", the final word goes to Pulis' former boss Harry: "It was just one of those days."

27/10/09 Portsmouth (1) 4 Stoke 0 (Carling Cup) – This should be easy-street against bottom side Portsmouth supposedly unable to pay its own players. But Stoke make 10 changes, and pretty much fall apart. For Portsmouth's third, Simonsen & Higginbotham collide, leaving the striker with an empty goalmouth all to himself. It's that silly. Even Whelan, Lawrence and Tuncay can't save this turkey.

31/10/09 Stoke (2) 2 Wolves (0) 2 - A typical game of two halves against newly promoted Wolves. An Etherington inspired first half - including his first Stoke league goal - sees Stoke 2-0 up & cruising. Joey Craddock pokes home immediately after the break, despite being miles offside. The normally goal-shy defender then heads the equaliser on the hour. Pulis throws on Lawrence, Tuncay & (back from injury) Mama Sidibe, but too little too late. Interestingly, Sidibe receives a standing ovation on his entrance, whereas Kitson is now conveniently airbrushed from history.

08/11/09 Hull (0) 2 Stoke (1) 1 - What a disaster! Stoke blow a unique opportunity to unseat beleaguered Phil Brown at Hull. Unforgivable! Also remembered for being Jimmy Bullard's long-awaited home debut (yawn), after a long recovery from injury. Etherington is on fire, thwacking home on the half hour. Then Olofinjana (now a Hull player) shows a lot of skill he'd forgotten to show at Stoke to equalise on the hour. After some frantic action, it all goes very silly: Tuncay comes on in the 81st minute, Faye is sent off six minutes later after taking out Barmby, and so Tuncay is immediately subbed again (for Wilkinson) fuming like a chimney. Subsequently, Hull poach a late late winner. "Horrible," cry the fans. But that's enough about Phil Brown.

22/11/09 Stoke (0) 1 Portsmouth 0 - There's 74 minutes on the clock and Tuncay is on the touchline, stripped & ready to replace a lacklustre Ricardo Fuller. Suddenly, Etherington supplies Fuller on the edge of the penalty area, and Ric brilliantly turns and curls the ball into the bottom left corner of the net. Bloody typical…albeit superb. Tuncay eventually comes on 10 minutes later, no doubt grinding his teeth. Up until then, things had been nothing short of shocking, particularly when playing against the bottom side. The turning point is the introduction of Lawrence on the hour as he virtually lifts the crowd all by himself (it's a good trick if you can do it). Oh, and Sorensen saves an early penalty (conceded by Delap).

Dave Kemp flummoxed by Towelgate, Tuncay, the Salif Diao selection algorithm, and, well, just about everything

28/11/09 Blackburn 0 Stoke 0 - "No one is expecting to see fans gambolling through the streets of Hanley kissing every fair maiden they pass." Martin Spinks spreads the good news for Hanley lasses after Stoke improve considerably on last season's 0-3 drubbing. Best chance falls to some guy called Steven N'Zonzi, who rattles Stoke's post late on. That's it, basically.

05/12/09 Arsenal (1) 2 Stoke 0 - Towelgate!!! Forget the score and the sparkling Arsenal display: This game should have been all about Tuncay who FINALLY starts a league game. For his pains, he's put up front with Mama Sidibe. Maybe he'd be better off on the wing, but Lawrence & Etherington are already there. It makes no difference as Arsenal are "dazzling", despite depleted by injuries (Wenger can't blame us for them, but no doubt tries). Delap gives away another penalty and Sorensen makes another amazing save. For the record, Tuncay plays "OK". But it's what happens AFTERWARDS that dominate the headlines for weeks to follow. Towelgate was the season's polarisation moment that shaped the club thereafter, a dressing-room bust-up over a planned Christmas party in the capital, with Pulis wanting them back for training with no hangovers. A standoff? Nakedness? Towels? Physicals? Uh?! What is worse is that details of the row are surreptitiously leaked by another player. The media have a field-day, and Beattie's career at Stoke takes a nosedive. Subsequently, everyone has a cold cold Christmas. Beattie starts only ONE league game after this, before moving to Rangers (somewhere in Scotland) in the summer.

12/12/09 Stoke (1) 2 Wigan (1) 2 - Tuncay's home debut is overshadowed by the rumbling repercussions of towelgate and THAT goal by Figueroa. After Wigan take an early lead, the world holds its breath on 37 mins as Tuncay breaks free on the left. He cuts in, blasts the ball between goalie & post, and the Brit goes bonkers. But the media quickly forgets that because on 72 mins Huth concedes a free-kick in Wigan's half. Instead of facing up, he and Delap turn their backs & Figueroa twacks it over everyone, including Sorensen for 1-2. Shawcross thankfully heads an immediate equaliser. Then, guess what? Sorensen saves ANOTHER penalty in the final minute (from Rodallega), his 3rd in 4 games. How does Thomas keep doing that?? And how the hell did we get him on a "free"?!

19/12/09 Aston Villa (0) 1 Stoke 0 - Anger! This is the game where Sidibe heads a perfectly good goal from an Etherington cross, and it's disallowed; then Carew scores one just like it, and it's given! Sidibe is penalised when climbing to head home because of a supposed dive by Warnock and by big club syndrome. Even BBC's Alan Hansen agrees, and so does Martin Spinks who refers to the ref as Lee Prohibit. Predictive text? I don't think so.

26/12/09 Man City (2) 2 Stoke 0 – Pulis vs Hughes Part…er, no. Hang on. Sparky was sacked last week. So, this is Roberto Mancini's first game in charge of Citeh and it's made dead easy for him. Faye & co seem unable to control Petrov and Tevez (who score on 28 and 45 minutes). With Collins, Diao, Sidibe and (it has to be said) Tuncay, it all looks a bit makeshift. Another Boxing Day defeat by a Manchester team.

28/12/09 Stoke 0 Birmingham (0) 1 - Beattie's last league start for Stoke, where he partners Tuncay to no avail. Like last season, The Potters are on a poor winter run; only one win since October's überfest at Spurs. But the game is all about goalkeepers: Sorensen is deemed to have "fumbled" Cameron Jerome's 50th minute snap shot, whereas Joe Hart has a blinder (which is staggering because no one remembers Joe Hart playing for Birmingham. Anyone?). Martin Spinks describes it as Stoke's "unluckiest" Premier defeat, then gives the game 8/10 for entertainment! Surely a misprint?

02/01/10 Stoke (2) 3 York (1) 1 (FA Cup) – Ex-Port Vale's Martin Foyle & Andy Porter come back to haunt Stoke from the technical area, and their Conference side even take the lead on 22 minutes. But Rory Delap's long throws immediately result in 2 goals in the next 3 minutes for 2-1 (own-goal & Fuller). Etherington's curling free-kick on the hour seals the victory for a strong-looking Stoke side…and Leon Cort. (Actually that's unfair, as Leon assists Fuller's goal in his last game before joining Burnley.)

05/01/10 Stoke (3) 3 Fulham (0) 2 - Snow & ice cripple the Premier League, but somehow The Brit stays open! Yes, the coldest, blusteriest place in the world sucks in the Sky cameras as there's nothing else in the world to film on a Tuesday evening, & boy do they get a cracker. Etherington's brilliant 2nd minute goal is given offside, & so Tuncay starts the ball rolling (into the net, that is) on 12 mins by slipping in Huth's goal-bound header (Stoke's first league goal for 5 hours!). Ab Faye slides in a 2nd, Sidibe (yes, Sidibe!) a 3rd. 3-0, and it's not even half time! A Duff deflection flies past Simonsen on the hour, and then a Dempsey cracker makes it a frantic 3-2 finish. Great TV, but hard on the nerves. Back in the Top 10.

16/01/10 Stoke (0) 1 Liverpool (0) 1 - Huth pokes in a late equaliser against a Liverpool side under fire for losing in the FA cup, with their manager Rafa Benitez looking increasingly vulnerable. With their first goal against the Reds for 100 years or so, The Potters could have beaten this rag-tag team easily, but don't. A bit dull otherwise.

24/01/10 Stoke (1) 3 Arsenal (1) 1 (FA Cup) – Finally Arsenal are smitten in the FA Cup, and it's Fuller and Delap smiting them down. Hasn't Arsene re-watched last season's game? Duh! It takes only 68 seconds for a Delap throw to find Ricardo for 1-0. Denilson equaliser before the break is another typical Gunners set-piece. But Sidibe crosses for Fuller in the 78th min for 2-1, and then Dean Whitehead scores his first for Stoke, getting on the end of an Etherington corker of a cross. Dunno what's up with poor Wenger – maybe his beta-max has broken down.

01/02/10 Sunderland 0 Stoke 0 - After the high of the Arsenal win, Stoke have a dreary Monday night TV game at the Stadium Of Light. Arsenal's nemesis, Fuller, is back on the bench, Tuncay having another go instead. But it's all pretty woeful though. Pulis has another look at Sunderland's Kenwyne Jones, and sees a big bloke with an unnaturally long pony tail, with loads of high-balls aimed at him. "Hm," he must have thought, "tasty!" (or words to that effect).

06/02/10 Stoke (2) 3 Blackburn 0 - Stoke win by 3 clear goals in the top flight for the first time since Frankie Goes To Hollywood dominated the pop charts. Sidibe scores his second goal of the season for the first time since Lily Allen was a little boy. And Tony Pulis leads out his Stoke side for the 300th time, the first time a Stoke manager has done that since The Beatles were still together. Who'd have bet on any of these things coming to pass?! Nuh, me neither. Even weirder, Higginbotham thinks he's a striker and volleys home from a corner on 4 minutes. Then after Samba is red carded on the hour, Etherington scores a brilliant solo goal for 3-0. Blackburn bruisers are outgunned, and even Wilko comes off with blood pouring down his forehead. But then this is the game notorious for the Blackburn fan who died after supposedly "heading" a 25lb bin thrown by a fellow supporter.

09/02/10 Wigan (1) 1 Stoke (0) 1 - Stoke seem welded to the 11th spot in The Prem. How they've done this without scoring an away goal in 3 months is beyond me. Tuncay puts this right by heading an equaliser on 74 minutes, after Wigan lead from an early goal. Fuller, who'd been arrested 2 days before for assault (charges later dropped), is Stoke's surprisingly inspirational 2nd half substitute.

13/02/10 Man City (1) 1 Stoke (0) 1 (FA Cup) – After Arsene Wenger is battered for not prepping up on Delap's throws, it's ironic that Shay Given admits that Citeh studied videos on them and then concede an equaliser on the hour from a Delap-Fuller special. But Citeh are obviously lulled into a false sense of security by the fact that Delap's on the bench. This all changes as Etherington, Lawrence and even Wilkinson are crocked. Stoke only go behind as a result of Shawcross and Sorensen playing Keystone Cops in the 11th minute for Wright-Phillips to score. But it's Ricardo Fuller who is the star. Is he really inspired by Kung Fu Panda?

16/02/10 Stoke (0) 1 Man City (0) 1 - Adam Cheshire reverently lists every referee for every game in his book until he gets to this midweek game where he names the ref as "Alan 'I should have gone to Specsavers' Wiley". He goes further: "An absolute travesty", "the most appalling refereeing of all time", and "This man should never referee a game of football again in his life. An absolute joke!!" What could Wiley have possibly done to upset everyone so? Well, for starters, Viera starts things off nicely by sticking his studs deep into Whelan's goolies, right in front of Wiley. Nothing. He then fails to give Fuller a clear penalty. He misses Ab Faye's supposed last-man professional foul on Adebayor, and has to rely on the linesman to red card Faye. But worst of all in the last seconds he disallows Shawcross's perfectly good headed winner from a Delap throw, which even keeper Shay Given admitted later wasn't a foul. Goals? Well, a very sore Whelan recovers to put 10-man Stoke ahead on 72 minutes from 25 yards, only for Gareth Barry to scramble a late equaliser. But from Stoke's point of view, and certainly Adam Cheshire's, it's "an absolute disgrace". Absolutely.

20/02/10 Portsmouth (1) 1 Stoke (0) 2 - "As we move into injury time, Fuller is loose down the right. He crosses and…A GOAL!! WHO IS THAT?? IT'S – I DON'T BELIEVE IT!! IT'S SALIF DIAO!! SALIF DIAO HAS SCORED!! Oh My God! Everyone will remember where they were when Salif Diao scored for Stoke City!!!" Well, that's the story of this one. Barmy. What on earth is Diao doing in the 6 yard box lashing home the winner from the brilliant Fuller. Even after the game Tony Pulis admits surprise: "I don't think he's ever got past the halfway line before." Disturbingly he adds: "I actually thought Sidibe had scored it - that's how bad my eyes are." Er, ha ha. Seriously?? Bottom and nearly bankrupt, Pompey are pegged back by a Huth header on 50 minutes, before Wilkinson is cruelly 2nd yellowed. But the headlines are all about Diao's first Prem goal since S Club 7 were Top Of The Pops. Weird, but a second away win of the season all the same.

24/02/10 Stoke (0) 3 Man City (0) 1 (FA Cup replay) – Both sides want this, but can't get it over the line…until Pulis brings on Tuncay and Kitson. Between them they combine for Kitson to make it 1-0 on 79 minutes, only for Bellamy to equalise 2 minutes later. Then the previously brilliant Adebayor lashes out at Shawcross just after the restart and is red carded. In extra time Ryan heads home a Delap throw, which Given should have seen coming a mile away, and a superb solo goal from Tuncay seals it at 3-1. Mancini hopes he never has to play Stoke in the cup again.

27/02/10 Stoke (1) 1 Arsenal (1) 3 - The game Aaron Ramsey breaks his leg in a 50/50 challenge with Shawcross. Campbell & Fabregas theatrically rage till the ref red-cards a distraught Shawcross. But it's Whelan who heroically cares for Ramsey until the medics get there, which judging by the angle of Ramsey's leg, I personally would have been too squeamish to do. So, Hail Saint Glenn. However, this game is *really* about Danny Pugh, who makes his ONLY start of the season, and heads Stoke in front after only 8 minutes. (This being Arsenal, of course it's from a Delap throw, via Shawcross.) Although, Bendtner heads an equaliser on 32, and Stoke are down to 10 men on 65, it's still 1-1 until Pugh is judged (harshly) to have handled in stoppage time. Vermaelen scores a further late late goal (well, this is Arsenal, afterall), but it's Arsene Wenger who rubs salt in the wound with some outrageous post-match comments about dirty Stoke. These would come back to haunt him. Ramsey finally returns to start a league game in December, whilst Danny Pugh has to wait till February 2011.

07/03/10 Chelsea (1) 2 Stoke 0 (FA Cup 6th) – Stoke are bundled out of the cup by soon-to-be-champions Chelsea, with a Lampard drive in the first half and a Terry header in the second. Best remembered for captain Robert Huth's free-kick that heads off towards Knightsbridge (almost as bad as the famous one he does years later). Actually, this game is best not remembered at all.

10/03/10 Burnley (0) 1 Stoke (1) 1 - Burnley officials move their advertising boards to thwart Delap in this midweek clash. Does it work? Does it begger! On 23 mins Sidibe heads on a Rory special, and Tuncay nods home. This rubbish Burnley side, on course for relegation (2nd from bottom, with only 1 win in 17), get a draw with David Nugent out-jumping Huth. What's most hard to believe though is that this is Sidibe's 14th consecutive start, whereas Tuncay only manages 9 in the same period. Weird or what.

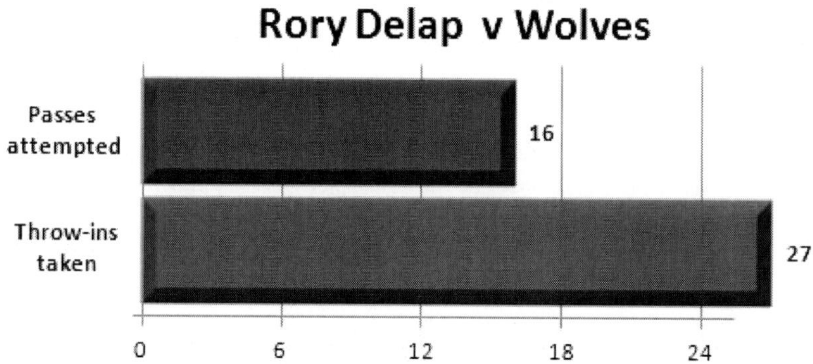

The science behind Rory Delap

13/03/10 Stoke 0 Aston Villa 0 - "And what kind of example was his stroppy behaviour to those young Stoke fans with 'Tuncay 20' on the back of their red & white shirts?" Yes, the only excitement of this game was Tuncay going off in a huff after his 54th minute substitution. Martin Spinks fills a whole column about his "childish tantrum", partly because the game's so dull, but particularly as Fuller comes on and does a lot better. And this against a highflying team that includes Friedel, Ashley Young, Milner, Downing, etc.

20/03/10 Stoke (0) 1 Spurs (0) 2 - Game ruined by Mike Dean choosing Whitehead as his weekly innocent victim for a 2nd yellow (he'd taken it out on Wilko in the Pompey game, remember?). Eidur Gudjohnsen shows off some of the skill that he fails to bring to us the following season. Peter Crouch sets him up to score after the break, Etherington equalises from the spot, before Kranjcar finishes off our 10 men. With Palacios on the bench, Pulis is so impressed with Spurs that he tries to sign the whole team! He's slowly getting there.

27/03/10 West Ham 0 Stoke (0) 1 - The game with THAT amazing Fuller goal. The last time he was here, he slapped Andy Griffin & was off. This time he comes on as sub, and within 2 minutes he's single-handedly beaten the entire West Ham defence and sent the keeper the wrong way! One of them is the "cumbersome" (says Spinks) Matthew Upson. Meow!! 3 games out of 4 in a row against claret-and-blue sides, & finally a win.

03/04/10 Stoke (1) 2 Hull 0 - Phil Brown has gone, & Hull are on their way out. They drop by the Britannia to get tonked by an early Fuller goal (headed on by an improving Kitson) and a late strike by Lawrence - his first goal for a year, and his last goal for Stoke. Wayward Tuncay comes on, but his overhead scissor kick poleaxes Boateng. Mundane.

11/04/10 Wolves 0 Stoke 0 - Bloody awful. A Sunday midday kickoff to supposedly avoid fans clashing. Well, what did they expect? 28,455 watch Mama Sidibe miss a sitter. Ugh!

17/04/10 Stoke (1) 1 Bolton (0) 2 - Daylight bloody robbery. Stoke are cruising against a dreadful Bolton side after Tuncay's lob sets Kitson up to round the keeper for 1-0 after 18 minutes. But after Tuncay AGAIN stomps off down the tunnel after being subbed on 77 mins (& boo-ed for his troubles), Stoke concede two late goals in 3 minutes. How did Stoke lose this game? One of life's great mysteries.

25/04/10 Chelsea (3) 7 Stoke 0 – Champions-elect are caught trying to show off. It all starts going wrong for Stoke when Faye is AGAIN subbed with his ankle, this time after only 8 minutes. (His star is definitely in the decline.) Then Kalou nods in the first. But the real turning point is on the half hour when Kalou goes in two-footed on Sorensen, and the ball goes in the net. Instead of being red-carded, Kalou is awarded a goal! How does that work?? Begovic replaces the bludgeoned Sorro to carry on the good work, but the goals start raining in as the Stoke defence freezes. Kalou (somehow still on the pitch) completes his hat-trick, Lampard bags a couple,...oh, you get the idea. At least it wasn't live on TV. It was?! Oh dear oh dear. Kitson throws a wobbly when substituted; Faye allegedly throws a punch at Whelan in the tunnel; and there's still a leak in the dressing room. Must be a faulty tap (although Whelan would probably claim it wasn't just a tap).

01/05/10 Stoke 0 Everton 0 - Best remembered for the recovery after last week's shenanigans. Pulis sets out his stall: Kitson & Beattie are remaindered (ie. don't figure for the rest of the season/ever-again), & even Tuncay is boo-ed when he replaces Sidibe late on. The players respond with a stirring performance, despite Rory missing a sitter. Everton have a late goal (rightly) disallowed, and David Moyes (wrongly) has a good moan.

05/05/10 Fulham 0 Stoke (0) 1 - Have you noticed that this season's visits to London have either been a total disaster (Arsenal - towelgate, Chelsea - 0-7), or brilliant 1-0 victories (Spurs, West Ham, Leyton Orient(!), and now Fulham!). But **Stoke have NEVER won FOUR times in London in a season in all of their history.** That's London 2 Stoke 4. (Interestingly, the only time they have ever won 3 in London is in 1990/91 when they beat Orient, Fulham & Brentford in Division 3 during their worst ever league season!) Player Of The Year Matthew Etherington rounds off a great performance by lashing home a late winner from a Fuller cross. Fulham don't look the least bit distracted by the fact that they are playing in the Europa Final next week against Madrid. Martin Spinks notes that Stoke are now only the 2nd club to "better their first season in the Premier". Wow. Also, the result propels Stoke off their constant 11th spot to the giddy heights of 10th. If only they can hold on to 10th place by winning their last game…

09/05/10 Man Utd (2) 4 Stoke 0 – Stoke fail to hold on to 10th place by losing their last game. They finish 11th (surprise surprise) with 47 points. This was the game that Stoke fans chanted for Chelsea. Why? Because down in London The Blues were beating Wigan 8-0 to win the Premier, and so United couldn't catch them, however many they put past Begovic. Stoke put up a fight, with 7 shots on target, but Fletcher, Giggs, an own-goal, & Parks put an end to any hopes of even a point. Almost all of Stoke's team that day remain loyal squad members for years to come:

Asmir Begovic;
Danny Higginbotham, Robert Huth, Ryan Shawcross, Andy Wilkinson;
Glenn Whelan, Dean Whitehead, Rory Delap, Matthew Etherington;
Ricardo Fuller, Mamady Sidibe

			Home					Away					Overall						
	Team	Pl	W	D	L	F	A	W	D	L	F	A	W	D	L	F	A	Pts	GD
1	Chelsea	38	17	1	1	68	14	10	4	5	35	18	27	5	6	103	32	86	71
2	Manchester United	38	16	1	2	52	12	11	3	5	34	16	27	4	7	86	28	85	58
3	Arsenal	38	15	2	2	48	15	8	4	7	35	26	23	6	9	83	41	75	42
4	Tottenham Hotspur	38	14	2	3	40	12	7	5	7	27	29	21	7	10	67	41	70	26
5	Manchester City	38	12	4	3	41	20	6	9	4	32	25	18	13	7	73	45	67	28
6	Aston Villa	38	8	8	3	29	16	9	5	5	23	23	17	13	8	52	39	64	13
7	Liverpool	38	13	3	3	43	15	5	6	8	18	20	18	9	11	61	35	63	26
8	Everton	38	11	6	2	35	21	5	7	7	25	28	16	13	9	60	49	61	11
9	Birmingham City	38	8	9	2	19	13	5	2	12	19	34	13	11	14	38	47	50	-9
10	Blackburn Rovers	38	10	6	3	28	18	3	5	11	13	37	13	11	14	41	55	50	-14
11	**Stoke City**	38	7	6	6	24	21	4	8	7	10	27	11	14	13	34	48	47	-14
12	Fulham	38	11	3	5	27	15	1	7	11	12	31	12	10	16	39	46	46	-7
13	Sunderland	38	9	7	3	32	19	2	4	13	16	37	11	11	16	48	56	44	-8
14	Bolton Wanderers	38	6	6	7	26	31	4	3	12	16	36	10	9	19	42	67	39	-25
15	Wolverhampton Wanderers	38	5	6	8	13	22	4	5	10	19	34	9	11	18	32	56	38	-24
16	Wigan Athletic	38	6	7	6	19	24	3	2	14	18	55	9	9	20	37	79	36	-42
17	West Ham United	38	7	5	7	30	29	1	6	12	17	37	8	11	19	47	66	35	-19
18	Burnley	38	7	5	7	25	30	1	1	17	17	52	8	6	24	42	82	30	-40
19	Hull City	38	6	6	7	22	29	0	6	13	12	46	6	12	20	34	75	30	-41
20	Portsmouth *	38	5	3	11	24	32	2	4	13	10	34	7	7	24	34	66	19	-32

2010-11 - The Cup-Final Season

14/08/10 Wolves (2) 2 Stoke (0) 1 - You know what it's like: the long awaited new season starts, your new £8m striker starts brightly by hitting the bar, and then (oh dear) Joey Craddock crocks him after only TWELVE minutes! Kenwyne Jones - for it is he of whom we speak - is yet another signing from Sunderland (Delap, Collins, Higginbotham, Whitehead, Lawrence, etc). Kenwyne hobbles off on crutches as Stoke crumble to two goals in 2 minutes. The other Jones (David) skillfully flicks the ball up from a free kick & loops it into the top of the net. The other is a deflection off Faye, who redeems himself by heading home a corner on the hour. "It's important we sign a fast right winger before the end of the month," instructs James Knowles. "And a new striker." Hm, let's see. “And…” Er, yes, thank you, James.

21/08/10 Stoke (1) 1 Spurs (2) 2 - The game Jonathan Walters (£2.75m) makes his debut in the "Sidibe role[tm]" behind Fuller. And-so-it-comes-to-pass that late in the game Walters heads home… only for a falling Peter Crouch (then with Spurs) to "chest" the ball clear from *over* the goal line. "Handball!" shouts Dave Harrison & thousands of others. Maybe. But Tony Pulis is clearly impressed by Crouch's defending. He knows he'll never be able to afford Gareth Bale, who scores a brilliant volleyed 2nd goal on the half-hour. Martin Spinks is saddened that Walters' "eventual resting place will no doubt be on the right of midfield" to accommodate the lively Tuncay. He’s sad because he sees goals in this guy, and he ain't wrong. This game is best forgotten then, particularly as Sidibe comes on, collapses in a heap a few minutes later, and is stretchered off again.

Peter Crouch, the best goalkeeper Spurs never had

24/08/10 Stoke (2) 2 Shrewsbury (0) 1 (Carling Cup) – This time Jonathan Walters really does score his first goal, heading home n 26 minutes from an Etherington left wing cross. He’s arrived! Tuncay copies Walters’ goal to make it 2-0 on 37, and Town get a late consolation as Nash & Shawcross get all mixed up. Yes, promotion hero Carlo Nash returns to make one last appearance, but he’s eclipsed by the new boy.

28/08/10 Chelsea (1) 2 Stoke 0 - It's official: this is Tony Pulis's worst start to a season as a manager EVER. Stoke play well...or as Martin Spinks puts it: "Stoke competed hard in the rucks and mauls, won their fair share of high ball in the line-outs, were never found wanting in the scrum, and did themselves justice in the loose." Nope, I have no idea what he's on about. (I think it's some sort of Rugby metaphor.) At least they didn't lose 7-0 like last time. This is probably down to Sorensen saving a 10th minute penalty from

Lampard to stem the flow. However, Malouda breaks free on the half-hour for 1-0, and a late penalty by otherwise luckless Drogba seals it, leaving Stoke 19th (of 20). Good news? £8m Kenwyne Jones is back from being "Craddock-ed" (yes, it's a new verb) .

13/09/10 Stoke (0) 2 Aston Villa (1) 1 - The turning point. This is the game that Pulis returns at half time. Stoke are heading for their 4th straight defeat after Downing nods a star-studded but managerless Villa 1-0 up on 35 mins. Then out of the blue, Tony Pulis appears for the second half after a mad-dash from Wales, where he has been mourning the death of his mother. The crowd go bonkers to see him, not a dry eye in the house. Suddenly, the previously luckless Kenwyne is causing all sorts of problems, eventually heading home in the 80th minute from a superb Etherington chip. THEN after 93 minutes, Huth stabs home another Etherington effort! 2-1! The Brit goes mad! We've done a late-late-one to Villa AGAIN! And with the help of new signings midfielder Marc Wilson (from a bizarre part-exchange including Lawrence & Kitson) & winger Jermaine Pennant (on as sub). Welcome, guys, to the barmy world that we call Stoke City.

18/09/10 Stoke (0) 1 West Ham (1) 1 - 4 defeats in a row, bottom of the league & turning up without their manager, but Stoke still can't beat the Hammers...despite Pulis starting with TWO wingers! First half comedy goal for West Ham is a result of Delap blasting a goal-line clearance straight into the face of Shawcross, leaving Parker an easy finish for 0-1. But in his first start, Pennant crosses for Jones to head the equaliser just after the break. Poor, really, although practically the same set of players would be playing Wembley-way a few months later. (Spoiler alert.)

21/09/10 Stoke (1) 2 Fulham 0 (Carling Cup) – Tony Pulis vs Mark Hughes Part 3. With tenacious Danny Murphy throwing his weight around, throwing the ball into Shawcross' face, and throwing his wayward shots out of the ground, one does wonder if he's on a mission from Sparky to wind up the Pulis boys. Well, it doesn't work, and he ends up with an early booking and a Kenwyne thunderbolt in the unmentionables (ooooo!). Whilst he's recovering, Danny Higginbotham heads home from a corner for 1-0. Then after Delap comes on for Diao, Rory's 78th minute long-throw is headed home by Kenwyne. But the game is best remembered for the very end. Andy Wilkinson is hacked at in Fulham's penalty area, and is somehow denied a penalty (which I'm sure he would have taken). So, he swings a harsh and unnecessary tackle on Dembele, who needs stretchering off. Sparky goes bananas, and as such doesn't shake Pulis' hand. Oh dear.

26/09/10 Newcastle (1) 1 Stoke (0) 2 - Another dreadful first half, with Stoke generously giving the opposition a head-start again. It's fine though if they're stupid enough to let us sucker-punch them in the 2nd half. Chris Hughton's newly-promoted United really are that stupid. Mind you, Fuller coming on for Diao after the break might also have something to do with it. Pulis experiments with Huth instead of Faye in the centre, only for the German to barge over Andy Carroll for a penalty. Not a good start. But in the 2nd half Huth sets up Kenwyne to head his 4th in 4 games. Then Huth pressurises defender Perch to head an Etherington corner into his own net in the 85th minute. Comical. "A game of two halves," says The Oatcake. "Our season's on fire!" exclaims James Knowles. Steady on.

02/10/10 Stoke (0) 1 Blackburn 0 - The dazzling Etherington sets up Walters just after the break to slip the ball past Paul Robinson for his first ever Premier League goal. Meanwhile, Huth, Shawcross and Faye (yes, all three!) look more than a match for the likes of Mame Diouf & Nzonzi. Despite Stoke hitting 7th spot and beginning to look a lot classier than the likes of Sam Alladyce's Rovers, only 25,515 people made it through this one.

16/10/10 Bolton (1) 2 Stoke (0) 1 - Dammit. Another late defeat to Bolton. Sorensen shoulders some of the blame for the conceded throw and subsequent Klasnic goal in the 92nd minute. Amusingly Klasnic is sent off 3 minutes later. Another poor first half, as a guy called Lee (cool name) is allowed to score for Bolton. Delap thwacks home a corner on 48, but unlike Newcastle, Bolton hold firm. Fuller comes on but lasts only 10 minutes with that floppy shoulder of his. Tuncay scurries off in another huff (well, in a taxi, actually) for not even making the bench. “Mugged again by Bolton,” grumble The Oatcake. And Martin Spinks thinks Bolton might be becoming our bogie side: "We are beginning to realise just how the Baggies must be feeling whenever they play Stoke." Hm, goodness knows what misfortune may occur next time we play away from home against Bolton. (Spoiler alert 2.)

24/10/10 Stoke (0) 1 Man Utd (1) 2 - The expression "butter wouldn't melt in his mouth" was invented for the charmed one they call Gary Neville. On a yellow card for a first half scything of Etherington, he then does it AGAIN just minutes later. Even Neville realises he's cocked-up big-style, and he’s got to go. But, hang on… the ref (Marriner) doesn't even bring him over for a stiff word! The whole world (& this game is being beamed round the globe) is bewildered. But hell, this is United we are talking about, so they are 1-0 up (Hernandez back-header) with 11 players still on the pitch. But despite Tuncay being in his bad-books, & barely figuring at all this season, Pulis sends the young turk on as sub. With 10 minutes to go he sways in from the right and whacks what can only be described as an earth-shattering thunderbolt past a dazed Van der Sar. A mega moment. If he'd managed to stop Evra crossing for Hernandez to score the winner 5 minutes later, he would be a Stoke legend. But, er, no, he can’t do that.

27/10/10 West Ham (0) 3 Stoke (1) 1 (Carling Cup) – Somehow Stoke lose this one. They lead from a Kenwyne header from a Pennant corner after only 6 minutes, and get within 6 minutes of winning. Pulis even subs Kenwyne & Pennant, and brings on loanee Eidur Gudjohnsen, who doesn’t look much like the ex-Chelsea & Barcelona player he once was. The Hammers equalise, and win it in extra-time. How? Well, it’s all down to Avram Grant whose Portsmouth also knocked Stoke out of the Carling Cup last season.

30/10/10 Everton (0) 1 Stoke 0 - Rumour has it that refs are being trained with videos of spurious Stoke manoeuvres. When Tuncay's prodded goal is unbelievably disallowed for his "contact" with Baines, people start believing the rumour. Yes, it's the Lee Probert Show again. But it's just more frustration for Tuncay - no wonder his Stoke career fails to take off. A few minutes later (67 minutes) Yakubu outsmarts Collins, and blasts past Begovic. Not such a good start for Begovic, particularly as this is the game that he officially takes over from (albeit injured) Sorensen. Spinks: “The scariest thing came in the toilets at half-time, confronting not just Fellaini’s beehive, but that of his younger brother as well.” That’s a grim image he could have kept to himself. Stoke drop to 14th.

06/11/10 Sunderland (1) 2 Stoke 0 - "Don't tell the editor this but events are getting so predictable that a chimpanzee could write Stoke's match reports!" admits the exasperated Martin Spinks (you can see why he's my favourite journalist). It's another lunatic of a game, in other words. An early goal & a late goal sink City, but despite Begovic saving a first half penalty (yes, this really DID happen!), any chance of a turnaround are scuppered by the ref: 20 minutes left and Kenwyne heads a certain goal from a corner...only for Lee Cattermole to scoop it clear with his arms, possibly from over the line. No goal, no handball, no red card, no penalty. Typical. And then 10 minutes later Shawcross is red carded for two yellows. Typical. Martin Atkinson (for it is he) then goes on to try and book the rest of the Stoke team. Card-wise, Sunderland walk away scott-free. Spinks generously awards Atkinson with a mark of 4/10 … for turning up and wearing black. What else he got right today is anyone's guess. Stoke now 17th!

09/11/10 Stoke (1) 3 Birmingham (0) 2 - Alex McLeish's team are 2-0 down and beaten...surely. Fuller is on fire as creator (for Huth 44 minutes) then scorer of a cracking drive (71 minutes), whereas even Pulis is chilled enough to bring off Pennant. Then it all goes pear-shaped. 2 goals in 2 minutes, and Birmingham, led on by the sprightly goalscoring Cameron Jerome (yes, HIM again), are moving in for the kill. Was it going to be a sixth straight Stoke defeat? Nope, Whitehead latches on to a deflected Etherington cross to pop home the winner 5 minutes from time. "Delirium," cry the fans. "Unexpected!" cry The Oatcake. The Sentinel rates this midweek game as a 9 out of 10, as, hell, it's better than losing 0-8 to Birmingham (as Stoke did in 1998).

13/11/10 Stoke (0) 2 Liverpool 0 - And talking of 0-8 games, it is 10 years (almost to the day) that Liverpool beat Stoke 8-0. They hit us at a low point, and now we do the same to them. Roy Hodgson is in charge (oh dear), & the players (we find out later) are not really behind him. Gerrard, Torres, Carragher, Kuyt etc aren't just beaten, they are ritually humiliated by the exuberant likes of Pennant, Etherington, Fuller and Whitehead. Stoke have 65% of possession!!! (Yes, you are reading this correctly.) They have over twice as many shots on goal!!! (And some even go in!) They have a lot fewer yellow cards!!! (1-3) They have more corners... (Yes, now we're reaching the bottom of this particular barrel.) Fuller finally scores after several attempts at poking it home on 54 minutes, and as Liverpool huff & puff, Wilkinson intercepts Gerrard's wimpy pass for Pennant to set up Kenwyne to finish the job in the last minute. As if Stokies aren't having enough fun, Lucas is then second-yellowed. Hodgson looks as close to expiry as it's possible to do. Six weeks later he's ousted and has to go and work at West Brom. And talking of West Brom…

20/11/10 West Brom 0 Stoke (0) 3 - You could see this one happening a mile away. It's almost too stupid to write about. Even ref Chris Foy gets into the "let's embarrass Albion" spirit by generously giving Stoke not one but TWO generous second half penalties. What a nice man. Etherington & his substitute Walters oblige tidily, before Kenwyne sets up Walters for a late piece of humiliation. Why do these Baggies even bother turning up?

27/11/10 Stoke (0) 1 Man City (0) 1 - The game with that brilliant injury time equaliser by Matty Etherington. Man City have already left it late when Micah Richards loses Collins, cuts in and blasts home on 81 minutes. Surely the millionaires have wrapped it up. But in the 92nd minute Begovic boots it downfield, Kenwyne heads it on, Tuncay back-heals and Matty overlaps to slide it home. WONDERFUL! It is Mancini's 46th birthday, & all he wanted was 3 points at the Brit. Well, Roberto, you'll just have to learn to live with disappointment.

04/12/10 Wigan (2) 2 Stoke (2) 2 - The Premier's lowest scorers play the Premier's most "boring" (as Stoke have been labelled of late). But instead of a bore-fest, it's rip-roaring stuff. Dave Harrison describes it as "like Shakespeare's Comedy Of Errors"...only with less dialogue...& fewer donkeys...& no players called Doctor Pinch. So, not much like Shakespeare's play at all really. Instead, Huth takes a free-kick from 35 YARDS!...and scores (ok, it takes a deflection, but they all count). The same thing happens the other end, the ball twanging off Collins. Immediately, Fuller baffles the Wigan defence, before sliding it across for Etherington to finish for 2-1. Then on 40 minutes yet another deflection, this time off Delap, flies past an otherwise brilliant Begovic. Yes, not even half-time. On it goes in the second half, except no more goals, although Fuller is incensed (yes, hard to believe) when he doesn't get a penalty. Well, all I can say is, it was just like Charles Dickens' A Tale Of Two Cities...except it wasn't a tale and Wigan isn't a city; it's a metropolitan borough. And a pier.

11/12/10 Stoke 0 Blackpool (0) 1 - It must be bloody December: Stoke's energy levels again hit a low. Newly promoted & right clever-dicks Blackpool FC are in town, with getting-loopier-by-the-day manager Ian Holloway in tow. You gotta love the little scamps, slickly passing the ball around with such aplomb and accumulating 22 points in 16 games. No, Stoke fans don't love them. Just after the break that midfield dynamo Charlie Adam sets up DJ Campbell to sink The Potters; by which time Stoke fans have started to get increasingly irritated with the cheeky chappies. "They have every right to anticipate possible salvation at the end of the season," suggests Martin Spinks. And sure enough 5 months later they are relegated.

26/12/10 Blackburn 0 Stoke (0) 2 - Not only Stoke's first Boxing Day Premier League point(s), but also Stoke's *first December win in the Prem*! And, interestingly, this is where Steve Kean's problems at Rovers really start. Kean takes over full-time from sacked Sam Allardyce, only to be confronted by - you'll never guess - Stoke attacking away from home! 51% possession! I know, unbelievable! 51 is also the minute that Huth's flick header from a corner gives Stoke the lead, as he out-jumps that not-really-a-defender Mame Diouf. Unmarked sub Marc Wilson (seen here with hair & playing in some vague midfield role) finishes them off in injury time, sweeping home from a snappy Fuller cross. This could mean trouble for Steve Kean in the long run (but he doesn't seem to care). "Bloody cold," observes The Oatcake, and getting colder by the game for away fans, particularly as Stoke don't win away again in the Premier for EIGHT MONTHS! OMG!

28/12/10 Stoke 0 Fulham (2) 2 – Pulis vs Hughes Part 4. Normal service resumes as December's standard dreadful form returns. Subsequently, Fulham's full back Chris Baird scores 2 goals in the first 10 minutes to sink Stoke. Baird's never scored a goal in his life! Typical. This is galling as Danny Murphy has slagged Stoke off in the week for their dirty play, which is good coming from HIM! & supporters want it shoving down his throat. But not today. After Mark Hughes doesn't shake hands after Stoke's Carling Cup win, Pulis makes a point by slapping Hughes' hand rather than shaking it. Hughes amusingly does his tragic "looks insulted" pose. Serves him right, really. Pennant waves goodbye - his loan deal is up - we will never see his like again...but luckily he then signs a 3 year deal. Knock-out!

01/01/11 Stoke (1) 2 Everton 0 - His name is Jagielka, and he scores regularly for Stoke. In 2008 it was a bewildered header from a Delap throw, but here he makes sure by wildly belting it in off the bar on 69 minutes. Why does he keep doing this? Bananas. Kenwyne Jones breaks his goal drought in the 1st half, heading home an awesome Etherington cross. Looks easy, particularly as the ref fails to send off Begovic for a foul outside the box, or impetuous Whitehead already on a yellow card. Stoke may be riding their luck, but who needs luck when Moyes keeps playing Jagielka. Stoke's first win against Everton in 28 YEARS!

04/01/11 Man Utd (1) 2 Stoke (0) 1 - Off to Old Trafford ("The Theatre Of Screams!" reckon The Oatcake) for the annual tonking by United, and Hernandez sets things rolling on 27 minutes. As Tuncay's only league goal of the season is the thunderbolt against The Reds at the Brit, Pulis decides (somewhat bizarrely) to recall him after 2 months. Wide-eyed he positions himself beside Kenwyne in a devil-may-care line-up. But amazingly it's Tuncay's inspired cross on 50 minutes that gives Whitehead the headed equalising goal that Stoke fans have waited 30 years for - yes, it's that long since they scored at Old Trafford. Amusingly the scoreboard briefly flashes up "United 1 Stoke 2", which to United fans it might as well be. Anyway 12 minutes later Nani smacks in from the edge of the box to ruin the party. Hell, it scared the pants off them, though.

08/01/11 Stoke (1) 1 Cardiff (1) 1 (FA Cup 3rd) – It's a pain in the neck, this FA Cup. Even Cardiff are more interested in gaining promotion than playing in the cup, but they take the lead on 8 minutes as Chopra has time to hit the post then put in the rebound. Can't blame Shotton (making his home debut) for that, as Ryan, Huth & Higgs are also on duty. Fuller sets up Tuncay to equalise on half-time, but Stoke huff & puff ineffectually, and now have to go all the way to Cardiff for a replay.

15/01/11 Stoke (1) 2 Bolton 0 - 30 point barrier reached by Stoke faster than previous Premier seasons despite poor start, and a total of 100 Premier goals notched up. Stoke are comfortably in 8th spot. Higginbotham finally deposes Collins at left back, and want-away Tuncay starts his second game in a row, shock-horror! But then Tuncay's corner sets up Higgs' first-half goal (squeezed in with the help of goalie Jaaskelainen), & a Tuncay pass results in Etherington being tumbled in the box on the hour. Matty's penalty is a bit weedy, but trickles over the line much to fully-stretched Jaaskelainen's annoyance. Oh, and Marc Wilson starts in midfield again - god knows why.

18/01/11 Cardiff 0 Stoke (0) 2 (FA Cup 3rd rpl) – It's like Night Of The Living Dead. Cardiff start with The Beast (Jon Parkin) & new-boy Danny Drinkwater, whilst Captain Higginbotham limps off after only 10 minutes to be replaced by Michael Tonge. Ghost of Xmas Past, Carlo Nash, sits on Stoke's bench, whilst Pugh, Soares, Shotton and Diao all decide to have a go. As if the nightmare can get any worse, it goes into extra time, but amazingly Walters scores twice and it's a happy ending. Maybe a cup run isn't so bad afterall.

22/01/11 Fulham (1) 2 Stoke 0 – Pulis vs Hughes Part 5, and part 3 of "Handshake-gate". Finally, Hughes & Pulis shake hands, & we're all friends again? Don't count on it. Stoke fans are still on Murphy's back for his "Stoke Dirty Play" talk, and he's subsequently booked on 22 minutes! Meanwhile, Fulham fans have it in for Wilkinson for his late late tackle on Dembele at the end of their Cup defeat to Stoke, and he's ultimately booked on 34 minutes. It just goes downhill from there. Shawcross is red carded for a professional foul on Dempsey just before the hour, & the resulting penalty makes it an easy 0-2 defeat. On comes lumbering loan-man John Carew for Stoke, & more surprisingly forgotten-man Abdoulaye Faye. Off goes Tuncay for the last time – he's off to Germany. The Oatcake award it The Worst Away Game Of The Season. "Shockingly poor." TP now VERY grumpy with Sparky Hughes, and understandably.

Mark Hughes & Tony Pulis scheduling their next strop

30/01/11 Wolves 0 Stoke (0) 1 (FA Cup 4th) – In Stephen Foster's book The Final he writes: "I count the matches out on my fingers, there's one missing. I ask the other Stokies what it is. They cannot remember it either, until one of them finally does: 'Wolves in the 4th round, 1-0. Huth with his head and then Sorensen saved the penalty late on, remember?'…I did. I picked up on a Stoke win bet. I owed my luck to a low dive to his left from the 34 year old Dane." Sky TV described the game as "awful", despite Pulis & Mick McCarthy fielding strong teams. But the goal – set up by Etherington – and the penalty – conceded by Huth – are all in the last 10 minutes. The rest is, well, "not great".

02/02/11 Liverpool (0) 2 Stoke 0 - You could have predicted this one before you even left The Brit. Shawcross is suspended, Kenwyne is dropped and so in come Faye, Diao & Carew! Are we being serious here? Roy Hodgson is gone, and now King Kenny Dalglish is stirring things up: he sells Torres for £50m, buys an injured Andy Carroll for £35m, but then sends some unknown new guy called Luis Suarez (£23m from Ajax) on as sub. At the same time, with Stoke 0-1 down, Pulis brings on Fuller (£0.5m in 2006) as a left winger. Yes, it's one of *those* games. Suarez rounds Begovic to score on his debut, although Wilkinson almost scoops it off the line. The Suarez legend is born here, and the legend reads: "Nobody likes you, Luis."

05/02/11 Stoke (1) 3 Sunderland (1) 2 - It's the comeback of the season! With wind & rain blowing the hell out of The Brit, it doesn't start well, with Kieran Richardson scoring in only the 2nd minute. On the half hour Carew, partnering Kenwyne up front (nope, God knows why), taps in a dodgy equaliser. Yes, it's offside, handball AND a push on the keeper, but jolly old Lee Probert is happy to give it (what a nice chap). But easily irritated Steve Bruce & his merry men casually go 2-1 up after the break. Pulis then does something very odd: he brings on an extra striker, Walters for Wilko - somebody else has clearly taken over Pulis' body. It pays off: 7 minutes from time, Pennant's free kick is "headed on" by Carew – "headed on" in the sense of using his arm not his actual head – and it bounces in off Huth's shin for 2-2. Same again 3 minutes into injury time, only without a Carew infringement. 3-2! Steve Bruce is understandably NOT happy, but Pulis is, for a change. Wonderful! With a win like that, who cares about walking home in the rain.

12/02/11 Birmingham (0) 1 Stoke 0 - THREE minutes into injury time, and Begovic spills a David Bentley rasper. Damn! Asmir has had little to do all day – get up, brush his teeth, catch the coach, get changed, watch Birmingham disappear up their own behinds for 90 minutes. But he makes up for his spillage by saving the rebound from the then Birmingham striker Cameron Jerome. Unfortunately, it sails up for 7 foot Zigic to head home. Lucky bleeders. Pretty forgettable, otherwise. "I thought we were on for a point," reckons Dave Harrison. You & all of Birmingham, Dave. Meanwhile Martin Spinks is concerned by the thinness of the squad; Tuncay has been sold, Marc Wilson is playing RIGHT back, and "Eider Gudjohnsen's departure remains a damaging blow for those wanting to see the 100 metres completed in minutes rather than seconds". Now really, Martin, that's a bit naughty!

19/02/11 Stoke (3) 3 Brighton 0 (FA Cup 5th) – A tough game against Gus Poyet's blazing leaders of League One…oh no, hang on. Stoke are 3 up by the break. Carew gets on the end of a Delap throw, Walters finishes a great move featuring Pennant & Wilson, and Shawcross scores from a corner from the right. Gus has something to sulk about.

23/02/11 Arsenal (1) 1 Stoke 0 - After a pretty positive start (3 away wins up until Boxing Day), Stoke's Premier away form is beginning to cause, er, ALARM! Five straight away defeats & more to follow. Thankfully, The Potters have a pleasant distraction in the FA Cup, with away wins at Cardiff & Wolves. Meanwhile, an early Squillaci goal sinks Stoke at The Emirates in this rescheduled game – remember it was cancelled at the last minute in December when a few flakes of snow fluttered over North London. In the end the Gunners hang on... just. But however much the 60,000 crowd barrack Shawcross (for last year's Ramsey challenge), it can't rattle our Ryan, who almost equalises. Shame,really. It would have caused a riot, although that's standard practice, I believe, for this part of North London.

28/02/11 Stoke (0) 1 West Brom (0) 1 - The game that The Baggies came back & almost sneaked it from us at the end. When Delap heads home a corner just before the hour-mark, it's time for West Brom to give up & go home. But Roy Hodgson won't let them, blast him! Carlos Vela squeezes home the eventual equaliser 4 minutes from the end, despite being woefully offside. (Is this really The Baggies' first Premier goal against Stoke?!) And then - get this - City are battered by Albion looking for a winner - what's that all about? That's not in their contract - they're here to lose like they normally do. Begovic performs miracles keeping them out, particularly a Vela strike in the last few seconds. In the end it's just a real sweat for not much reward.

05/03/11 West Ham (2) 3 Stoke 0 - Stoke's season hits a low point, particularly on the road, and their away fans are revolting (steady on!). Soon to be relegated West Ham with their striker Demba Ba make Stoke look shambolic. "So much for his dodgy knee," notes Dave Harrison – Stoke were due to sign Ba before that knee failed a medical. Ba scores on 21 minutes during a Wilson/Begovic mixup. Then 8 minutes later, little da Costa out-jumps Stoke's giants, & the game's effectively over. Until today Stoke are the last Premier club not to concede more than two goals in a game this season. So much for that. Next week Stoke will take on The Hammers in the FA Cup quarter-finals, and everyone begins to doubt their chances. Martin Spinks even notes some calls for "Pulis-out".

05/03/11 Stoke (1) 2 West Ham (1) 1 (FA Cup 6th) – But it all turns around at the Brit with a gutsy performance from the likes of Whelan, Pennant, Kenwyne, and in particularly ex-Hammer Etherington. Just when you think Delap's throws have become old-hat, Huth scores from one in the 12th minute. But Piquionne handles whilst equalising on the half-hour, which winds up The Brit to full-volume. So, right at the start of the 2nd half, the ref gives Etherington a soft penalty, but Walters grabs it & misses. But on the hour, Pennant's free-kick is handled in the wall. Higginbotham thumps the next one, the keeper touches it on to the post, and it trickles over the line for 2-1. Matthew Upson hits the post late on, but Stoke are back at Wembley. All's well that ends well.

19/03/11 Stoke (1) 4 Newcastle 0 - It's not just the score, it's the quality of the goals. Even taking into account that United have just sold Andy Carroll for a ludicrous £35m, this is still monumental. And Stoke's biggest Premier win. But more importantly it's yet another opportunity for Joey Barton baiting! Yippee! Apparently he kicks like a girl, or so they say. Walters' glancing near-post header from a luscious Pennant cross is perfect for 1-0 on the half-hour. Just after the break, goalie Harper generously just gives the ball to Kenwyne, resulting in a slick finish by Pennant for his first Stoke goal. Higgs then rockets a free kick past a motionless Harper for 3-0 three minutes later. Finally, super-sub Fuller comes on in the 88th minute, and in the last four minutes does what we expect him to do: wind up Joey Barton a bit more, and get on the end of a Walters header to rush through and belt in a scorcher. New manager Alan Pardew does not look a happy bunny.
Stoke's cracking team that day: Begovic; Wilson, Huth, Shawcross, Higginbotham; Pennant, Delap, Whelan, Etherington; Jones, Walters

02/04/11 Stoke (1) 1 Chelsea (1) 1 - Now, listen carefully. In the 8th minute Jonathan Walters picks up a Whelan clearance on the halfway line, left-hand touchline. He sneaks past David Luiz like he's not there, leaving him for dead, and tears towards the penalty area. Most expect a cross to Kenwyne or the incoming Delap, but instead he cuts inside to give him the edge over floundering defenders Essien & Terry, and whacks the ball past Cech. The Brit goes wild. It's a wonder goal against a top side, a club that have just splashed £50m on Torres, and who field superstars such as Ashley "air-rifle" Cole & Frank "moon-gazing" Lampard. "Best performance of the season, brilliant & exciting," enthuses Sue Bryan in The Sentinel. This is despite Drogba heading an equaliser after 33 minutes. Wilson then hits the bar from a superb freekick, and from the resulting corner so does Huth. Drogba hits the post and then the bar. Sub Fuller almost pinches it in the last seconds, but heads the ball across the goal when heading it in looks easier. Stoke more than a match for this lot. This time last year they were losing 0-7 to them. Makes you think. However, in the final minutes Higginbotham's season comes to a premature end with a cruciate knee ligament injury …ouch.

Tony Pulis celebrating 40 points...oh, and winning 5-0 at Wembley

09/04/11 Spurs (3) 3 Stoke (2) 2 - Yes, this is the SEVENTH Premier away defeat in a row, so Pulis decides this is the time to try something odd, like putting Marc Wilson at LEFT back. Bizarrely, it works...if you forget the first 20 minutes. After 10, Peter Crouch heads Spurs' first, with Modric's magic making it 0-2 several minutes later. Might as well go home. So what is Etherington thinking when he picks up the ball on the halfway line? Off he nonchalantly goes towards goal losing Dawson & Huddlestone along the way. Finally, he reaches the goal line and pokes the ball home from an impossible angle through Gomes's legs. Smart. The players celebrate like they haven't scored an away goal for 5 games, which, of course, they haven't. Sadly, that man Crouch (or "Nobbly Knees" as Martin Spinks calls him) beats Shawcross (yet-again!) to make it 1-3. But the goal of the game is scored shortly before half-time: Wilkinson robs dopey Bale and feeds Kenwyne. Jones decides this is the moment to unleash an unstoppable shot, stunning everyone. The big guy celebrates like he hasn't scored for 13 games, which, er, he hasn't. Actually, he just turns away like the cool dude he is. The Potters give Spurs a hard time in the second half, much to the concern of Spurs coach Joe Jordon (or "Jaws" as Martin Spinks calls him, remembering what "fun" it used to be to interview the former Stoke manager). Hm, thinks Pulis, maybe I'll try Wilson at left-back again next week...at Wembley.

17/04/11 Stoke (3) 5 Bolton 0 (FA Cup Semi-final, Wembley) – Shock horror! Stoke keep a clean sheet away from home for the first time in months! And suddenly, after years everyone's interested in the FA Cup again rather than just The Prem! Even Spinks gives it a 10 in The Sentinel! But Stoke start nervously, and Owen Coyle clearly thinks he's got Stoke rattled. Well, for 10 minutes, then Etherington hits a loose ball on the edge of the box, and the Boothen End of Wembley goes completely ballistic. 6 minutes later it's 2-0, with Huth also hitting a loose ball from the edge of the area. But 2-0 is never going to be enough, say all the folk who remember 1971, so Pennant grabs the ball and feeds it (through Gary Cahill's legs) to Kenwyne to slide home for 3-0 on the half-hour. Jon Walters finishes Bolton off on 68 minutes by running the length of the pitch, cutting inside, and firing home for 4-0. The fifth goal should have been Wilko's, but he misses, and Walters makes it 5 in the 81st. Conspiracy theorists come forward as all 5 goals go to Jaaskelsinen's hitherto-secretly-vulnerable left! Really we should feel sorry for Bolton. One of Stoke City's greatest days. Who says the semi-finals shouldn't be played at Wembley?!

23/04/11 Aston Villa (1) 1 Stoke (1) 1 - The game that Fuller comes on as a late substitute, scores the fastest disallowed goal ever, and then ruptures his Achilles tendon. With Higgs already out for the season, Stoke's FA Cup ambitions start to unravel. However, the team are still on a high, and get their first Premier away point in 8 games! This is all thanks to a Kenwyne headed goal on 20 minutes from (you'll never guess) a Delap throw. Bent equalises before the break, which somehow manages to kill off this game.

26/04/11 Stoke (2) 3 Wolves 0 - ...and then there were three. Injured, that is. Higgs, Fuller, and now, on the half-hour, Matty Etherington. Twisting slightly as he runs unchallenged on the far touchline...Matty collapses after tearing his hamstring. Wolves fans are less than sympathetic, so the Boothen bays for blood and gets it! Pennant's cross finds Kenwyne's head (1-0), Whelan's deflection finds Shawcross ("with time to light a fag" - Spinks) to poke home (2-0), and Walter's cross is casually guided in by starman Pennant with a dipping deflection (3-0). But despite rubbing the smiles off the Wolves fans' faces, this mid-week game is really only remembered for poor stretchered Matty.

30/04/11 Blackpool 0 Stoke 0 - My mate paid extra for Platinum membership just to ensure he got a ticket for this game beside the seaside. Oh dear. Apart from Kenwyne missing a sitter after rounding the keeper ("Miss Of The Season!" scream Match Of The Day), and Wilko scaring everybody by going off injured (thankfully just a dead leg), it's a bit of a dirge. Even Charlie Adam tries more of his long-range stuff to no avail. But, hell, it's another away point! More noticeably, Stoke come down to Blackpool's level, and Blackpool are going down; just as Spinksy predicted (sort of). Get this: this is the first game this season at Bloomsfield Road where BOTH sides haven't scored. Tony Pulis sees the positive, and celebrates being the first Premier manager to keep a clean sheet here. Think about it.

08/05/11 Stoke (2) 3 Arsenal (0) 1 - Stoke's Game Of The Season! Well, in the league anyway. Just edging out the defeat of Liverpool and the draw with Chelsea. Arsene

Wenger ups the ante by referring to Stoke as having rugby tactics. For once he takes it well(-ish) when the crowd start singing "2-0 to the rugby team" (to the tune of Go West) and Swing Low Sweet Chariot! How does it get to 2-0, you ask? Well, in the first half Kenwyne chests in a Pennant free-kick and then Jermaine powers through to thwack the ball into the top of the net (albeit with a teeny deflection). Van Persie starts a late resurgence with a powerful goal, but a minute later Walters makes it 3-1 from close range. Scares? Well, Pennant almost gets a red card (and a subsequent suspension) after reacting to Jack Wilshire hacking him down. But worse, it's ANOTHER bloody injury, and only a week till the Cup Final: Alex Song carelessly drops on Huth's knee, and realistically Bob should be out for the season. Abdoulaye Faye comes on for an impressive but what (curiously) turns out to be his final appearance for Stoke. If only the season ended here...

Leaping for joy! The lesser-spotted-flying Kenwyne & the spread-eagled Hart at Wembley

14/05/11 Stoke 0 Man City (0) 1 (FA Cup Final, Wembley) – ...but sadly it doesn't. Nice day out, though. In truth, many of the Stoke players are carrying injuries and shouldn't be playing, but Pulis feels loathe to trust Collins, Diao, and Faye (although Danny Pugh gets 5 minutes at the end). Somehow Huth does play, although he almost gets red-carded for that forearm across Balotelli's throat. Sorensen is the star for his finger-tip saves particularly from Balotelli. Kenwyne has a one-on-one with Joe Hart on the hour, but Citeh finally finish the job in the 74th minute, with Yaya Toure blasting home, despite Tevez offside in from the keeper. It's gutting, particularly as it's hardly a thrilling cup final. But to hold the millionaires at Wembley with this makeshift side is pretty remarkable.

17/05/11 Man City (1) 3 Stoke 0 - Dreadful, but could have been worse. This could have been the cup final, with a seriously depleted Stoke side outclassed from fairly early on. After controversially playing injured Huth and Etherington in the FA Cup final, Pulis rightly leaves them in the treatment room. But then he bewilderingly plays left-back Collins at centre-half instead of Abdoulaye Faye, which just sounds mean to Ab. Tevez scores two blinders, the second a curling free kick, and Lescott out-jumps Sorensen for another. As for the smirking Man City fans, thankfully they're actually quite generous; well, as generous as Stoke's defence.

22/05/11 Stoke 0 Wigan (0) 1

- 8 days after the FA Cup final, a full house welcome a full strength team (well, and Danny Collins). Even Etherington is back. And the task? To beat Wigan and send them down on this final day of the season. Surely this is going to be fun. But despite every effort and an early disallowed Walters goal, Stoke are turned over by a Rodallega (pronounced Roddie-ai-ger) header on 78 minutes. Wigan fans, players, manager, chairman and any passing Wigan urchin are overwhelmed with joy at the end, although actually a draw would have been enough for them in the end. A bit deflating for Potters' fans, but hell, we're the ones in Europe next year.

			Home					Away					Overall						
	Team	Pl	W	D	L	F	A	W	D	L	F	A	W	D	L	F	A	Pts	GD
1	Manchester United	38	18	1	0	49	12	5	10	4	29	25	23	11	4	78	37	80	41
2	Chelsea	38	14	3	2	39	13	7	5	7	30	20	21	8	9	69	33	71	36
3	Manchester City	38	13	4	2	34	12	8	4	7	26	21	21	8	9	60	33	71	27
4	Arsenal	38	11	4	4	33	15	8	7	4	39	28	19	11	8	72	43	68	29
5	Tottenham Hotspur	38	9	9	1	30	19	7	5	7	25	27	16	14	8	55	46	62	9
6	Liverpool	38	12	4	3	37	14	5	3	11	22	30	17	7	14	59	44	58	15
7	Everton	38	9	7	3	31	23	4	8	7	20	22	13	15	10	51	45	54	6
8	Fulham	38	8	7	4	30	23	3	9	7	19	20	11	16	11	49	43	49	6
9	Aston Villa	38	8	7	4	26	19	4	5	10	22	40	12	12	14	48	59	48	-11
10	Sunderland	38	7	5	7	25	27	5	6	8	20	29	12	11	15	45	56	47	-11
11	West Bromwich Albion	38	8	6	5	30	30	4	5	10	26	41	12	11	15	56	71	47	-15
12	Newcastle United	38	6	8	5	41	27	5	5	9	15	30	11	13	14	56	57	46	-1
13	**Stoke City**	38	10	4	5	31	18	3	3	13	15	30	13	7	18	46	48	46	-2
14	Bolton Wanderers	38	10	5	4	34	24	2	5	12	18	32	12	10	16	52	56	46	-4
15	Blackburn Rovers	38	7	7	5	22	16	4	3	12	24	43	11	10	17	46	59	43	-13
16	Wigan Athletic	38	5	8	6	22	34	4	7	8	18	27	9	15	14	40	61	42	-21
17	Wolverhampton Wanderers	38	8	4	7	30	30	3	3	13	16	36	11	7	20	46	66	40	-20
18	Birmingham City	38	6	8	5	19	22	2	7	10	18	36	8	15	15	37	58	39	-21
19	Blackpool	38	5	5	9	30	37	5	4	10	25	41	10	9	19	55	78	39	-23
20	West Ham United	38	5	5	9	24	31	2	7	10	19	39	7	12	19	43	70	33	-27

2011-12 - The Europa Adventure

28/07/11 Stoke (1) 1 Hajduk Split 0 (Europa League) – Blimey, Potters-Fortnight has only just ended, the kids have only just broken up from school, and suddenly Stoke begin their unlikely Europa League adventure. Charmingly innocent, Pulis plays a full strength team and so there's high expectation against the hot Croats from Split, with their rabid-looking (in the nicest possible way) fans. But Pulis' preparation is extraordinarily thorough. A 3rd minute goal from a Walters header settles things nicely, although the only thing that shuts up the Split fans is the sight of Delap's long-throw - they have never seen the like. Kenwyne & Huth should make it 2 or 3-0, but the 26,322 crowd is satisfied with this win.

04/08/11 Hajduk Split 0 Stoke (0) 1 (Europa) – Many thought the Europa dream might end here, in front of the intimidating cacophony of 30,000 Split fans. But Pulis sides are nothing if not tough & resolute, and give as good as they get. (They also get a record THREE yellow cards for "time-wasting"; who'd have thought.) Walters takes a lot of abuse and stick – probably for that first-leg goal. Jon is eventually replaced in the 86th minute by Ryan Shotton, but it's Shotton who gets on the end of a Deano cross to score in time-added! Oh, the look of delight on the Fenton-boy's face. OK, so it's credited as a Milicevic own-goal, but what do they know? Woodgate makes his debut in this devil's pit, but the real heroes are the 600 delirious Stoke fans who faced up to this malarkey on that day.

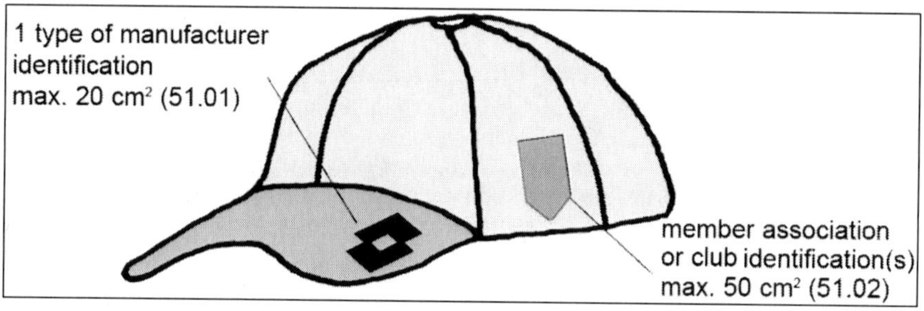

UEFA had cap restrictions for coaches at Europa League games…& ignored by Tony Pulis

14/08/11 Stoke 0 Chelsea 0 - In fact, Split is excellent preparation for playing a less than prepared Chelsea. But it doesn't matter who is managing The Blues – this week it is boy-wonder AVB (Andre Villas-Boas) – they're always tough nuts to crack, with a team stuffed full of household names (if you read OK Magazine). They may knock the ball around with aplomb on the floor, but they look ludicrously small in the air. After last season's monster 1-1 draw with the Walters wonder goal, this performance is commendable albeit a little disappointing. With Wilko & Shotton on the bench, Pulis punts for Huth as right-back (!) with newboy Jonathan Woodgate successfully partnering Shawcross in the middle. Amusingly everyone waits with baited breath for Woody to go down injured, but in fact it's Etherington with an attack of dodgy-Fuller-shoulder who's the victim. Loads of penalty appeals on each side. Terry surely handling in the box is a good one. The funniest though is Woodgate shoving Torres; but then that's a sport in itself.

18/08/11 FC Thun 0 Stoke (1) 1 (Europa) – After Split, this is weirdly tranquil. Thun's new stadium only holds 10,000 (today there are 7850), the pitch is plastic, and as this is Switzerland, everything's running as clockwork as a cuckoo-clock. In come Pugh, Tonge and new-boy old-boy defender Matthew Upson, but who would have bet one of these three would hit a left-foot drive into the corner of the net in the 19th minute? Yes, it's Danny Pugh's big moment. Mind you, head-bandaged Walters should make it safe late on, before & after he is pulled down by keeper Da Costa. I say "after" because AFTER the keeper is red-carded, Thun's winger goes in goal and saves a one-on-one with Jonathan. Fun fact: Stoke are forced to wear their old blue away strip, and this is the ONLY win they ever have wearing these shirts.

21/08/11 Norwich (1) 1 Stoke (0) 1 - His name is Jonathan Walters, City hero from 2010/11. But to newly promoted Norwich playing their eagerly awaited first home game, he is ex-Ipswich, and boy do they remind him. So, on the hour, after being tripped on the very edge (ie. outside) of the penalty area (& seeing Leon Barnett sent off), he has the chance to silence the baying crowd from the penalty spot. But no. Ruddy saves to his left, and Walters starts a slow but steady spiral downwards into what will become a frustrating season. To add insult to injury, former Stokie De Laet puts Norwich on course for their first Premier win with an unchallenged first half header. Stoke look sluggish after winning in Thun only 3 days before. But a sickener for Delia's mob: a whopping FOUR minutes into stoppage time Kenwyne heads in Whelan's cross. How do we get away with this? Well, their manager is one Paul Lambert, who can't believe his bad luck at not being able to hold on to 3 points. (Spoiler alert!)

25/08/11 Stoke (3) 4 FC Thun (0) 1 (Europa) – Martin Spinks compares Tony Pulis to Napoleon for his ruthless approach to the Europa League (& his odd looking hat, probably). Here, Stoke take no prisoners: Upson heads home Pennant's early corner, and Kenwyne heads in Pennant's cross for 2-0 by the half-hour. Even Whelan gets in on the act for 3-0 before the break. Sub Tom Soares crosses for Kenwyne for 4-0, before Wittwer hits a late consolation. Split & Thun are no easy-meat, so many are impressed by Stoke's progression – many better clubs have fallen by this stage. Stoke fans start renewing their passports and the Stoke Board go looking for their wallet.

28/08/11 West Brom 0 Stoke (0) 1 - Now let's be serious. Nope, let's not! Ha ha ha ha ha ha ha ha ha ha ha ha ha ha ha ha ha ha ha ha ha...well, you get the idea. No, really, get this: It's literally the 90th minute of this rather average tie (or "toss game" as the 500th edition of The Oatcake describes it). It's only 3 days after flattening Thun, and Pulis hasn't even started blaming extra Europa fixtures yet. Meanwhile, Roy Hodgson's WBA look unable to knock the skin off a rice pudding - so nothing new there. This really should be the end for Roy, but strangely isn't. A few months later, he's England's manager! Anyway, 90th minute, and Walters lobs the ball nonchalantly towards the penalty area. Shotton, a late sub for Pennant, lollops after it like a frolicking puppy. But surely goalkeeper Foster will gather – his hands are practically on the ball – or defender Tamas will clear – he's ready to hoof it. As the ball bounces between them, and they remain undecided as to what to do (duh!), Shotton nips between them with his foot suspiciously raised, robs them, and smugly prods the ball into an empty net. It's got to be one of the funniest moments against West Brom yet. "Bonkers," says Martin Spinks. It's now only one defeat for Stoke in their last 28 league fixtures against Albion over the last 23 years. "Cheeky," says The Oatcake. "Terrible...Fabulous." Laugh? Stopping me is a real, real problem.

10/09/11 Stoke (1) 1 Liverpool 0 - Stoke have a week off, which is bad news for the pockets of the Coates family. Tony Pulis somehow manages to sign Peter Crouch for £10m! He also picks up another striker (yes, this is Pulis we are talking about!), Cameron Jerome for £4m. What is going on?! Wilson Palicios (£6m?) seems to be the booby prize for Pulis taking Woodgate and Crouch from Spurs, but surely the gaffer will find a use for him. Eventually, Dalglish's side roll into town, and get beat by a 21st minute penalty. Jamie Carragher had thrown his arms lovingly around a striker once too often for referee Clattenburg, and victim Walters blasts it down the middle to make up for his Norwich miss. New boy Crouch does ok, Matthew Upson also makes his Stoke league debut, and a rather unfit Palacios even makes a late appearance. But they all spend most the game heroically defending, even against one Charlie Adam.

Peter Crouch unveiled to the press & found to be not much taller than Tony Pulis

15/09/11 Dynamo Kiev (0) 1 Stoke (0) 1 (Europa) – Not at the huge Olympic stadium, but at Kiev's dinky little stadium round the corner. Serves them right, as Stoke look just as much a home there as they do. As proof, new boy Cameron Jerome, bought if only to stop him scoring against Stoke, slots home from a Shotton cross on 55 minutes. Despite the efforts of Shevchenko and Da Silva, Stoke hang on till time-added when Vukojevic scores a dodgy-looking equaliser. But Stoke's squad is using its depth well, with Diao and Palacios pulling their weight.

18/09/11 Sunderland (3) 4 Stoke 0 - After only conceding a miserly 3 goals in 9 games (including the one in Ukraine just 3 days before), the heavens open on Stoke. It literally pours down with goals. Now, c'mon, only Shawcross, Huth & Jerome started both this & the Kiev game, and Whitehead & Walters were only late subs in the Ukraine. The other 6 of the starting 11 *DIDN'T EVEN GO*. So why the likes of Woodgate and Begovic perform so poorly is anyone's guess. Although the game is particularly dreadful, it's the first half hour that goes down as horrifically inept. The first goal goes straight through Begovic like a red hot poker. Then Woodgate decides it's time to head home an impressive own goal. Finally, Shawcross deflects a shot past his own keeper. Manager Steve Bruce basks in the glory, which makes a change from the normal abuse he gets (he's lost 8 of his last 9 home league games and is on the way out). A fourth goal on the hour from a free kick conceded by the particularly tardy Huth is fair enough. How does The Oatcake describe this game? A "horror show", a "real dog", and "..." er, oh dear, I don't think I can repeat that!

20/09/11 Stoke 0 Spurs 0 (Carling Cup) – Stoke win 7-6 on penalties. Yes, ANOTHER, cup game, and this despite a "bye" to the 3rd round. The depth of Stoke's squad is really paying off, as despite several changes, Pulis can safely start with the likes of Sorensen, Shotton, Upson, & Palacios, and even when Kenwyne hamstrings after 10 minutes, Crouch is on hand to give his old club a hard time. By a hard time, I mean a gruelling 0-0, extra-time, and then a lengthy penalty shoot out. Spinks: "Like a Ken Dodd routine, it threatened to go on all night". Despite Pennant hitting the bar with his spot kick, it reaches 6-6. Shotton then sinks his, and Luongo's is saved by Sorensen. Pulis looks at his watch and wonders how he's going to keep this up.

24/09/11 Stoke (0) 1 Man Utd (1) 1 - Stoke's first Premier point against United, and Crouch's first goal for Stoke in only his 3rd start. Pete is particularly pleased as it's his first EVER goal against United in his 14 games against them for 14 different Premier teams (actually it's only 6 teams, it just seems like 14). On the half-hour Nani drives a shot into the corner for 1-0. Amazingly Andy Wilkinson nearly equalises with a pile-driver that goalie de Gea can only tip on to the bar. But suddenly, Crouch heads home an Etherington corner on 52 minutes, and the place erupts. What's more this Stoke side press for a winner - yes, a winner! - hitting more shots overall and more on target than The Reds, who have been storming it in the league till now. Rooney is already out with a hamstring, and Hernandez goes off after only 11 minutes after a playful push by Woodgate that embarrassingly goes unpunished. This is only 6 days after losing so badly at Sunderland, and only 4 days after beating Spurs on penalties in the cup. But it does show that - tired or not - Stoke players can raise their game when the time fancies it. More importantly, this supposedly-bankable game is the one that later costs Alex Ferguson's United the Championship to Aguerooo. Well, probably.

29/09/11 Stoke (1) 2 Besiktas (1) 1 (Europa) – Stoke's SEVENTH cup game, and it's still September! Are the 23,551 crowd exhausted yet? No way. Even when Hilbert gets the better of Huth to score on 13 minutes, Crouch equalises 2 minutes later after Shawcross heads down for him from a Deano corner. Pennant comes on to help pound the Turks with their wobbly keeper, and after Crouch is molested, sub Walters sinks the 78th minute spot-kick winner. Stoke are motoring on their Grand Tour.

02/10/11 Swansea (1) 2 Stoke 0 - Despite fielding the same side that got a draw against Man Utd (well, minus Etherington), it looks more like the barmy side that started so badly against Sunderland. And this against Brendan Rodgers' newly promoted high-flyers, whom everyone thought were easy-meat. Could this be another Stoke-weary performance, caused by playing Besiktas 3 days before? Dozily conceding an early penalty (here we go again), and then a late second, this says more about Stoke's defence (Shawcross & Woodgate respectively) than is worth saying. Jerome livens things up after replacing Delap - Delap is today's idea of a left winger. Whelan hits the post, curling the ball around the wall from a free kick, and...oh dear, I've run out of things to say about this game. Thank God.

15/10/11 Stoke (0) 2 Fulham 0 - A surprise in store for fans: Stoke actually do have a midfield! After a frustrating first half, Pennant turns Fulham inside out on the right, whilst Whelan slogs away in the middle, quelling the extremely irritating Danny Murphy. Then there's Etherington who assists two late goals, although the first on 80 minutes is a shot heading off god-knows-where until Walters diverts it in. But the star is Rory Delap, who heads powerfully past Schwarzer from a Matty free kick. It's the 2nd of only SEVEN league goals that come from midfielders for the whole season! Despite fewer appearances, Delap will score more than Pennant & Whelan put-together. Mention should also go to another midfielder, the very late substitute Salif Diao, if only for Martin Spinks describing him as "Auditioning for The Phantom Of The Opera" just coz he's sporting a face mask for a fractured jaw. Nah, surely, he's "Diao-Man", maverick superhero returning from saving the world. You think not?

20/10/11 Stoke (3) 3 Maccabi Tel Aviv 0 (Europa) – Forget that Stoke are 3-0 up in half an hour. Forget Kenwyne's header from Deano's corner, Jerome's header from Matty's free-kick, & Jermaine rounding the keeper to set up Shotton. Forget that Jerome is 2nd-yellowed before half-time. Forget all that. This is the game where pantomime villain, Yoav David Ziv, is sent off for kicking his boot at the linesman, after it comes off in a clash with Shotton. You can't buy comedy like this. It makes up for his contribution towards Jerome's red-card. Actually, this is the game that sub Palacios does that killer through-ball to Kenwyne...and then never does it again.

23/10/11 Arsenal (1) 3 Stoke (1) 1 - Outmanoevered by Arsene Wenger, it's another away defeat after a Europa win. Stoke run around genuinely thinking they're at least on for a point, only for Wenger to unleash the Van Persie goal-machine from the side-lines on 66 minutes. And 7 minutes later it's all over. Stoke's moment of joy comes on the half-hour, when Crouch scores from a disputed free-kick, but the 60,000 crowd know how it's going to end: predictably.

26/10/11 Stoke (1) 1 Liverpool (0) 2 (Carling Cup) – With Stoke on a run of 9 home games unbeaten, Dalglish's Liverpool don't look too sure of themselves. After having a decent goal disallowed, Jon Walters then sets up Kenwyne just before the break for 1-0, & that could be enough. But along comes Suarez to ruin things, curling one in the corner on 53 minutes, and even heads in the winner 4 minutes from time. After facing Spurs &

Liverpool, Stoke would have next faced Chelsea then Man City! Liverpool beat both, then are taken to penalties in the final by Cardiff. It's a strange old world.

31/10/11 Stoke (0) 1 Newcastle (2) 3 - That Demba Ba game. Pulis passed on £9m Ba in the January window as his medical threw up an injury. As a result Ba goes for a song to West Ham & then the Toons for a pittance. A dozen goals later, he turns up with the remarkably over-achieving Newcastle, and crucifies The Potters. Stoke fans are bitter with him for some reason, despite Ba repeating in the press that he was all set (& happy) to be a Stokie several months before. He runs rings round Shawcross, Woodgate, Upson, Huth, Wilson...well, just about everybody. A flying header on 12 minutes and a well-worked finish on 39 mins for 0-2 leave Stoke fans infuriated. To make things interesting, or maybe just out of boredom, Ba then tries pushing Crouch over in the penalty area on 75 minutes, with Walters scoring from the spot. But 6 minutes later, just as Stoke look like they may make a comeback, Robert Huth gives Leon Best a hearty shove, naively hoping that no one will notice. Ba gets his hat-trick from the subsequent penalty. Yes, a hat-trick. Salt, wound, ... well, you know the rest. As for Demba, well, nobody loves a smart arse. Stoke are 11th.

03/11/11 Maccabi Tel Aviv (0) 1 Stoke (0) 2 (Europa) – You go all the way to Israel, and it pours down with rain for the first time in 6 months. The Stoke fans must have brought it with them, reckon some, whilst others go in search of Noah just in case. Meanwhile, Higgs is back in a sturdy-looking back-five, and Deano has another blinder. Whitehead even scores just after the break, and then sets up substitute Crouch (a local celebrity) just after the hour. Maccabi pull one back, but what chance have they against this mystical rain...I mean, against this Stoke side.

06/11/11 Bolton (2) 5 Stoke 0 - No, Begovic didn't fly all the way to Tel Aviv like half the team did. So, what reason does he have for picking up Whelan's mis-kick into his penalty area with only a minute gone? Ref Howard Web reckons it's a back-pass, and the Stoke players stand around aghast. So, what reason does Begovic have for letting Klasnic grab the ball, take the free kick for Kevin Davies to score in an empty net? On 23 minutes he's still not quite in the land of the living, with the ball rolling to his feet. So what reason does he have for clearing so carelessly straight to Eagles, who blasts it back and past him for 2-0. The defence looks rocky without Shawcross and his groin strain, but even the strike-force with Cameron Jerome, who also didn't go to Israel, looks weary. After SEVEN straight home defeats, Bolton are happy to throw in three more second-half goals to make Stoke look completely ridiculous, giving the same scoreline as that cup semi-final only months before. Revenge? Listen, six months later Stoke send Bolton down on the last day. THAT'S what I call revenge.

19/11/11 Stoke (1) 2 QPR (2) 3 - This is Stoke's fourth league defeat in a row. And it's to Joey Barton's newly promoted QPR. Damnit! It starts well enough with Crouch setting up Walters to score on 8 minutes; c'mon, surely this'll be a doddle. But then Higginbotham, making his ONLY league start, loses Heider Helguson for 1-1. After Pulis bows to supporter pressure, and finally plays Huth & Shawcross together at the back ("The one issue that Stoke fans have been talking about, with good reason," grunt The Oatcake) ...he finds they're not much better, and soon Stoke are 1-3 down. Crouch heads on for Shawcross to make it 2-3, but it's a waste if time, even with Fuller making a late comeback appearance or Sorensen's recall in goal. The ref even misses two clear penalties (on Pennant and Huth). After this game, QPR spiral downwards till they sack Neil Warnock. Helpfully, Martin Spinks writes "Walters continues to look clinical in front of goal", which in fact is the kiss of death as he doesn't score another outfield league goal till the very end of the season.

26/11/11 Stoke (1) 3 Blackburn (0) 1 - Thankfully the civil-war they call Blackburn Rovers rolls into town. Amazingly, Steve Kean is still in charge, but a Delap header, a Whelan deflection and a Crouch route-one volley makes everyone wonder why. It keeps Stoke mid-table at least. A late albeit impressive consolation goal goes Rovers' way, and Kean thinks he's a hero. Embarrassing, really. Blackburn are bottom of the league.

01/12/11 Stoke (0) 1 Dynamo Kiev (1) 1 (Europa) – As Kiev made Stoke play in their mini-stadium, so Stoke should make Kiev play at Newcastle Town. Sadly, it doesn't happen, and 23,774 watch Stoke progress to the knockout stage, the only British side to do so this season. Upson deflects in an own-goal on the half-hour, but Stoke wake up in the 2nd half, even bringing on Ricardo Fuller. Eventually, Kenwyne heads in Pennant's cross with 10 minutes left, and a point will see Stoke through. Begovic makes a brilliant save late on as he tries to regain his first-team place (after Bolton), but the likes of Upson, Palacios and Diao looking a little jaded.

04/12/11 Everton 0 Stoke (1) 1 – It's a miracle! With only ONE away league win ALL YEAR (and that was at West Brom, so it doesn't really count), this result was NOT expected. Betting companies all over the world lose their shirt on this one. Whitehead's volley is diverted by Huth past Tim Howard after only 15 minutes. It's Stoke's first win at Goodison since 1981, when Adrian Heath scores a late winner in front of only 15,000 supporters, before going home to celebrate Bucks Fizz winning the Eurovision Song Contest. In contrast, 33,219 watch this rainy encounter. How times have changed. More Moyes moaning: "I thought the ref had a poor game." Oh dear, here we go again. "What wins games is goals and they got the goal and we didn't." Really? How has he got away with this sort of twaddle all these years?!

11/12/11 Stoke (2) 2 Spurs (0) 1 - Massive! A superb win against a star-studded Harry Redknapp side who've just won 10 out of 11 games. And who is charged with stopping this torrent of talent? Yes, Woodgate and Shotton!! Yes, Redknapp reckons they're a liability on Stoke's right, and throws the rampant Gareth Bale, and then Aaron Lennon, and then finally substitute Jermain Defoe at them. But the City boys hold firm, and reborn Etherington slots home two first half goals to punish the not-as-clever-as-it-thinks Spurs defence. They can't even deal with Shotton's long throws; he's noticed drying his balls with his designer towel-vest (spotted by wee Lee Dixon on MoTD2). Ref Chris Foy's decisions for once go Stoke's way, much to the annoyance of Redknapp & his animated side-kick Mr Joseph Jordan ("His arms outstretched like some kind of rabid extra from Highlander," observes Mr Spinks.) Adebayor has a perfectly good goal ruled out; Shawcross handles off the line; and then a luckless Kaboul even gets himself a second yellow late on. Add to that Walters sticking his fingers up a defender's nose & Crouch's handball before setting up Matty... ah, bliss. But these are balanced out by Modric tumbling down after Whelan's boot barely nicks Luka. Look carefully at the replay, and you'll see Modric already falling down long before Whelan taps his shin. Adebayor sinks the penalty past the otherwise brilliant Sorensen for 2-1. When it comes to the ex-Spurs players Redknapp can't believe his eyes: Woodgate plays a whole game uninjured, Crouch & Etherington tear his defence apart, & to add serious insult to injury (!) Pulis sends on Palacios as a sub! Harry flashes Tony a look that seems to say "Are you taking the michael?" I think he is, Harry, I think he is. To cap it all, Spurs are eliminated from The Europa League, whilst Stoke progress. Mint.

14/12/11 Besiktas (0) 3 Stoke (1) 1 (Europa) – Playing in the Europa League isn't all laughter & flowers, & can get ropey. Here in the incendiary Turkish stadium, Fuller hits a beauty (his last ever Stoke goal) to make it 1-0 on the half-hour. But on the hour, Upson (captain for the day) concedes a penalty & is red-carded. Soon it is 1-3, and Stoke players even have to avoid flying debris from the crowd. But Pulis is satisfied. He starts Diego Arismendi, and only really has one substitute (Pennant on early to replace Wilko). The other subs are Nash, Michael Clarkson and Lucas Dawson.

ESPN have their say on Stoke's successful formula

17/12/11 Wolves (1) 1 Stoke (0) 2 - TWO AWAY WINS IN A ROW? Yes, you are reading this correctly! What is going on?! Pulis starts with a strong 11, none of whom went to Turkey. But he soon realises he's made a terrible mistake at right back. Here we find Mr J.Woodgate, "A disaster waiting to happen," warn The Oatcake (after the event). He is being annihilated by Matt Jarvis, and is amazingly not second-yellowed for tripping Jarvis in the box (Hunt scores from the penalty). Woody is only too happy to be subbed for Pennant, who is "mysteriously" out of favour behind the scenes, but who inspires a right royal comeback, despite playing in Turkey 3 days earlier. However, it is Robert Huth who turns out to be the unlikely hero as he takes a free kick from miles away that deflects past Hennessey for 1-1 on the hour. Mick McCarthy's mob begin to panic, & 10 minutes later Crouch heads the winner. "And stats not all," says Martin Spinks; apparently Stoke haven't won at Molineux in the top flight since just before Waddo was forced out in 1977. Makes you think.

21/12/11 Man City (2) 3 Stoke 0 - Now this is something we do really well: turn up at the Etihad and lose. Stoke could do this all day everyday. Without Shawcross, Whelan & Crouch - arguably the backbone of the side - we'll say they were injured - it's a waste of time. Woodgate, Upson & Palicios start a game together for the first time. In fact

Upson & Woodgate have only ever played together for the defeats at Bolton (0-5) & home to Newcastle (1-3). Man City have Hart, Richards, Kompany, Lescott, Toure, Nasri, Silva, & Aguero. Amazingly, Stoke last 29 minutes before Aguero scores a marginally offside goal. And when Whitehead & Palacios each lose the ball in midfield, it's soon 3-0. But wait, an icon comes on as sub in the 68th minute. It's Ricardo Fuller. The millionaires are so rattled they immediately throw on Balotelli. Are they serious? Is Pulis, for that matter??

26/12/11 Stoke 0 Aston Villa 0 - Dreadful. Changing the kickoff time to 7.45 for the benefit of Sky TV winds-up the fans, and is savaged by the critics. Pulis isn't impressed either. But this is nothing to the atrocity of mind-numbing proportions that unfolds to those dumb enough to turn on SkySports1 on a Boxing Day night. Even Pennant FINALLY coming on in the 71st minute to help out Kenwyne can't transform this turkey. "Forgettable," reckons Martin Spinks. "Forgettable," reckon The Oatcake. It was, well, ...oh, I can't remember.

31/12/11 Stoke (0) 2 Wigan (1) 2 - More of that same Boxing Day forgettableness – despite recalls for Pennant, Wilko and Crouch – until the last 15 minutes, when it goes completely mad. Up until then, the only thing to happen is Rodallega crossing for Victor Moses to put Wigan 1-0 up on half-time. But Pulis eventually turns things round by finally putting on Jerome in the 74th minute. A couple of minutes later he's effectively won a penalty & got Caldwell sent off for hand-ball! Talk about impact. Walters sinks the spot-kick for 1-1, before Jerome races clear minutes later to brilliantly slip it home for 2-1. Sadly, Shotton then concedes an unlucky penalty, and Wigan waste enough time bringing on a sub to take it that it ends 2-2. Dave Kemp thinks Palacios is man of the match for completing a whole game, but the jury is still out on him. (Out of their minds, probably.) Stoke are 8th.

02/01/12 Blackburn (0) 1 Stoke (2) 2 - Steve Kean is STILL in charge of Blackburn! How? Maybe it's the points he's just brought home from Man Utd and Liverpool. The home crowd even give him a huge cheer, albeit ironically, when Pedersen accidently barges into him like a ton of bricks, knocking him flying. Comedy gold. Two smashing goals by Crouch in the 17th & 45th minute kill the game off, till a guy called Goodwillie pulls one back after 69 minutes. In fairness, Crouch's first is against the run of play. (Blackburn have already had a goal disallowed.) He chests Whitehead's lob, blasts it home, then does some funny shapes with his fingers. Turns out it's his 100th league goal. His second is thwacked in from an Etherington cross. It's noted that Delap comes on late ("Thrown on to add late solidarity," purrs Martin Spinks.), followed by Diao ("Ditto the old fella." Ditto the old fella??? You can't say that!)

07/01/12 Gillingham (1) 1 Stoke (2) 3 (FA Cup) – Oh dear. However much Paul Scally – Pulis' ex-boss & arch-enemy – tries to turn Gillingham fans against TP, the more they seem to like the capped-crusader. Against all Scally's instructions, they give Pulis a hearty welcome, whereas Scally tries to ban him from most areas of the club, apart from the technical-area. And from that area Pulis ensures this doesn't turn into Hartlepool because he REALLY wants to win this, probably more than any game this season. So, the first half-hour are uncomfortable with The Gills taking the lead, redeemed when Walters fires home for 1-1. And the other Pulis-boys combine to make it 2-1 on the stroke of half-time: a Shotton long-throw headed on to the bar by Shawcross for Jerome to volley in. The players are spared a rant at half-time, and Huth even heads in a Palacios corner after the break for 3-1. For some reason Scally isn't so chatty after this game.

14/01/12 Liverpool 0 Stoke 0 - Getting a draw against Kenny Dalglish's Liverpool isn't what it used to be. Even Blackburn got a point there on Boxing Day. The Pulis plan seems solely to be Walters deserting Crouch to play on the right in a crowded midfield. Withering Dalglish eventually slings on Carroll, who falls over whenever Huth looks at him. Ref Howard Webb is suitably unimpressed. There is a poignant strategy moment when Dalglish throws on rampant Bellamy, only for Pulis to send on Wilkinson to snuff him out. Check-mate to Pulis in his 400th game as Stoke manager.

The BBC have their say on Stoke's successful formula

22/01/12 Stoke (0) 1 West Brom (1) 2 - The last time The Baggies won at Stoke, Michael Foot was leader of the Labour Party, no one had heard of the Falkland Islands, and most of the Stoke team hadn't even been born. Mind you, 30 years ago Roy Hodgson is very much as he is now. With everyone dreaming of going to Valencia in the Europa League (or the cheap ticket, Derby in the FA Cup), this fixture seemed to disappear under the radar...until we lost it. Firstly, James Morrison strolls through the midfield to hit a "possessed" swerving shot past a startled Sorensen for 1-0 after 35 minutes. Then Walters misses a typically dubious second-half penalty. Then after Jerome heads a tumultuous late equaliser, West Brom have the bloody nerve to hit an injury-time winner from a "possessed" free kick past a startled Sorensen! Cheeky or what! Finally, Martin Spinks goes completely bonkers: "No true football fan could deny Albion their moment of glory after so much heartache down the years, particularly after patently looking the better team"!! Nonsense! True football fans love stuff like Albion cocking it up time & time again... (continued on page 274)

28/01/12 Derby 0 Stoke (1) 2 (FA Cup) – Stoke's squad stretched even further for more cup action, but this strong and assertive team aren't giving mid-Championship Derby any breaks, particularly in front of 5,500 travelling Stokies. Hell, no. Jerome, reckoning Huth is taking too long to shoot, blasts in after only 5 minutes. Robert finally gets his goal from a late volley from a Pennant corner. Nine away wins this season. For a Pulis side. Sobering.

21/01/12 Man Utd (1) 2 Stoke 0 - In the absence of Salif Diao (a human sacrifice for impossible-to-win games), Pulis decides to recall Pennant (supposedly out-of-favour for unknown reasons from around the time of The Goodison Park game, probably car-related), Palacios (supposedly dropped from the WBA game as it was too "windy"), & Kenwyne Jones (in the supposed dream-team coupling with Crouch). Although this "team" battle away commendably (yeah, one shot on target), two dodgy penalties sink The Potters. But then if you do allow your own forwards into your own penalty area, then you are just asking for trouble. In this case Pennant & Walters are the offenders. After 5,500 Stokies cheered on the cup win at Derby 3 days earlier, only 500 bothered for this inevitably depressing (& expensive) evening fixture.

04/02/12 Stoke 0 Sunderland (0) 1 - The snow comes down, Huth is sent off, the Black Cats sneak a winner, and Stoke's home record is beginning to look calamitous. There's little else to say. Martin "Mr Red Card" Atkinson is probably at fault for dismissing Huth, particularly when the replays all clearly show Huth's foot DOWN in the fateful challenge with David Meyler, who "rolls around on the floor as though he's been hit by a bus" (The Oatcake). But what Huth is doing lunging towards a player in these poor conditions so far up the pitch is anyone's guess. Instead the fans barrack Pulis for taking the beloved (but underperforming) Pennant off to put on a replacement defender (& it doesn't help that it's Woodgate). James McClean's solo goal, carving through Stoke's defence, is the only impressive thing on show. His new manager, Martin O'Neil seems jolly pleased.

11/02/12 Fulham (2) 2 Stoke (0) 1 - Fourth league defeat in a row. Well, Stoke are rubbish in London this season. Newboy Russian Pogrebnyak (and that's just the abbreviated version) picks up a Riise mis-kick, and it's 1-0 after 16 minutes. Dempsey's super strike on the half hour hits the crossbar then bounces in off Sorensen for 2-0. After an hour of this nonsense, although it seems longer, Pulis brings on Fuller, Pennant & long-thrower Shotton. Stoke awake as if from a dream, and Fulham start to panic. Fuller wins a corner, and Shawcross heads it in from Pennant with 12 minutes left for 1-2. Stoke should equalise, but don't. "Why didn't we start the game with the team we finished with," question The Oatcake, quizzically. Coz Sparky's not still their manager. But then Crouch misses enough chances for Martin Spinks to start to question his goal ratio for a £10m player ("a goal every 5 hours"?!). C'mon, cut him some slack. Stoke are 13th with 30 points, 9 points above relegation. Surely no need to panic?

16/02/12 Stoke 0 Valencia (1) 1 (Europa) – Squeezed out of the Champions League by Chelsea, Valencia drop into the Europa League. How fair is that? Here they turn up at The Brit well prepared for all Stoke can throw at them (Delap included). However, they're almost caught out in the first few seconds as Walters races through and just slides the ball wide. But Valencia gain control, and Topal drives in a cracker on 36 minutes. Stoke struggle to get a grip on the game, even with the likes of Pennant, Etherington, Crouch, Walters plus a strong bench. The choice of Palacios over the likes of Whelan or Whitehead is the only curio. Never mind. Anyone fancy a trip to the return game?

19/02/12 Crawley 0 Stoke (1) 2 (FA Cup 5th) – Three days after Valencia, it's a trip to League Two side Crawley Town in Sussex. Never a dull moment. A mixed bag of Stoke players – Danny Collins even gets a start – are no match for giant-killers Crawley. They need a kick up the butt, so Delap is sent off on 17 minutes, as Hunt over-eggs his tumble. But it backfires for Crawley as Stoke start to play like they've got 12 men when they only actually have 10. Shawcross is unexpectedly floored in the box, and Walters sinks the penalty just before the break. Crouch seals it with a header from a Whelan free-kick on 52. Another cup-run, and Delap's red card is rescinded. Win-win.

23/02/12 Valencia (1) 1 Stoke 0 (Europa) – Truth is, I've never met anyone who can remember where they were when JFK was killed, but every Stoke fan remembers where they were when they heard Pulis' Valencia team. What?? Arismendi, Woodgate and Diao haven't played for weeks; Fuller, Kenwyne & Collins are relative strangers; Sorensen gets this game, which means relinquishing his first-team spot to Asmir; they're joined by Palacios, Delap and Jerome, but it's only Huth who is a regular first-teamer, and the bench (only 4) is Shotton, Pennant, Begovic and Lucas Dawson from Kidsgrove. The several thousand Stoke fans enjoying the sunny trip to Spain are bemused by the choice. But the team gamely give it their all in Valencia's imposing Mestalla stadium to the strains of "Delilah". Kenwyne's chances come & go, and Jerome & Fuller stir up trouble, but Jonas (not Jones) buries the gig on 23 minutes, breaking away when Stoke should have had a free-kick. Pennant & Shotton come on to make it 4-4-2, but it ends 0-2 on aggregate, and the Europa dream is finally over (more down to UEFA's rules than Stoke's ability). But nothing ruins the fun of the merry Stoke fans singing their way through The Mestalla. Valencia go on to be knocked out in the semi-final by eventual winners Atletico Madrid, an original Europa side, who started their campaign in July just like Stoke.

26/02/12 Stoke (2) 2 Swansea 0 – Stoke turn over flighty passing Swansea in a "must-win" game. (League wins, particularly at home, are alarmingly scarce.) The starting line-up only has Shotton from the Valencia away game (he was a late sub) 3 days earlier. Martin O'Neill pulled this stunt with Villa, and didn't get away with it, remember. Some of the rest of the odds'n'sods team that played in Spain watch from the bench. After an early scare, the Swans obligingly roll over to an Upson header from an Etherington corner on 24, and a Crouch header before the break from (get this) a long throw, albeit from Shotton not Delap. Happy days are here again…

03/03/12 Stoke (0) 1 Norwich 0 – It's Paul Lambert's first ever visit to The Brit, and the question is, does he feel lucky? Matthew Etherington puts in an unexpectedly good performance & an unexpectedly good goal. With back-to-back wins, there is no more talk of relegation. What else? Well, the goal is on 72 minutes. Tony Pulis surprisingly subs Walters for Jerome who steers a throw into Matty's path. Ethers then sweeps past a defender down the left of the 6 yard box, before blasting a left-footer past goalie Ruddy. Ruddy looks dazed as if he'd forgotten Matt was left-footed. Duh! Norwich complain it wasn't Stoke's throw. Well, it's a bit late now, chaps. Afterwards, Lambert goes on & on about it, but Pulis just says, "I haven't seen it, but if that is right & we got a little bit of luck then I think we deserved it with our overall performance." So, Lambert not so lucky then.

10/03/12 Chelsea (0) 1 Stoke 0 - The game in which Ricardo Fuller stamps on pain-in-the-arse Ivanovic after less than half an hour. Curiously, the ref doesn't think this is so funny. Nor do Stoke fans, who think he should know better (particularly as John Terry is a perfectly acceptable alternative). Ivanovic stays down pretending he's been impaled to the ground liked a vampire. (Maybe Ric noticed something we didn't.) 10 man Stoke lose to a Drogba goal; he rounds the keeper in the 2nd half. But everyone's missed the point: and that is, what the hell is Ricardo doing starting ahead of Crouch, Jerome & Pennant for the 1st time in 11 months?! And in such a big game at Chelsea, who under Di Matteo are on the march to win the European Cup?! Well, the clue is that Salif Diao (yes, he's still with the club!) starts in midfield, which means this is one of those games that Pulis has written off, and in some ways you reap what you sow.

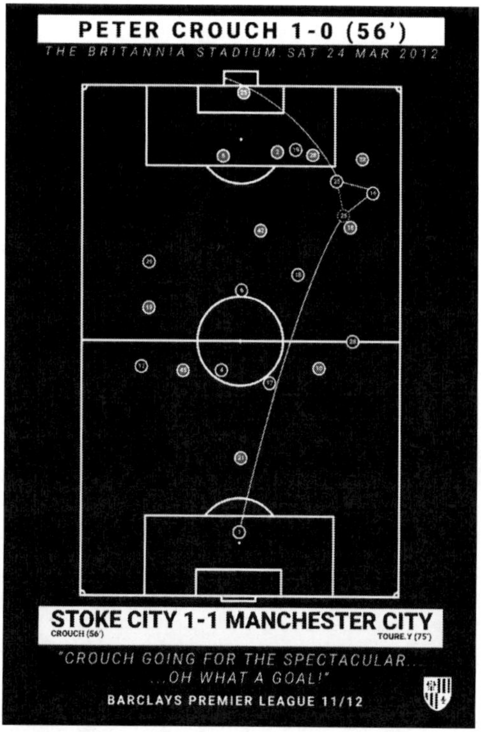

18/03/12 Liverpool (1) 2 Stoke (1) 1 (FA Cup 6th) – Stoke go out of the cup by 2-1 thanks to Suarez, after Stoke's tall centre-forward scores a first-half goal to put the wind up The Reds. Hang on, haven't we done this one before? No, that was the Carling Cup, and anyway, this one's at Anfield. Suarez hits the first on 23, but it's Crouch this time (not Kenwyne) who startles his ex-club 3 minutes later heading in from a Matty corner. Downing drives home the winner just before the hour, and finally after EIGHTEEN cup games, Stoke get to concentrate on the Premier League.

21/03/12 Spurs (0) 1 Stoke (0) 1 - Oh hello, Tony is at it again. After fielding a full-strength squad at Anfield, Pulis mixes it up at White Hart Lane. In come Jerome, Palacios, & (you guessed it) good ole Salif Diao. You can't help but fear the worst. But then something weird happens: Diao goes off injured early on, and Palacios is withdrawn soon afterwards. Almost by accident Harry's Spurs have been hoodwinked, and are now playing a full-strength Stoke side with FOUR strikers (& of these only Walters started at Chelsea). Eventually, one of them (Jerome) grabs a hit-&-run goal. With Spurs in crisis, mainly because the FA are furtively eying Harry Redknapp to take over the England job, it looks like Stoke may hang on...until Van Der Vaart converts Gareth Bale's cross in the 93rd minute. A 1-

1 draw at White Hart Lane, but nobody seems particularly happy with this outcome. No doubt Harry's 2 defeats & a draw against Stoke this term go against him when it comes to managing his country.

24/03/12 Stoke (0) 1 Man City (0) 1 - Yes, the game with THAT goal by Peter Crouch. On 58 minutes, Begovic aims a long clearance at Crouch, who duly heads it on to Pennant. Jermaine "with possibly his first header as a Stoke player" (says Mr Spinks) nods it back for Crouch to tee it up. Then he volleys the ball home from miles away & an impossible angle. OH…MY…GOD!!! One of the greatest goals ever! England's No.1 goalie Joe Hart is left fuming whilst the Stoke fans do a hilarious Poznan celebration at the stunned Man City fans, and boy do they look stunned. 20 minutes later Yaya Toure shoots from the next county, and the slightest deflection off Shawcross puts it just beyond Begovic for 1-1. Mancini's expensive bunch go on to win the title on the last day in dramatic style, but they never score a goal this good. "Crackerjack!" beams The Sentinel, "Wonder goal!" rave The Oatcake. "Oh my Godddddddddd!" (me). Well, at least it stops everyone talking about Pulis avoiding a driving ban. Ah.

31/03/12 Wigan (0) 2 Stoke 0 - "A serious contender for the 'Worst Performance Since We Got Promoted'," enthuse The Oatcake. "It really was that bad." Pulis plays a strong side, but two silly second half goals sink Stoke (including a last minute goal by that man Victor Moses). The Oatcake sum it up bluntly: "We had to wait until Palacios & Fuller came on as late subs before any Stoke player managed to do anything right."! Bloody hell, *that* bad, eh? Wigan are on the seemingly impossible road to survival. So, where the hell are Stoke going?!

07/04/12 Stoke (1) 2 Wolves (1) 1 - The game that Tony Pulis spots Wolves' Michael Kightly (probably!). Whilst everyone is raving about striker Matt Jarvis, Pulis can see Kightly fitting in nicely at The Brit, thank you. On the half hour his lob into Stoke's box is missed by everyone, and rolls gently into the net. Pulis is thus smitten - golly, he scores goals as well! Huth soon tucks in an equaliser thru' the keeper, and Crouch heads in Pennant's free kick on the hour for 2-1. But who cares? Tony is in love again, Stoke surpass his target of 40 points, and his golden boy £10m Crouch is up to 9 league goals in 26 games, so worth every penny. TP sleeps well tonight.

09/04/12 Aston Villa (1) 1 Stoke (0) 1 - End-of-season run-of-the-mill game. "Certainly no Thriller-at-the-Villa," observes The Oatcake. Even Crouch is left on the bench. Weirman puts a beaut in the top corner. But Huth equalises again (a header from Pennant's free kick), increasing any bid for an improved contract that, er, could just be round the corner.

21/04/12 Newcastle (3) 3 Stoke 0 - Stoke's 52nd game of the season, and the players look jaded. Well, Stoke's do, whilst Alan Pardew's Newcastle's are on a roll to grab a Champions League spot. To make matters worse Pulis puts Wilkinson on the left and Marc Wilson on the right, + Palacios in the middle for good measure. Stoke are 0-2 down within 20 minutes. "Are you Sunderland in disguise?!" chant the Toons. Oh dear.

28/4/12 Stoke (1) 1 Arsenal (1) 1 - Mancini and Ferguson are playing mindgames, Redknapp is being talked up as the new England manager, Di Matteo is performing miracles at Chelsea, and Steve Kean is STILL manager at Blackburn! Poor old Arsene. His team may be up to 3rd, but nobody's interested in poor old Mr Wenger…until his annual visit to The Brit. Suddenly he's getting all the attention he could possibly want, and the rest of the rather bewildered media haven't got a clue why. And even then it's more to do with Shawcross-Ramsey. To cap it all, Crouch heads his 10th league goal in the 10th minute, and The Brit is rocking. OK, so Van Persie soon equalises, but amusingly Stoke almost win it late with a (you-guessed-it) Delap long throw. It's like they're never seen this throw-thingy before (again).

01/05/12 Stoke (0) 1 Everton (1) 1 - Stoke miss the chance to do the double over Everton for the first time since The Summer Of Love (that's 1967, kids). In come Upson, Delap and Jones, with Kenwyne partnering Crouchy up front. Nikica Jagielka is notorious for scoring own goals against The Potters, but this time it's Peter Crouch's turn, with the ball bouncing in off the-tallest-boy-in-the-park just before half-time. More embarrassingly, it turns out to be the Premier League's 1000th goal this season. Thankfully, Jerome comes on for Jones, charges down the middle, and belts in what turns out to be Stoke's 100th Premier goal at The Brit. However, if you check the replay, his shot takes a deflection off...(and no, I'm NOT kidding) Jagielka! Not again! What is he on?!?

06/05/12 QPR (0) 1 Stoke 0 – Pulis vs Hughes Part 6. Tony Pulis is totally dejected at losing this game, particularly with the chance of sending QPR down. It's not Rangers, it's their latest manager Mark Hughes, who's taken over from Neil Warnock. When asked before the game by a Sky reporter about his "fellow-Welshman" Hughes, you can almost hear Pulis' teeth grinding. And after fielding some odd line-ups away from home this season he chooses to start with FOUR strikers?!?? (Walters, Jerome, Fuller & Crouch). So afterwards I ask him: "Who are you, & what have you done with the real Tony Pulis?!" But they miss their chances, particularly Jerome, and when Pulis brings on Kenwyne for Fuller, The Oatcake actually has a dig at the manager for being defensive, despite there still being 3 strikers on the pitch, with two over 6'5"! If Stoke had got a draw, it would have been fine, but Cisse scores in the very last minute to bring the Loftus Road house down. Pulis is doubly disgusted, particularly as Stoke face Owen Coyle's Bolton next week, and he has a soft spot for the sanguine Scot rather than the fellow-welshman.

13/05/12 Stoke (1) 2 Bolton (2) 2 - "A mini end-of-season classic" reckons Martin Spinks describing this somehow unsatisfying game. Bolton need to win to stay up, assuming QPR will lose at desperate Manchester City. [Citeh need to beat Rangers to pip United to their first title in over 40 years.] So at halftime when Bolton are 2-1 up and Rangers 1-0 down, Wanderers fans are particularly cocky. Ricardo Fuller is given a standing ovation on 10 minutes as a special tribute after the news that he will be leaving Stoke at the end of the season. 2 minutes later it's 1-0, with Walters blundering the ball out of goalie Bogdan's hands. No one can believe (or seem to care) that it's given. Bolton fans look very glum. Then on 40 minutes, Huth blasts a clearance right at Mark Davies and it weirdly cannons back past Sorensen. 1-1. Is it going to be one of those days? Yes, yes it is. On the stroke of halftime Kevin Davies hits a cross/shot from Stoke's left, and Sorensen flaps around as it swings in between him and the post for 1-2. Bolton fans look very happy. Not for long, as QPR miraculously equalise at Citeh. Then some great news comes through from the Etihad that pleases everybody: Joey Barton has been sent off! C'mon everyone, lets party! Bolton fans don't have the stomach for it as QPR then take the lead!! What is going on?! Oh, of course, Man City are cocking it up again. Meanwhile, Fuller is given another ovation when substituted for Jerome, but the fun-and-games aren't over as on 77 minutes, Crouch falls over the goalie, and Walters cracks home the penalty for 2-2. Well, by now Bolton fans have given up as even a win won't help them now, & so the game ends. And so does the season. A fair result in front of a capacity crowd, and we all applaud politely. It is only now, as we descend the steps that Man City equalise. And by the time that Stoke fans reach the railway bridge, Aguerooooo (as he will always be called from now on) scores the late late winner for Man City, and they win the Premier League. For a brief moment we feel part of history. However, it suddenly dawns on Bolton fans that a win would have kept them up afterall…and that basically they wuz robbed. And to think, if Walters had missed that penalty, Mark Hughes would've been relegated & probably would never have managed in the Premier League again. Ah, football: it's a funny old game, which is why we all carry on walking home along the canal, with a smirk on our faces. We are bad people.

			Home					Away					Overall						
	Team	**Pl**	**W**	**D**	**L**	**F**	**A**	**W**	**D**	**L**	**F**	**A**	**W**	**D**	**L**	**F**	**A**	**Pts**	**GD**
1	Manchester City	38	18	1	0	55	12	10	4	5	38	17	28	5	5	93	29	89	64
2	Manchester United	38	15	2	2	52	19	13	3	3	37	14	28	5	5	89	33	89	56
3	Arsenal	38	12	4	3	39	17	9	3	7	35	32	21	7	10	74	49	70	25
4	Tottenham Hotspur	38	13	3	3	39	17	7	6	6	27	24	20	9	9	66	41	69	25
5	Newcastle United	38	11	5	3	29	17	8	3	8	27	34	19	8	11	56	51	65	5
6	Chelsea	38	12	3	4	41	24	6	7	6	24	22	18	10	10	65	46	64	19
7	Everton	38	10	3	6	28	15	5	8	6	22	25	15	11	12	50	40	56	10
8	Liverpool	38	6	9	4	24	16	8	1	10	23	24	14	10	14	47	40	52	7
9	Fulham	38	10	5	4	36	26	4	5	10	12	25	14	10	14	48	51	52	-3
10	West Bromwich Albion	38	6	3	10	21	22	7	5	7	24	30	13	8	17	45	52	47	-7
11	Swansea City	38	8	7	4	27	18	4	4	11	17	33	12	11	15	44	51	47	-7
12	Norwich City	38	7	6	6	28	30	5	5	9	24	36	12	11	15	52	66	47	-14
13	Sunderland	38	7	7	5	26	17	4	5	10	19	29	11	12	15	45	46	45	-1
14	**Stoke City**	38	7	8	4	25	20	4	4	11	11	33	11	12	15	36	53	45	-17
15	Wigan Athletic	38	5	7	7	22	27	6	3	10	20	35	11	10	17	42	62	43	-20
16	Aston Villa	38	4	7	8	20	25	3	10	6	17	28	7	17	14	37	53	38	-16
17	Queens Park Rangers	38	7	5	7	24	25	3	2	14	19	41	10	7	21	43	66	37	-23
18	Bolton Wanderers	38	4	4	11	23	39	6	2	11	23	38	10	6	22	46	77	36	-31
19	Blackburn Rovers	38	6	1	12	26	33	2	6	11	22	45	8	7	23	48	78	31	-30
20	Wolverhampton Wanderers	38	3	3	13	19	43	2	7	10	21	39	5	10	23	40	82	25	-42

2012-13 - The End Of An Era

18/08/12 Reading (0) 1 Stoke (1) 1 – After all the Europa League excitement, it's time to start again. And it's all looking good when new signing Michael Kightly (ex-Wolves) mis-kicks a debut goal on 34 minutes; Huth miraculously recovers from meningitis, only to run headlong into a goalpost; even Palacios comes on as sub (what???). Then as Pulis' substitutes park the bus, it all unravels. In the dying minutes, Whitehead brings down McCleary in the box...only for the ref to play advantage, allowing Reading a shot which Begovic saves brilliantly. But then the ref calls it back, sends off Whitehead for a 2nd yellow, & gives a penalty! Is he just making the rules up now?? An away point on the opening day, but Pulis is livid already. Hope the season isn't all going to be like this.

26/08/12 Stoke 0 Arsenal 0 – Tame. Walters has a goal disallowed for offside early on, and then taps a late chance weakly at the keeper. American idol Geoff Cameron makes his debut, Pennant makes his only league start, & Palacios comes on late...again (oh lord). Famous for being the only game that Stoke fail to win a single corner! At home! Arsenal win 11.

During the Swindon game, Tony Pulis wished the ground would open up & swallow him

28/08/12 Stoke (0) 3 Swindon (2) 4 (League Cup) – THIS was the game that ultimately cost Tony Pulis his job. With a large Europa squad of players all requiring games, a cup run is essential to keep harmony behind closed doors. Despite Pulis making 6 changes, surely nothing can go wrong? But no one can predict what will happen playing crazy Paulo Di Canio, & soon Swindon are 2-0 up, though it could've been more. Although Sorensen spills a cross to concede the first, the back-4 of Shotton, Huth, Upson, & Wilson are simply dreadful (whilst Shawcross & Wilko look on in horror from the bench). Kenwyne heads one back on the hour from Kightly's cross, before Pulis makes a triple substitution with Crouch, Walters & debutant Jamie Ness on with 12 mins left. Jonny Walters looks like he's saved the day equalising with 5 minutes left. But Swindon head home in extra time, and Ness limps off (Rangers fans warned us that he does this a lot) leaving Stoke down to 10 men. Amazingly, Crouchy heads home Walters' cross, with 8 mins left for 3-3, before the Robins' James Collins puts Stoke out of their misery, completing his hat-trick in the last minute of extra time. It's a costly defeat to a League One side. Pennant & Ness never play for Pulis again, but even Upson is only allowed one more game before disappearing. The peasants are revolting.

01/09/12 Wigan (1) 2 Stoke (1) 2 – A game so non-descript that Sentinel Spinksy spends his whole report gushing about how new boy Charlie Adam will transform

Stoke from "egg chasers" into a team of "Alan Hudsons". Adam's arrival "signals a significant change in their style", although arguably he's the second nail in Pulis' coffin. Of all the Stoke players, Adam probably ends up instrumental in undermining Pulis' attempts to "move on" from long throws and long balls. He looks like quality, but no one seems to be on the same wavelength as him. He's all over the place. Anyway, Adam comes on for head-banged Wilko on the half-hour, by which time Stoke are 0-1 down to an early penalty (Huth handball). Walters equalises from the spot on 40 (more handball). Di Santo makes it 2-1 in the second half, before Jerome sets off Walters to cross for Crouch to head home for 2-2. Stoke finish strongly, should win it but don't; however the big question is: what the hell are "egg chasers"?!

15/09/12 Stoke (1) 1 Man City (1) 1 – Man City must hate this fixture. The League Champions are soon behind to a cheeky Crouchy goal, "accidently" handled before he slips it past Joe Hart. Shortly before half time, Mario Balotelli falls over, & Garcia heads home the subsequent free kick. Pulis' new loan striker, some kid called Michael Owen comes on late as a sub, & he DOES NOT TOUCH THE BALL ONCE. He does witness Shawcross miraculously scooping Dzeko's lob off the line in the *very last second.* Commendable performance. But forget all this, as today is the debut of Steven Nzonzi, a lad who can actually pass the ball. What on earth is Tony Pulis going to do with him? Nope, no idea.

22/09/12 Chelsea (0) 1 Stoke 0 – Real evidence that Pulis' side has moved on from long throws & set-pieces, with Stoke matching a multi-millionaire side (Torres, Mata, Hazard, etc) with skill & flair. Yes, hard to believe, isn't it. In fact, it's Roberto Di Matteo (who's clearly not long for this world/job) who has the dodgy tactics, vainly pleading innocence for diving Ivanovic & Oscar, booked for "simulation". (They are later humiliated with constant TV slow-mo replays.) Spinksy even sees them in Speedos, "giving Tom Daley a run for his money". Ugh! But they are only the warm up act for David Luiz, who is forced to apologise for his late late tackle on Walters for which everyone but the ref thinks he should have walked. The Potters have 50% of possession (huh??) & a fair share of chances in front of 41,000 supporters. Even Walters should score but his header typically hits the bar. In fact, the only goal comes 5 minutes from time, with Ashley Cole finishing from close range. Curiously, the winner comes from a counter-attack – yes, Stoke were attacking at the time, not parking-the-bus. No wins this season, but the plaudits are out.

29/09/2012 Stoke (2) 2 Swansea 0 – A WIN! A bread & butter game for Pulis, as Crouch sinks The Swans with 2 first half goals. Just as well, as journos are saying this is Stoke's worst top flight start since 1973! Now they're saying this is Stoke's first win in 6 months. Critics, eh? Crouch's first is a header from a Whelan corner, the second from a cross from Kightly - nice to see him making himself useful - which Crouchy eventually pokes home. Swans defender Ben Davies is booked for diving, much to Pulis' satisfaction, after last week's Chelsea dive-fest. Sentinel reports Stoke possession as low as 26%...nationals reckon 39% - either way, The Potters control this all the way.

07/10/2012 Liverpool 0 Stoke 0 – Pulis' THIRD draw at Anfield. To put that in perspective, Tony Waddington only managed ONE in 17 years worth of relentless Anfield defeats. And over 50% possession! But then new manager Brendan Rodgers is struggling with a side that features Suarez, Gerrard & Sterling. Even some guy called Assaidi comes on as sub, but can't make an impression against The Potters. Highlights? Dean

Whitehead legally flattening Suarez, & then Suarez doing such an appalling dive that everyone just ignores him. (Oh, he hates being ignored.) Amazingly, he's not booked, nor any of his teammates; 6 Stoke players see yellow.

20/10/2012 Man Utd (2) 4 Stoke (1) 2 – Media & Potters' fans genuinely impressed with Stoke's evolving style, with Charlie Adam leading by example for a change. Stoke even take an early lead as Shawcross pressures Rooney into heading home an own goal. However, Wayne and the dreaded Van Persie soon re-address the balance. Kightly heroically charges through to bring it back to 2-3 on the hour. Despite all the passing play, & the inevitable appearance of Michael Owen, Stoke concede a fourth with unexpectedly poor defending, which is something you just don't expect from a Pulis side.

Michael Owen explains how to park the bus

27/10/12 Stoke 0 Sunderland 0 – Spinks: "A game slipping so far down the MotD running order that it almost popped up in the Football League Show instead". Marc Wilson breaks his leg, and Andy Wilkinson gets up from being pole-axed by Craig Gardner to shake his hand! Ha, you DO remember it! Wilko is a God.

03/11/12 Norwich (1) 1 Stoke 0 – There's a problem. No, it's not Nzonzi. It's "How do you solve a problem like Charlie Adam?" Pulis plays him "in the hole" behind Crouch (where he's all over the shop), because he has the more defensive Whitehead, Walters & Whelan in the more appropriate midfield positions, and he's not going to drop Nzonzi. Tricky. Then on half time, the ref ignores Adam being tripped, and the ball goes down the other end, and well you can guess the rest. Mr Spinks paraphrases Morecambe & Wise: "TP has all the right players, but not necessarily in the right order." Nice, but I prefer my Sound Of Music analogy.

10/11/12 Stoke (0) 1 QPR 0 – Pesky Mark Hughes is back in town with his bottom-placed Rangers side without a win since May (when they beat Stoke), and without an away win for 12 months (when they, er, beat Stoke). But Pulis is having none of it, and nor is a full & very loud Brit Stadium. With Adam on the wing for some reason, Walters moves up alongside Crouch, despite a nasty head gash requiring 5 stitches. SJW casually tosses his bandage aside in order to head Huth's free kick into the penalty area where it finds Adam who thwacks it home before the hour. His first Stoke goal secured, Adam slides legs-apart towards the corner flag, which thankfully doesn't end in tears. On the verge of the sack, Sparky has a good look round mainly in envy. The Oatcake helpfully observe before the game: "Mark Hughes - Dead Man Walking. Hopefully Stoke won't do their usual charity trick, thus giving QPR's under-fire manager the lifeline he needs to extend his failing reign a few weeks longer.

All we can do is hope that we break the habit of a lifetime & actually hammer a nail into someone else's coffin for a change." The next time the Dead Man is back, he's in the home dug-out. "Ropey," declare The Oatcake, although it's unclear whether they are referring to Stoke's performance or a hangman's noose!

19/11/12 West Ham (0) 1 Stoke (1) 1 – The words "high-flying Sam Allardyce side" don't sound like they go together, but surprisingly promoted West Ham are 6th. Curiously, it's Stoke who look like the high-flyers (13th), showing off in front of the cameras in this live TV game. "Superb!" say The Oatcake. Walters is as surprised as anyone finding himself sweeping home from an early Whelan corner. The Hammers equalise after the break, and The Potters hang on for a deserved draw with astonishing 46% possession. Big Sam thought his side deserved to win, but he is clearly deluded. Walters' injury of the week is to his calf, and as Pulis has used all the subs (yes, even Palacios is on for half an hour!), SJW has to hobble around like a lame pony.

24/11/12 Stoke (1) 1 Fulham 0 – Stoke's results are looking suspiciously binary, particularly as they've only conceded one league goal at home this season (Man City), and only scored more than once (that Swansea game). But in fact Fulham took-one-hell-of-a-beating, and should have lost by more. Martin Jol reckons they got a physical beating too, but that's sore losers for you. As Pulis is running out of full-backs - even Wilko is out after being chopped-up by Andy Carroll last week - he gamely starts Shotton, whose superb cross for Crouch sets up Adam on the half-hour. Yes, Crouch & Adam are an item again, awkward though it may be. Fulham's Berbatov is the only scary thing in their arsenal, and Begovic sorts him out. Sub Kenwyne pokes one through Schwarzer's legs right at the end, but the Binary Gods decide it should be unfairly ruled out for offside. Well, you can't argue with the Gods, can you.

28/11/12 Stoke (0) 2 Newcastle (0) 1 – Holy cow! Stoke concede a goal at the Brit! Take 60% of possession! Come from behind! Climb to 9th in the Prem! Fail to get mugged by Demba Ba! Give Shotton another 90 minutes! And Crouch gets his teeth kicked out! Bloody hell! Actually Ba does cause problems as it's his shot that Begovic parries for Cisse to score off the post just after the break. But just as the "useless-United" think it's their lucky day (yeah, in yer dreams!), on comes killjoy-Jerome whose awesome cross from the right is glanced in by dogged Walters with 10 minutes left. SJW then returns the favour, when his long ball forward is headed down by sub Kenwyne for Jerome to smack home in the 85th. "Thrilling!" exclaim The Oatcake, noting that it wasn't very thrilling for the first 70 minutes. Yeah, all very well, but I bet Jerome is back on the bench next week.

01/12/12 West Brom 0 Stoke (0) 1 – Oh look, Cameron Jerome is back on the bench this week, and it's as an unused substitute; my, he must be pleased! In fairness, he did twist his ankle in the warm-up, so instead it's Kenwyne who replaces the recovering toothless Crouch. If Mr Jones gets crocked, Pulis will have to try and remember which cupboard he locked the invisible Michael Owen in, or else put Shotton up front (which you wouldn't put past him). ANYWAY, Stoke get their first away win in almost a year - was this ever in doubt against Albion, who've only won 2 out of the last 30 Stoke derbies? Unbelievably, Albion were 4th before this game!! In the 74th Kenwyne helps win the ball back, sub Kightly crosses low, and the other sub Whitehead pokes home. Even Stoke fans can't believe they've scored, and that it's Deano! Steve Clarke's subs (Lukaku and a certain Peter Odemwingie) fail to make the same impact.

08/12/12 Aston Villa 0 Stoke 0 – A horror show of tedium. 40 quid a ticket and hardly a shot on goal. Well, that's a Paul Lambert side for you. This game is only remembered by Ryan Shotton who received two grossly unfair yellows, the second for clearly pulling out of a challenge THREE minutes into injury-time. He is seen iconically standing like a demented duck as he pleads his innocence to ropey ref Roger East. A grim game with only 5 corners, but an away point all the same. "They could use the video highlights of this game to torture terrorist suspects in Guantanamo Bay!" reckon The Oatcake. What a horrible thought.

After unjustly being red-carded at Villa, Ryan Shotton does the "demented duck"

15/12/12 Stoke (0) 1 Everton (1) 1 – Nasty Marouane Fellaini, he of weird sticky-out hair, gets a retrospective 3-match ban after head-butting Shawcross, before trying to rip his face off! And he doesn't even get a yellow card! The unjustly-suspended Shotton watches all this from the sidelines in disbelief. But thankfully, unlike Tom Cruise in Mission Impossible, Shawcross doesn't have a different face underneath, like for example Denis Smith's, otherwise Fellaini might have left the pitch with no teeth or hair (which frankly would have been an improvement). Shawcross does turn a Pienaar cross from the left into his own net just after the half-hour, but Kenwyne beats Jagielka to the ball just after the break to head home off the post. It's his first Prem goal for 16 months; pickings are that slim.

22/12/12 Spurs 0 Stoke 0 – No No No, this 0-0 is not what it seems! Stoke have 43% possession away from home and also the three best chances (fluffed by Kenwyne (twice) and Shotton). In fact, in the first half Stoke just about stole it (51% possession!), with star-studded 4th-place Spurs (Bale, Adebayor, Defoe, Lennon) huffing and puffing to no avail in the second. But although Stoke are impressive almost across the board (keeper, defence, midfield), goals are what count. Well, maybe next week.

26/12/12 Stoke (2) 3 Liverpool (1) 1 – Game of the season is this crackerjack mother of a Boxing Day clash! A full house at The Brit witnesses THREE goals in the first 12 minutes, and the game rocks along nicely after that. Luis Suarez struggles with Shawcross until he's in the penalty area, then falls over. It's a penalty after only 33 seconds! Gerrard naturally sends Begovic the wrong way - well, penalty-saving is not one of Asmir's strong points, and even The Sentinel are sympathetic, saying "He had no chance with the goal." It's a penalty, for goodness sake! Of course he has no chance! At the Liverpool end a massive smoke bomb goes off, engulfing the ground with a red mist, not unlike the one engulfing the Stoke fans towards the world-famous diving Suarez. As things reach fever pitch, Shawcross makes all things better again by floating a free kick forward that finds Walters who fires home superbly after only 5 minutes! 1-1. Seven minutes later, and Shawcross bamboozles a certain Glen Johnson as Kenwyne heads Stoke 2-1 into the lead from a Whelan corner. The Brit, as TP would put it, is rocking! Brendon Rogers throws on Raheem Sterling at half time, but a few minutes in Kenwyne lays off a beaut to Walters to chest-and-volley for 3-1. It's end to end stuff, but Suarez gets yellowed for sending Begovic flying, much to everyone's amusement (although it should have been a red). Nzonzi is brilliant, and Whitehead comes on to nonchalantly take out keeper Pepe Reina, much to everyone's amusement...again. Suarez gets the ball in the net on the hour...but the whistle had already gone for Henderson's handball, much to everyone's amusement...yet again. Not a bad Boxing Day night's entertainment. "Made Steven Gerrard look a very ordinary player," claim The Oatcake. Ah, if only all games were like this. Stoke go above Liverpool to 8th place; half-way through the season and they have 28 points already! What could possibly go wrong?!

29/12/12 Stoke (1) 3 Southampton (3) 3 – The neutral's Game Of The Season. Even Martin Spinks gives it 9/10 for entertainment! Where do you start?? Upson comes in for Shawcross (suspended after his yellow for conceding that Suarez penalty 3 days earlier). But although the Stoke defence goes to pot, it's Huth and Wilko who need their heads banging together. To oblige they do it for us, and there's literally blood everywhere - like they care. Rickie Lambert sweeps in unseen on 10 minutes, but Kenwyne back-heels on the quarter-hour for 1-1. Rodriguez makes it 1-2 after 24, from the rebound of Huth hitting his own bar. Wilko then fumbles an own goal for 1-3. Pulis sends on Jerome on the hour, but just as Stoke are getting back into it with Upson (of all people) popping up to make it 2-3, Nzonzi is unfairly red-carded for stamping when he wasn't! Although it's rescinded by the FA later, it leaves a rabid Stoke side pulverising the Saints for the rest of the game. The ref misses two stonewall penalties, and a Jerome goal is disallowed for offside. Then in the last minute, the FOUR strikers (is this really a Pulis side???) combine to create the Goal Of The Season. Kenwyne flicks on for Crouch to set up Jerome 33 yards out. He hits a dipping thunderbolt past Davis that blows the top off The Brit. It's 3-3!! It's not a win (although Crouchy almost heads a winner in time-added), but it's 10 matches without defeat, and two superb games in 3 days. No complaints here.

01/01/13 Man City (1) 3 Stoke 0 – Aguerooo tears Stoke apart, with help from Zabaleta (42 mins), and Dzeko (56). In fact, Aguero's only actual goal is a 74 min penalty, although Silva is actually tripped OUTSIDE the box by Nzonzi, who looks unlikely to recover from last game's rescinded red card incident. Stoke's unbeaten run (10 games) is over, unsurprisingly. In other news Jerome makes his first league start, and Charlie Adam returns after a family tragedy. Both must have wondered if it was worth it.

05/01/13 Crystal Palace 0 Stoke 0 (FA Cup) – Tony Pulis finally starts the old England partnership of little Michael Owen alongside big Peter Crouch...but to no avail. Crouchy's still got it (i.e. missing a couple of sitters), but Owen looks a shadow of his former self as he crabs sideways across the pitch. Ian Holloway's Palace are merrily on their way to promotion, although "Ollie" has a dicky-fit when Shotton accidentally poleaxes his star winger Wilfred Zaha. In fairness (really? here?!) our Ryan keeps Zaha in his pocket all match. Pulis doesn't look too impressed with Zaha or Palace, which is ironic because the next time he washes up on their touchline he's their manager.

12/01/13 Stoke 0 Chelsea (1) 4 – Oh, you must remember THIS one. The Jonny Walters nightmare game! He starts by almost knocking himself out hitting a volley straight into his own face! But then everything's going tickety-boo, with Stoke giving as good as they get, when suddenly Walters heads home an own-goal under pressure from Mata on the stroke of half-time. Stoke then get a penalty...until the referee changes his mind and gives an offside. Then on the hour Walters does it again, heading home another own-goal under pressure from Lampard for 0-2. Lampard's penalty and Hazard's mega-strike soon make it 0-4. But the icing on the cake is in injury-time when Walters is taken out by John Terry, and Walters grabs the ball genuinely thinking he can gain some sense of redemption from taking the subsequent penalty himself. It clips the top of the bar on its way off towards Jupiter. This is the thanks you get for playing a record 73 consecutive Premier League games. That, and the whole stadium (Chelsea fans & all) singing your name at the end of the game. You could'ner make it up!

15/01/13 Stoke (0) 4 Crystal Palace (0) 1 (FA Cup rpl) – Cold??? One of the coldest games at The Brit! Grown men froze where they stood!! Even Martin Spinks spots Stokie-hero-hardman Mike Pejic wearing...GLOVES!!! A more tasty Palace side (with subs Bolasie & Murray) are let down by Zaha being booked for diving. But Zaha then wins a dubious penalty which Sorensen dives left to save! Pulis takes against the lad, one suspects, and is glad to see the back of him when he's subbed at half-time. Kightly is not happening either, and is replaced by Jerome. But the game only really takes off when Kenwyne comes on and teams up with Walters like it's the good old days. Jones heads home on 70 mins, but Shawcross gives away ANOTHER penalty on 85 minutes, taken by Glenn Murray. 1-1. With the temperature dropping further into extra time, Walters finishes Palace off with a header from an Etherington cross, a piledriver from a Kenwyne through-ball, before Jerome rounds the keeper for 4-1. But by then most of the 11,613 crowd have died of hypothermia.

19/01/13 Swansea (0) 3 Stoke (0) 1 – Michael Owen scores for Stoke! But not something to write home about. The peasants are restless, namely newcomers Adam, Nzonzi and Owen. Frustration is creeping in. As Swansea appear interested in signing Kenwyne, TP instead starts with scary mouth-guard wearing Crouch to little avail, until Swansea sweep into a 2-0 2nd-half lead. And by the time Kenwyne, Jerome and Owen are on, it's 0-3. Jerome misses from 3 yards, somehow getting the ball over the bar! No wonder he drives Pulis mad. But in time-added he crosses for Owen to flick-head his 150th Premier League goal...almost 2 years since his last one. Despite 50% possession, there's nothing to see here. Somehow Stoke remain 10th.

26/01/13 Stoke 0 Man City (0) 1 (FA Cup) – Surely this is just a replay of the 2011 FA Cup Final? Seems like it. Hardly inspiring from either side, apart from a late-ish winner for Citeh, this time by Zabaleta, aided by substitute Aguero-oooooo! Stoke sub Jerome in-turn puts his big chance way up into the Boothen End as per normal. Just as well; no one really fancied a replay up at the Etihad. But then, for the rest the season seems over, and it's only January.

29/01/2013 Stoke (1) 2 Wigan (0) 2 – Can they do it on a cold Tuesday night at Stoke? Clearly not, despite Pulis FINALLY finding a perfect spot for Charlie Adam (no, not working the scoreboard) as part of an effective 3-man midfield. Noticeably only 24,421 turn up, which sets alarm bells ringing upstairs, and will undoubtably be another nail in Pulis' coffin. Stoke strikers don't even win a single corner all game (mind you, Wigan only manage one!), so it's the defenders to the rescue! Almost immediately Huthy gets his obligatory bandage round his head after being horizontal for a whole 4 minutes. Then the more erect Shawcross is in the right place at the right time when Wigan cock up a clearance on 23 mins, volleying home for 1-0. Previously barren Crouch finally gets one (2-0), also banging in a rebound after the break...and then Wigan wake up and suddenly it's 2-2. Crowd have a lot to moan about, particularly as star-player Adam (who'd set up both goals) and the seriously-all-over-the-place Nzonzi are replaced by the likes of Jerome (just as naff), who naturally (or naff-urally) misses a chance to win it. Wasteful.

Brek Shea, man of mystery...& a tongue

02/02/2013 Arsenal (0) 1 Stoke 0 – Our Tone has one last go at getting Stoke a result at The Emirates, and in typical Durban-style (ie "Go watch a bunch of clowns!") his side last 78 minutes (thanks to brilliant Begovic) before a deflected free-kick off Cameron gifts 3 lucky points to Wenger. The game is typically physical: Shawcross gets a gashed shin; Walters' head needs 6 stitches, & he joins Huth wearing a by now obligatory head-bandage; and Michael Owen even takes a swing at Arteta! Meanwhile The Sentinel reckon Pulis' Stoke side get 53% possession (away at Arsenal??) - when in fact it should be 35%, which although low, shows progression - Stoke's possession never drops below 42% for the rest of the season. (In fact, Stoke possession only drops below 40% on one other occasion all season; at the Etihad.) But for most of the match everyone (including Arsenal) is wondering where on earth Geoff Cameron is supposed to be playing. Inside-left? Outside-right? In-the-hole? He's given a free reign to pop up all over the place. He'll be the next Doctor Who at this rate.

09/02/2013 Stoke (0) 2 Reading (0) 1 – Rubbish Reading – arguably the worst Premier team to visit The Brit – are amazed to get in at half-time still at 0-0. They're not the only ones. Huth's header and super-sub Jerome's stunner address this in the 2nd half putting Stoke 2-0 up, but Rubbish Reading somehow make it 2-1 late on, and Pulis is embarrassed that his side have to panic-defend for their 3 points. Shotton is lucky not to concede a late-late penalty (bit of a dive spotted by the ref), and Huth is lucky not to get a black eye for his tweet: "Felt good to get height on my jump for the goal yesterday. Looking down, Shawcross is definitely thinning on top". He's a bad lad.

23/02/2013 Fulham (1) 1 Stoke 0 – Things are getting so weird that even Brek Shea & his haircut comes on as sub to make his debut. He wins a penalty...and Jon Walters fluffs it! Marc Wilson is back from injury at left-back, Cameron is back in his wondering-all-over-the-place role, and Nzonzi just seems angry this time from having his nose split by goal scorer Berbatov. Although Nzonzi gets away with his retaliation, Huth gets a post-match ban for taking out Senderos. Stoke still in the top-10, but without Huth the club could now pay dearly for not allowing Pulis to buy a replacement central defender in the January window; someone like, er, Scott Dann. Instead, he signs a goalkeeper! Some kid called Jack Butland...

02/03/2013 Stoke 0 West Ham (1) 1 – Another huge nail in Pulis' coffin, as Stoke concede the only goal in the first-half injury-time, and fans lay into the manager. Even without Huth, and even with Kightly (who plumbs a new low today), this Stoke side should pulverise West Ham with the likes of Shawcross, Begovic, Walters, Nzonzi, Crouch, Jerome and sub Adam (whose brilliant volley thumps the bar late on).

09/03/2013 Newcastle (0) 2 Stoke (0) 1 – Cisse was "too ill" to travel to Moscow for United's Europa League game 3 days before, but here he is beating the offside trap in injury time to sink Stoke. Or maybe Alan Pardew was trying to pull the wool. The Toons don't deserve this win. Stoke had taken the lead in the 67th with a Walters penalty (surprisingly still the taker after missing 3 of his last 6 spot kicks). Pegged back to 1-1 by a Cabaye free-kick goal off the bar, and Stoke should have got a point. Consolation? Newcastle were hammered out of the Europa in the next round.

16/03/2013 Stoke 0 West Brom 0 – Fourth league game in row that has failed to get a crowd near 27,000, but the 26,317 present turn the volume up to 11. Albion sport one Odemwingie and a guy called Lukaku, but their equivalents, Nzonzi (in a mask) & Kenwyne (not in a mask) are a better combination. Somehow it doesn't bring any goals. Crowd bays when Pulis chooses Whitehead instead of Adam to replace Whelan at halftime, but when Charlie does come on later he's more than a bit "rusty" (says Martin Spinks) or "poor" (says The Oatcake), as his free kicks sail off into the sunset. A point is worth celebrating, but a goal would also be useful.

30/03/2013 Everton (1) 1 Stoke 0 – Huth is back, and although Stoke's performances continue to improve, the results don't. When your luck is not in, then it's not in. With Stoke pounding the Everton goal, Mirallas breaks, runs the full length of the pitch, outwitting Nzonzi and Cameron, and slips home the only (& rather dazzling) goal on the half-hour. Everyone (except, amusingly, Michael Owen) comes on to turn it around, but Everton hang on. Not a defeat "to have the more fair-minded fan reaching for a loaded pistol and heading to the nearest woods" (as Martin Spinks puts it), but not far off.

06/04/2013 Stoke (0) 1 Aston Villa (1) 3 – Paul Lambert's Villa are in the relegation zone before this game; afterwards they are one point behind Stoke. That's the state of things. Lowton's wonder-volley goal on 87 minutes just about sums up Stoke's luck. A full house at The Brit cheer on Stoke to get a smashing 80th minute equaliser (by sub Kightly, whom the crowd are not initially pleased to see). But with Lowton's flukey strike, Benteke's late-late breakaway goal, and the ref failing to spot penalty hand-balls and a foul-throw that lead to a Villa goal, what hope is there? Just where is the next point coming from, anyone?

Even Begovic can't believe how lucky Lambert's Villa are as Lowton's winner flies past him

14/04/2013 Stoke 0 Man Utd (1) 2 – Well, the next goal isn't coming against United, who are on their way to winning the league by a mile in Fergie's last season. It's all Rooney, Van Persie, Welbeck, Ferdinand, Valencia, Vidic, Evra - Giggs can't even get on the pitch! Stoke battle bravely (despite conceding scappily after 4 minutes), with bandaged-head Wilko barging through to shoot (sadly blocked), and Charlie even getting 90 minutes. But Van Persie's penalty on the hour ends the game. Owen gets a cameo for a quarter hour ("He's still alive then?" queries The Sentinel), but thankfully Palacios doesn't. (Is he still alive??) Pulis is asked if there's anything positive to take out of this game: "Yeah, we don't have to play Man Utd again this season!" Those were the days.

20/04/2013 QPR 0 Stoke (1) 2 – After ditching Mark Hughes, QPR had somehow managed to crawl off the bottom spot under Harry Redknapp (albeit only by goal-difference to Rubbish Reading, who are merely conceding more goals than Rangers!). But with only 24 pts and 5 to play, they're as good as gone. (or, as TP would say, they can't mathematically get 40 pts now). So, wouldn't it be nice if Harry got them to roll over and gift the points to Stoke and his old mate Tone? Well, get this: QPR have 25 goal attempts (11 on target), more than any team against Stoke. This is no gift. But Stoke power their way past Rangers, personified by Marc Wilson with his superb tackle just before halftime, following it with an inch-perfect pass to Jerome, who crosses for ex-Redknapp favourite Crouch to tap home for 1-0. Then when ex-Stokie Clint Hill "tangos" with Crouch in the box, Walters blasts the penalty high-centre-right for a change...only to have ref Chris Foy make him take it again for a QPR encroachment! As he's missed a few this season, the peasants are nervous. His 2nd attempt is his normal low-bottom-left, and the keeper guesses right, but thankfully can't reach it, which is just as well. Rangers get only one more point before relegation, but this is probably the game that sinks them (& Harry). It's also probably the game that saves Stoke.

27/04/2013 Stoke (0) 1 Norwich 0 – After only 6 points from a possible 42 before the QPR game, suddenly Stoke think they're supermen and win 2 in a row. "Stoke's Premier League status now looks like one less item on the agenda," enthuses The Sentinel. However, The Oatcake worry that "we may not be mathematically safe yet"! Ah, come on, guys, that's Tony's 40 pts, and anyway Wigan, Reading and QPR are too poor to stay up. Another full house cheer on a sluggish first half, but in the second Pulis' men (the likes of Shotton, Huth, Nzonzi, Jerome, Whelan etc) make Norwich look as poor as their zero-shots-on-target indicates. Special mention to Charlie, who charges through to score 52 seconds into the 2nd half, with a goal he dedicates to his dad (who'd died so tragically a few weeks before). Special mention also for Crouchy, who comically mis-kicks a sitter from an Adam cross when it seems easier to score. Oh, we can laugh now as his giraffe legs go off in all directions. And so we will.

06/05/2013 Sunderland (0) 1 Stoke (1) 1 – Once upon a time this was billed as a bottom-of-the-table 6 pointer. But now this is merely a chance for Pulis to stick the knife into Paulo Di Canio (who's taken over from Martin O'Neill) as revenge for his Swindon side knocking Stoke out the League Cup. Paulo's Black Cats have just lost hilariously 1-6 to fellow strugglers Villa. In this one, top-scorer Walters makes it 11 for the season after 9 minutes, before Craig Gardner takes out Charlie twice: once over the advertising hoardings (oooo!), and once rather nastily right in front of the dugouts. Pulis & Co comically jump around like fleas in the Di Canio style, and Gardner is sent off. It's like watching a puppet show. Walters gets another head injury - what with face-masks and head-bandages, it's like watching The Walking Dead this season! Inevitably, O'Shea volleys an equaliser on the hour, and Stoke miss a chance for 3 points against 10 men. But sending Sunderland to the brink (they survive, just), and being another nail in Di Canio's downfall (he lasts 6 more games), this is as good as entertainment gets at this level.

12/05/2013 Stoke (1) 1 Spurs (1) 2 – It's May, it's FREEZING, it's Stoke's 150th anniversary game (free t-shirts all round), and Spurs are rampantly going for Champions League football as they're just one point behind 4th place Arsenal. So, Wenger is no doubt ecstatic to hear of Nzonzi flick-heading his first Stoke goal after only 150 seconds. But after that Spurs (fronted by that irritatingly talented Gareth Bale) pulverise Stoke almost as much as QPR (!), making it 1-1 after 20 mins due to a defensive mix-up, before scoring late with Adebayor. Pulis waves goodbye - everyone later wonders if he knew he'd not be back. And Spurs have to wave goodbye to the Champions League - they fail to catch Arsenal. Tragic, really.

19/05/2013 Southampton (0) 1 Stoke (0) 1 – The hot sun shines down on what turns out to be Tony Pulis' last Stoke game, although on the day it was all about little Michael Owen's last ever game; he gets 20 minutes at the end, which is all he really deserves particularly when he fluffs his big chance late on with an "air-shot" from Shotton's brilliant cross. Duh! What a difference HE'D have made if he'd been fit for more games this season. Ha! Crouchy shows how it should be done, heading home 79 seconds into the 2nd half from a Cameron cross. However, Rickie Lambert equalises from a rebound off Begovic 10 minutes later, and this proves quite expensive: if Stoke had won, they'd have finished a fairly respectful 11th, but instead slip down to finish 13th (losing a couple of million in revenue as a result). It would also have been more controversial for Stoke to dismiss Pulis after their best finish (11th) for nearly 40 years! (Well, equal-best with 1981 & 2010.) Put another way, Owen's miss probably ensured Pulis' departure, so maybe baby-Michael does have something to smile about. 2 days later Pulis & Stoke go their separate ways, and Owen joins BT Sport (MO: "If there's a bit of rain about, it makes the surface wet"). Pulis later signs three of the Southampton side: Puncheon, Lambert & Rodriguez. Un-used Stoke-sub Cuvelier is never heard of again.

	Team	P	Wh	Dh	Lh	GFh	GAh	Wa	Da	La	GFa	GAa	W	D	L	GF	GA	GD	Pts
1	Manchester Utd	38	16	0	3	45	19	12	5	2	41	24	28	5	5	86	43	+43	**89**
2	Manchester City	38	14	3	2	41	15	9	6	4	25	19	23	9	6	66	34	+32	**78**
3	Chelsea	38	12	5	2	41	16	10	4	5	34	23	22	9	7	75	39	+36	**75**
4	Arsenal	38	11	5	3	47	23	10	5	4	25	14	21	10	7	72	37	+35	**73**
5	Tottenham	38	11	5	3	29	18	10	4	5	37	28	21	9	8	66	46	+20	**72**
6	Everton	38	12	6	1	33	17	4	9	6	22	23	16	15	7	55	40	+15	**63**
7	Liverpool	38	9	6	4	33	16	7	7	5	38	27	16	13	9	71	43	+28	**61**
8	West Bromwich	38	9	4	6	32	25	5	3	11	21	32	14	7	17	53	57	-4	**49**
9	Swansea City	38	6	8	5	28	26	5	5	9	19	25	11	13	14	47	51	-4	**46**
10	West Ham Utd	38	9	6	4	34	22	3	4	12	11	31	12	10	16	45	53	-8	**46**
11	Norwich City	38	8	7	4	25	20	2	7	10	16	38	10	14	14	41	58	-17	**44**
12	Fulham	38	7	3	9	28	30	4	7	8	22	30	11	10	17	50	60	-10	**43**
13	Stoke City	38	7	7	5	21	22	2	8	9	13	23	9	15	14	34	45	-11	**42**
14	Southampton	38	6	7	6	26	24	3	7	9	23	36	9	14	15	49	60	-11	**41**
15	Aston Villa	38	5	5	9	23	28	5	6	8	24	41	10	11	17	47	69	-22	**41**
16	Newcastle Utd	38	9	1	9	24	31	2	7	10	21	37	11	8	19	45	68	-23	**41**
17	Sunderland	38	5	8	6	20	19	4	4	11	21	35	9	12	17	41	54	-13	**39**
18	Wigan Athletic	38	4	6	9	26	39	5	3	11	21	34	9	9	20	47	73	-26	**36**
19	Reading	38	4	8	7	23	33	2	2	15	20	40	6	10	22	43	73	-30	**28**
20	QP Rangers	38	2	8	9	13	28	2	5	12	17	32	4	13	21	30	60	-30	**25**

2013-14 - Enter The Sparky

Not everyone was happy to see Mark Hughes, particularly this capped driver

17/08/2013 Liverpool (1) 1 Stoke 0 – Stoke fans seem singularly unimpressed with the appointment of Mark Hughes, whom they don't see as much of an improvement on departed Tony Pulis, whose time (it seems) has come and gone. Hughes couldn't even hold down a job at QPR, they reason. What the hell does HE bring to the party? But they are reassured that Sparky will take Stoke "to the next level", improve the style of football, bring back disgruntled supporters, and play the transfer market more wisely. Hm, little early sign of that. So, for this first game, he buys left-back Erik Pieters (whom Pulis would have signed in January if the Viking hadn't just put his fist through a window after being sent off in his come-back game from injury!). He tries to start Palacios (no kidding!!?!), but he breaks down in the warm-up (somewhere in his "nether regions", says The Sentinel, delicately) just minutes before the start! No, really! Hughes then riskily re-signs bad-boy Jermaine Pennant, and even brings him on as sub! Meanwhile, Shawcross has clearly been told to pass the ball out of defence and not hoof it, and the look of fear on his face is comical. Thankfully, Nzonzi has been persuaded to stay, so Ryan can always give the ball to him (as Huth religiously just gives the ball to Ryan). Begovic stays too, which is just as well as he is "superb" in this game. But 48% possession at Anfield in front of the BT TV cameras doth not a successful season make (particularly as it's actually LESS than last season!). Sturridge puts The Reds ahead before half-time with a shot through Huth's legs, but an 88th minute Walters penalty should make it 1-1. Keeper Mignolet saves to his right (even the BT commentators knew it was going there) and he also saves the rebound shot from Kenwyne. Watching on the bench is the new boy, one Marc Muniesa, wondering what on Earth is going on; and Wilko who is watching

Stoke's full-backs playing in the opponent's half! How does that work? Tony Pulis (hired by BT as a pundit for the day) can't explain it either. Palacios & his "nether-regions" end up in hospital! Stay tuned for more weirdness!

24/08/2013 Stoke (0) 2 Crystal Palace (1) 1 – Sparky's home debut against newly-promoted Olly-managed relegation-doomed Palace only attracts 25,207, which isn't much of a welcoming committee for Hughes. Mind you, for the first half we can all see why. It's crud! Shawcross is particularly awful, responsible for Chamakh bursting forward on the half hour for 0-1. Sparky has a half-time "word" with his team, but it's not until Palace fans ring out with "sacked in the morning" that The Brit crowd wakes up. Two "scrappy goals" on the hour from Adam and predator Shawcross suddenly make it 2-1 in this – strangely described by The Oatcake as – "must win match". No one is sacked in the morning, but then Ian Holloway only lasts another EIGHT weeks...but then who could possibly replace Olly?

28/08/2013 Stoke (2) 3 Walsall (0) 1 (Capital One) – Time for passing practice against lowly Walsall, but it's clear Sparky hasn't explained it right. Passes go all over the place: into the Boothen, down the tunnel, up the Khyber... Kenwyne's first goal of his hat-trick is typically hilarious: he passes to Walsall, they bewilderingly pass it back, & he belts it home, 1-0. He then makes it 2-0 on the half-hour after a Pennant cross from the left. At the break Sparky tries to rectify things by replacing Palacios ("Rusty," say The Sentinel) & Shea ("Tentative") with lively-loanee winger Oussama Assaidi. But Kenwyne loses the ball again and suddenly it's 2-1. Andy Wilkinson then scores (it's judged offside, damnit!), Huth then scores (it's also offside), before Kenwyne gets his hat-trick in the 83rd min (Stoke's first trio since Lawrence's 6 years ago). Muniesa makes his debut at left back, but it's a bit of a shambles really; Stoke only manage 46% possession! A guy called Butland watches from the bench.

31/08/2013 West Ham 0 Stoke (0) 1 – Re-signing Pennant seems like a great idea! After setting up the goals against Walsall, he comes off the bench and bends an 82nd minute free-kick over the wall for the only goal. Wilson and Nzonzi are brilliant in midfield (not a sentence you expect to hear), and as such The Hammers literally don't get a shot on target all day. Big Sam is not amused, but Stoke are 5th, sandwiched between Arsenal & Spurs. "We're Stoke City, we're passing the ball!" the Stoke fans merrily sing.

14/09/2012 Stoke 0 Man City 0 – Hughes definitely doesn't want to lose to the millionaires' club that sacked him 4 years previously. But he has no worries here as Stoke easily match the likes of Hart, Toure and Aguero, even matching them shot-for-shot (11 with 3 on target). In fact, The Oatcake can't believe Stoke don't win. However, this is best remembered for the substitutes: New signing Marko Arnautovic comes on for Charlie with the swagger of a Hudson or Fuller. Other new boy Stephen Ireland (on for Etherington) is more restrained. Left on the bench is last game's winner Pennant (grinding his teeth) and Wilson (still-here) Palacios. NOT substituted is Huth who is knocked unconscious whilst sandwiched between Begovic & Negrado, but then is allowed to play on for the last 10 minutes as Sparky has used all his subs! Heroic, but dumb. It is later pointed out that he should really have gone straight to hospital with possible concussion. Germans, eh?

22/09/2013 Arsenal (2) 3 Stoke (1) 1 – Austrian Arnautovic (or "Arnie") starts, and Geoffrey Scott Cameron (previously with the Rhode Island Stingrays) scores a GOAL! His first for Stoke. Apart from that it's the Gunners showing the new-passing Potters how it's done, despite Stoke having an unproductive 50% of possession. Ramsey puts in a rebound on 5 minutes, Geoff puts in a rebound on 26, Mertesacker heads in a corner on 36, and Sagna heads in a free-kick on 72. Actually, all 3 Arsenal goals are from set-pieces, which speaks volumes about Wenger & Hughes: Arsene is clearly more Pulis-like than Sparky is!

The Three Wise Men arrive at The Brit, minus the dodgy haircuts

25/09/2013 Tranmere 0 Stoke (1) 2 (Capital One) – A chance to see Sparky's 4 new boys, 5 if you include Pennant (!?), as Hughes makes 7 changes. Arnie puts Ireland through to score on the half-hour, Muniesa slices a shot off towards Greenland and almost gives away a late penalty, and loanee Ossie Assaidi comes on to spur on Crouchy to seal the win in time-added. But this should have been done & dusted before Coronation Street has finished.

29/09/2013 Stoke 0 Norwich (1) 1 – Chris Hughton's struggling Norwich side think Xmas has come VERY early as Stoke fail to turn up at all. So poor are they that Sparky subs Adams AND Walters at half-time! Yes, SJW! Even Begovic looks sluggish diving for Norwich's first-half goal. Nearly 60% possession, but Stoke's shooting & passing are laughable; just ONE shot on target at home to a team destined for relegation. "Powder puff!" exclaims Martin Spinks, inexplicably, but no doubt well-deserved. And things were going so well.

05/10/2013 Fulham (0) 1 Stoke 0 – Martin Jol's struggling Fulham side think Christmas has come VERY early...too. Only it's ref Roger East who's playing

Santa, failing to hand out a couple of penalties (as Ireland and Walters are victims of attempted murder inside the box) nor any red cards (despite Pieters and Ireland getting a good slapping). And that's just the first half! When Darren Bent scores a late winner, the cross is from a Fulham player who should have had an early bath. The result saves Jol's job...well, for just a few more weeks. But the big mystery is why Arnie is playing centre-forward.

19/10/2013 Stoke 0 West Brom 0 – This week it's Jon Walters' turn to be centre forward, with Assaidi & Arnie lobbing in the crosses. Not a sausage, & it's now 5.5 hours since a Stoke league goal - you remember, that one by Stingray-Geoff at Arsenal. Mind you, Albion fronted by Saido Berahino aren't much better, with star-man Asmir "I'm going to the World Cup with Bosnia, me!" Begovic thwarting them. The Baggies bleat that they should have had a penalty on the hour (well, Charlie Adam was playing), but ref Howard Webb laughs it off. And so should we. Attendance a dodgy 25,904 for this dodgy local derby.

26/10/2013 Man Utd (1) 3 Stoke (2) 2 – The return of Peter Crouch. Seemingly snubbed by Sparky, Crouchy is finally recalled and takes only 4 minutes (& two attempts) to break Stoke's goal drought (he goes on to be the season's top-scorer). David Moyes' side is already losing touch with the leaders (and reality), but Van Persie claws an equaliser on 43 mins, only for Arnie's free kick to make it 2-1 at break-time. Sadly, with Arnie having to go off, joined soon after by the tired figure of Palacios (yes, you read that correctly, WilsonP played this game), after dominating the first half, Stoke can't hang on in the second. Two late goals in 2 minutes by Rooney and Hernandez steal it for United. Stoke will have to wait a little longer to sink a telling nail into Moyes' coffin...so stay tuned.

29/10/2013 Birmingham (1) 4 Stoke (1) 4 (Capital One. Stoke win 4-2 on penalties) – Goals, penalties, red cards, cock-ups...you couldn't buy a game like this (unless you were a far-eastern betting syndicate, of course). Assaidi lets fly and blasts Stoke 1-0 up, but at 1-1 he gets an elbow in the face & Birmingham are down to 10 worried men. Ossie then crosses for comeback-Crouch to make it 2-1, but when Pete tries it again with a theatrical scissor kick, he can only thwack the bar. Arnie hits a cracker for 3-1, and it should be all over. Should be. But two sloppy late goals mean extra-time, and Kenwyne has to come on to quickly make it 4-3, and nearly 5-3. But, blow-me, Palacios hands sub Olly Lee a late equaliser - there's a surprise. Brum miss their first 2 penalties, but Kenwyne, Ryan, Muniesa and Nzonzi sink theirs, thankfully. "One of craziest & scariest games we've ever seen!" claim The Oatcake. The "inexcusable" vs the "bedraggled", reckons The Sentinel. Mark Hughes, who is frightened out of a year's growth by this Halloween Horror, turns 50 three days later, though it probably feels like 60 after this. He describes the game as a "dog's dinner", but for the neutral it was the "dog's bits"(?).

02/11/2013 Stoke (1) 1 Southampton (1) 1 – Yes, the one where Begovic scores! It's five seconds after The Saints kick off and Erik back-passes to

Asmir, who (on 7 seconds) belts it clear as if Tony Pulis was still monkeying about on his back. The wind catches it, and so Southampton's two dozy centre-backs both decide to leave it for the keeper. Stupified, Artur Boruc immediately knows he's in trouble, and it bounces over his head into the goal on 13 seconds. Pieters jumps all over embarrassed Begovic, no doubt delighted to get a goal "assist" that he certainly wasn't expecting. Despite this nonsense, Pochettino's expensive Southampton side equalise through a Jay Rodriguez header on half-time. Noticeably the second-half drags as Hughes brings on Palacios despite all the wind, and as the crowd drift away nobody notices him being blown away, as Pulis used to fear. Begovic - now Stoke's joint top-scorer in the Premier - is given a target by Sparky. He's told to stick it on Palacios' back...

10/11/2013 Swansea (0) 3 Stoke (2) 3 – Just daft really. 72 hours before, Swansea were playing in Russia. Suddenly, they're 2-0 down, with Walters (playing his 100th consecutive game) scoring on 7 minutes and Ireland on 25. But some guy called Wilfried Bony scores 2 in the second half, plus one by Nathan Dyer, leaving Stoke with 4 minutes to get back from 2-3 down. With Swansea kicking seven bells out of Stoke players, it is poetic that 5 minutes into time-added that the ball tenuously hits Routledge's arm, and sub Charlie sinks the penalty equaliser to Stoke fans' extreme delight. This Sunday point dinks Stoke out of the relegation zone (!!) that they'd dropped into the previous day, but then it has been only 4 points from 24. Stoke desperately need a win; if only we can find the perfect victim...

23/11/2013 Stoke (1) 2 Sunderland 0 – Sunderland fans hate Mark Hughes. No, they REALLY hate him. His record against them is formidable (9 wins in 11 games), far better than Stoke's (3 wins in 11). So, this is the sort of game the Board expect Sparky to deliver. Instead, ref Kevin Friend dolls out the goods for him, red-carding Wes Brown on 36 minutes for launching into Charlie, who'd scored 6 minutes earlier. Initially, play goes on, and Adam casually hops off the pitch for tea and sympathy from the bench. But a few seconds later, Friend stops the game and red-cards Brown. Gus Poyet (this month's Black Cats manager) goes completely barmy, and rips off his gloves and clothes as if preparing for a punch-up! The Pulis old-boys Cameron, Adam, Crouch and finally Nzonzi combine nicely to make it 2-0 late on to give Hughes his 100th Premier victory, whilst Poyet grumbles incessantly until Brown's red card is finally rescinded a few days later. Sentinel's Martin Spinks swears he sees Nzonzi crack a smile after scoring, but isn't sure ("maybe he was just passing wind").

30/11/2013 Everton (1) 4 Stoke 0 – Let's play a game. Let's replace injured Robert Huth with league debutant Marc Muniesa against Roberto Martinez's high-flying side. Hughes learns early that he needs at least one more big burly central defender in the January window. AT LEAST one. A goal either-side of half-time are enough to sink Stoke, but even Lukaku (an inspired Martinez signing) later pokes one home to ensure Sparky gets the message. Whether he will or not is another matter. Rubbish.

04/12/2013 Stoke 0 Cardiff 0 – With Huth out for the season with a knee injury, it's Marc Wilson's turn to fill in. And bizarrely, after 100+ consecutive games, Walters is "rested" for less impressive Arnie & Assaidi. Geoff Cameron's first-half goal is wrongly ruled offside, and that's about as exciting as it gets for the 25,014 Brit crowd. Could have been worse: Cardiff could have had a penalty, Charlie could have got a second-yellow, and the late Cardiff-sub (some guy called Odemwingie) could have scored. But to put this wasted opportunity in context: declining Cardiff later finish bottom of the league.

Assaidi looking for any opportunity to rip off his shirt & wave it in the air

07/12/2013 Stoke (1) 3 Chelsea (1) 2 – Yes, here it is. That brilliant last-minute curling goal from Assaidi, Stoke's most iconic win since Boxing Day's demolition of Liverpool, and the Potters' first Chelsea league win since 1975. Ossie gets yellowed for "ungentlemanly conduct" for ripping off his shirt and waving it in the air like he just doesn't care. Walters and Ireland are similarly yellowed for ungentlemanly behaviour, so clearly this is no gentleman's game. Schurrle scores early, but the now re-established Crouch equalises from a corner on 42 minutes - the ball dropping conveniently at his feet. Substitute Ireland makes it 2-1 on 50 with a curler off the post, but that-man Schurle bullets in the equaliser for 2-2 only 3 minutes later. But just when everyone thinks Chelsea are going to steal it late as normal, Wilson makes another cracking tackle, Ireland picks it up and he lays on Assaidi on the left. Obviously, Ossie (who's only been on for 7 minutes after replacing Man Of The Match Jon Walters) is going to kill time in the corner. Not a bit of it, and off he sets to lose Ibranovic and unleash a classic past Cech for an unbelievably mental 3-2. Even Mourinho pats celebrating Assaidi as he goes past. He knows his 3 subs (Demba Ba, Lampard & Eto'o) are no match for Ireland, Assaidi and, er, Palacios.

14/12/2013 Hull 0 Stoke 0 – And Ireland pokes the ball home, but it's offside! And if you can remember ANYTHING else from this game, then you're a better man/woman/organism than me. Centre-back Marc Wilson is MotM again, closely followed by other pre-Hughes players like Begovic, Crouch, & cracking Cameron. Assaidi, Arnie, & Muniesa not quite there, but amusingly The Sentinel say of sub Erik Pieters "Thrown On for his attacking potential..." (really?!) "...but couldn't quite produce the killer ball" (no, really?!?!).

18/12/2013 Stoke 0 Man Utd (0) 2 (Capital One QTR final) – More famous for that hail storm that had the players running for cover on the half hour. "Was that necessary?" tweets Edward, a stoic Stokie; "I've seen worse." God, we're hard up here. Only major change is Palacios (who nobly battles on in the high winds without being blown over once) for Nzonzi (who seems to have disappeared altogether this week along with Wayne Rooney - no rumours there). A decent 26,000 crowd (a thousand more than saw Chelsea in the League) witness Moyes' classy United cope better on slush, and Ashley Young & Evra sink Stoke in the second half. Sparky can only stare longingly at the star-ridden United side, and wonder if he could only sign just one of them. Just then Darren Fletcher comes on for Welbeck. "Hm," he thinks.

21/12/2013 Stoke (0) 2 Aston Villa (0) 1 – Despite leaping over miserable Paul Lambert's weedy Villa (minus Agbonlahor & Benteke) into the Premier Top-10, Sparky is frowning. Arnie just isn't delivering and goes off at the break, Muniesa is stuck on the bench, an invisible Assaidi is subbed, and Erik's feeble header back to Begovic is easily intercepted for their equaliser. But Stoke's old guard are thriving: Charlie comes on for Arnie at half-time, and Crouch immediately sets him up for 1-0; Cameron's cross eventually reaches Crouchy to make it 2-1 in the 70th; and the impressive Whelan, Adam and Begovic lose out to man-of-the-match Crouch, who could have had a hat-trick. He then rushes down to London to catch Abbey Clancy as she leaps into his arms on winning Strictly Come Dancing. "The most perfect experience I've had," she gasps, no doubt talking about beating Susannah Reid than her union with Crouchy. "The Big Fella isn't getting any younger at nearly 33," chips in Martin Spinks. 33? That's no age. Grand-dad could be here for years. If only all days could be this magical!

26/12/2013 Newcastle (1) 5 Stoke (1) 1 – The one Whelan got sent off. Oh, and Marc Wilson. Er, and Mark Hughes. And only then did it get completely ridiculous. But let's start with the referee: yes, it's Martin Atkinson - need we say more? Then there's the smug Alan Pardew and his over-achieving Newcastle. Neither can do anything about Stoke's impressive first 30 minutes, culminating in Assaidi hitting another cracker for 1-0. Then out of the blue - just like towards the start of the first Pirates Of The Caribbean movie when the dubloon lands in the water - the wind changes mysteriously. Whelan is booked twice in 4 minutes and walks! Sparky explodes, throws his coat in the air, and he also walks. Then 3 minutes later the last-man Wilson tugs Remy very professionally and he walks too. At this rate of dismissal all Stoke's players and coaching staff could be having an early bath together in 15 minutes! Hang on though, we haven't even got to the ridiculous parts yet. Remy takes the subsequent penalty, and Sorensen (in for Begovic's broken finger) saves it! It's still 1-0 in goals, but 9-11 in players. But wait. The cleared ball blatantly hits Williamson's waving hand, it comes back through to Remy, whose ricocheted shot somehow beats Soro for 1-1. What's left of Stoke's bench (and everyone on TV) go mad, but Atkinson thinks everything is tickety-boo. Then just after the break, Ben Arfa crosses a ball that is clearly out of play (now even the pundits are tearing their hair out!) and Gouffran makes it 1-2. Palacios comes on to switch Stoke to 4-4-0, and soon it's 1-5, with even sub Papiss Cisse sinking a late penalty. Well, that's Boxing Day television for you. Pardew celebrates like he's already qualified for Europe (Newcastle are 6th). Hughes is naturally apoplectic. And Stoke's season, which was beginning to settle down nicely, goes seriously off the rails and careers into an exploding firework factory. But chin up: Pardew later has to explain why Stoke go on to finish above United. So, ha ha haaaaa!

29/12/2013 Spurs (1) 3 Stoke 0 – If some big guy does a scissor kick with his boots several feet off the floor inches from your face, then you're entitled to put up your hands to protect your head from serious injury. If the ball, which would have hammered you squarely in the face, is deflected off your protective arm, then you should be commended, not have a penalty given against you. But on 37 minutes Adebayor almost kills Shawcross and wins himself a penalty. Curiously, Ryan isn't yellow carded, but the damage is done, and Stoke whither away to only 32% possession and one shot on target. With Whelan and Wilson suspended, Palacios makes one of his last starts but is "Caught on the ball too often for comfort before being relieved of his duties" (Sentinel) or just plain "AWFUL!!" (tweets PhilBoot). Things are so thin on the ground that, yes, that really is Jamie Ness on the bench!

01/01/2014 Stoke (0) 1 Everton (0) 1 – Poor old Mark Hughes feels he has to learn everything the hard way. He's clearly been told to put Wilson Palacios in the shop-window for the January transfer-window, but enough is enough, surely. After finally reducing the Honduran to bench-only work, he then finally understands why Pulis lost his faith in Pennant. With Stoke leading 1-0, late-sub Pennant comes on and needlessly hacks down Osman in the 92nd minute to concede a Baines penalty, and lose Stoke 2 precious points. No one else remembers Assaidi's cracking goal just after the break, or newbie Jack Butland coming on at half-time for injured Sorensen. And unsurprisingly Pennant never plays for Stoke again. I don't want to say "I told you so", but "I told you so".

04/01/2014 Stoke (1) 2 Leicester (0) 1 – (FA Cup 3rd) The return of Arnie, whose New Year resolution "I Must At Least Look Like I'm Trying" rewards him (from today) with a steady run in the first team. But even he's eclipsed by the on-form powerhouse that is, er, Charlie Adam (really?) who swaggers through to make it 2-0 on the hour from 25 yards; plus also by debutant Jack Butland who saves a Nugent header that is surely a certain goal. Kenwyne heads the opener on 16 mins, but despite the Championship's leaders grabbing a consolation, Stoke march on in the cup. Hopefully the draw will be kind. (Bet we get something like Chelsea away.)

12/01/2014 Stoke (2) 3 Liverpool (2) 5 – Sparky's Xmas hangover continues, as the "S"s (Suarez, Sterling, Sturridge, Skrtel & Cissokho) take on the "Ex"s

(Crouch, Adam & Walters (who's really not an "ex-Liverpool", but just an Everton fan)). The Brit finally attracts 27,000 for the first time since May to see an 8 goal feast (for "feast" read "nightmare"). Jack's Prem debut is a hoot (for "hoot" read "nightmare") as Cissokho's early shot (expertly aimed at the corner flag) cannons off Ryan for 0-1, and creepy Luis Suarez nips in as Stoke's defence dithers for 0-2. But suddenly just before halftime ex-Reds Crouch (header) & Charlie (25 yarder) make it 2-2. The ref then unfairly gifts Gerrard a spot-kick after the break (moments after denying Stoke a clear penalty), and Sturridge (an ex-Sparky player) sets up Suarez for 2-4. Walters scores his regular goal against his arch-rivals to tighten it to 3-4, but Sturridge finishes off a Suarez move, giving all the points to the "S"s. Well, says everyone, THAT was enough entertainment for two games, which is just as well, given whom Stoke are playing next...

18/01/2014 Crystal Palace (0) 1 Stoke 0 – Yes, it had to happen eventually: it's Pulis vs Hughes...again. That's all this game is about. Tony has galvanised Ollie's recent signings, and is pulling Palace slowly away from relegation (& soon above Stoke!). But more than this, he SO wants to win this game. So, despite his modesty before, during and after the game, he has fired his players to 11 out of 10. Sparky, meanwhile, has (curiously) only fired his players up to 6, as if resigned to defeat. This is ironic as Stoke play this game partly as a Pulis side (with not much chance of winning away) and partly as a Hughes side (with a record 57% possession, supposedly Stoke's highest Premier away possession ever), which is a recipe for disaster. Stoke fans generously wave Pulis-thankyou flags, then watch their side being ambushed by him. As The Oatcake poetically put it: "We still fell for it." Charlie is "taken out" early, which might explain why Hughes decides to protect Arnie on the bench, but Adams recovers enough to be Stoke's only threat. Puncheon hits the only goal on 51 minutes after Wilson hesitates from a dodgy Assaidi pass - this is the same Puncheon whose penalty miss last week against Spurs is still the funniest thing on the telly. And some guy called John Guidetti (a loanee from Man City) comes on for Walters. Even Shotton (who doesn't get on the pitch all season) is given a spot on the bench. But the real mystery is The Sentinel's Martin Spinks, who sounds like he's smoking something odd: "Shawcross may have had a case for a penalty late on had he possessed black hair, big teeth and a Uruguayan passport...", "Stoke suffered a Puncheon to the ribs...", "Puncheon was suddenly the hero after standing in the stocks and being pelted with rotten tomatoes" and "There were rumours of motorway police pulling over a Welshman on Saturday evening for allegedly zig-zagging at high speed across all 3 lanes of the M3, but we have no absolute proof of this". What is he on??

Charlie Adam celebrating a goal

26/01/2014 Chelsea (1) 1 Stoke 0 – (FA Cup 4th) Begovic is back, and clearly in Chelsea's sights here, despite being beaten by a tricky Oscar free-kick on the half-hour. Apart from that, it's standard Stamford Bridge stuff, with Stoke yielding

gracefully. "Not embarrassing," reckon The Oatcake, although they were puzzled why Stoke didn't really press for an equaliser. This is the game that Guidetti blots his copybook by complaining to a Swedish paper about being left on the bench. Oh well; easy come, easy go.

29/01/2014 Sunderland (1) 1 Stoke 0 – Peter Odemwingie arrives from Cardiff (swapped for Kenwyne) as Stoke sink to 16th spot. Nzonzi then leaves on 53 minutes after a second yellow. The New Year slump continues at joint-bottom Sunderland, whose 17th minute strike and PhilBardsley-esque defending earns them the 3 points in this "vital 6-pointer" (The Oatcake). Spirited performance, despite only having 10 men, but the best news is 52% possession and Guidetti getting 4 minutes on the pitch. However, it is stretching things to call it "best" news.

01/02/2014 Stoke (1) 2 Man Utd (0) 1 – Who'd have thought it would be a super fit Charlie Adam (yes, really!!) getting all the plaudits for seeing off United for the first time since, er,... [put outrageous figure here]. Nobody, that's who. With Stoke briefly sinking into the relegation zone, and little to show from the transfer window, even the neutrals see David Moyes' stuttering wastrels (like Mata & Rooney) wiping Stoke off the map. Instead, United lose their 2 central defenders in quick succession (total accident, honest), and Charlie-boy pings a long-range free-kick off a bewildered Carrick for 1-0. Van Persie gets his obligatory goal after half-time (that's EIGHT games in a row against Stoke, damnit!), before Adam hits the stunning winner 5 minutes later. He runs round with his arms out like Biggles about to take off. As City hang on for a famous victory, Martin Spinks gives the game (& Adam) an unprecedented 9/10, and bounce up to 12th spot! Downside? Stoke only have 38% possession, the crowd is only 26,547, and the ref is only worth 5/10. What am I talking about?! Of course there's no downside! Brilliant.

08/02/2014 Southampton (2) 2 Stoke (2) 2 – Artur Boruc looks suitably nervous in goal in case Begovic tries to lob him again. But it's Charlie they need to be worried about. After Lambert fools Begovic with a narrow free-kick on 6 minutes (also fooling the ref into moving the kick 3 yards in his favour), Adam sets up Odemwingie with the mother of through-balls to make it 1-1. Then after Asmir is fooled by a cross that slips in, Charlie's corner touched in (barely) by Crouch. 2-2 is fair, but questions still linger about Stoke's away form; this is only their 6th point from 39 this season! Sure, everyone's going on about Odemwingie, but Charlie is my darling, or as The Sentinel put it "the manager's new slimline tonic". Oh dear.

12/02/2014 Stoke (1) 1 Swansea (0) 1 – Oh, these Swansea games can be so DULL. This one is very windy, so instead of bringing on blow-away Palacios, Hughes gives Guidetti a whole 25 minutes at the end to try and break the deadlock. The Sentinel call him "rusty", but The Oatcake politely refer to him carrying "excess timber" (which might mean he's made of wood (& therefore a witch) or that he's rotund (& therefore in need of a diet) or just mid-spelt (& therefore could mean anything). Meanwhile, Crouch pokes home on 17, and Flores glances an equaliser on

52. Crouch should have a late penalty after being tripped by Flores, but then Bony misses a couple of golden chances (well, that sounds like Bony) particularly thanks to brilliant Begovic. Swansea have a remarkable 64% possession (they must hide the ball up their shirts or something), but only 24,822 turn up to groan at this missed opportunity. With the Early-Bird season-tickets soon on sale, the jury is still out on Sparky's appointment.

Sparky in talks with his tailor

22/02/2014 Man City (0) 1 Stoke 0 - Six Premier games at The Etihad, and Stoke still haven't scored?? Charlie and sub Ireland have a quick go to change this, but otherwise Citeh dominate with 74% possession. Kompany and Fernandinho are somehow not red-carded for wasting Cameron, Odemwingie and, well, most of Stoke's team; that's what money buys. But the Stoke lads switch off on 70 minutes, and Ya Ya Toure sweeps in for 0-1. The only joy is watching Asmir's Bosnian mate Dzeko casually miss an open goal with a back heel; yes, a real open goal! Cocky git. Aguerooo is thankfully back next week, or Pellegrini Citeh (currently 3rd) would miss out on being League Champions next May. Stoke sink to 16th, 2 points off relegation. Sobering.

01/03/2014 Stoke (0) 1 Arsenal 0 - This game is the turning point for Mark Hughes. Walters sweeps home a penalty ("It should never have been a penalty," grunts Arsene) in the 76th minute - unbelievably sending Szczesny the wrong way (the wrong way?? for a Walters penno??). Time to dust off "Swing Low Sweet Chariot" and "1-0 To The

Rugby Team". Wenger has a good moan about how rough Stoke are, although number of fouls are roughly equal. Brilliant Arnie has finally arrived, although it's taken him half a season to get here. Ozil - signed for more than the whole Stoke squad put together plus the cost of the coaching staff etc - comes on as sub, & can only sweep one shot wide; & the rest of their star-studded team aren't much better (making Arnie look a complete bargain). Arsenal drop from 2nd to 4th, & subsequently fail to climb back up again - yes, their crash-&-burn is all Stoke's fault. But the real story is Charlie being post-match-banned for allegedly stamping on Giroud! Everyone thinks he's innocent - the video shows it to be a complete accident - except the bloomin' FA panel of old refs, & subsequently the internet goes into meltdown. Hands off our Charlie, yer beggers!

08/03/2014 Norwich (0) 1 Stoke (0) 1 – I'm sorry? "Stoke's best away day all season", as The Sentinel describe it, is a 1-1 draw at soon-to-be-relegated Norwich?! Really?! Sure, Stoke come from behind to score against the stoic Canaries, & then survive 20 mins with just 10-men, but it's sad that this supposed 6-pointer is "a good day for Stoke, with West Brom, Fulham & Palace losing" (The Oatcake). "Any away point with our record is most welcome." (!) Is this really what Mark Hughes signed up for? Norwich lead from a header on 56, but 15 mins later sub Guidetti is floored, & Walters' penalty makes it 1-1. Just 4 mins later, Walters is red carded for the first ever time for waving his legs around, and amusingly sub Guidetti is then subbed himself! He takes it better than, say, Tuncay, but effectively, that's the last we ever see of him. Maybe that's what makes this the "best away day"?

15/03/2014 Stoke (1) 3 West Ham (1) 1 – Finally, Stoke move into top gear overwhelming this mid-table claret & blue side whilst completing the double over them; this despite conceding early to their burly centre forward. Yes, Andy Carroll heads in a free-kick on 4 minutes, but after that it's Odemwingie's day. Crouch's wild swipe ricochets off Wingie on the half-hour to make it 1-1. Little Pete then sets up reborn Arnie to lash home on 69, before Ireland's counter-attack is swept in beautifully by Wingie for 3-1 just 10 mins later. "It's like watching Brazil," reckon the crowd, despite Big Sam bemoaning a disallowed goal & a possible penalty. Oh dear. If only we could do this every week.

23/03/2014 Aston Villa (1) 1 Stoke (3) 4 – Finally, Stoke move into top gear overwhelming this mid-table claret & blue side whilst completing the double over them; this despite conceding early to their burly centre forward....Hang on, didn't we do this one last week?!? Yes, but this time Stoke are away from home, and this time it's Benteke not Carroll who scores on 5 minutes, but it's still Odemwingie who waltzes around like he owns the place. It's infectious, as even Martin Spinks awards every player 8/10, even Palacios (yes, really!), who gets a game as he's Sparky's only spare midfielder. Things are so thin on the ground that Shea, Guidetti, Shotton and, er, youngster Charlie Ward are on the bench! Meanwhile, Odemwingie nutmegs the keeper for the equaliser, Crouch slots in Pieters' cross, and Nzonzi finishes a superb passing move for 3-1 by halftime! With the game killed off, fans have to wait till the last minute for full-back Cameron to finish off Arnie's run. Amazing. Why? Right, here we go: first away win since August, first double over Villa since 1966, biggest ever victory at Villa, 4 goals away in the top-flight for first time since 1982, etc etc... Hm, any other claret & blue sides we can play? Burnley, where are you when we need you? "We were second best if truth be known," reckons Paul Lambert. Really? I think it was a bit more obvious than that.

29/03/2014 Stoke (0) 1 Hull 0 – It's all Odemwingie, as he intercepts a naff Hull pass, and drills in for 1-0 on the hour. Meanwhile poor old Kenwyne (swapped for Wingie) who'd scored the winner on his debut for Cardiff is now on a goal-drought as his side determinedly slide to relegation. Looks like good business for Sparky (Cardiff are fuming!), although pundits reckon he's just lucky. Anyway, Begovic saves the points late on after a deflected shot off Cameron is somehow stopped by his outstretched paw. Geoff looks mightily relieved. Stoke are safe in 10th, although Crystal Pulis aren't too far behind!

05/04/2014 Chelsea (1) 3 Stoke 0 – And the reason Crystal Pulis aren't too far behind is that they've just beaten Chelsea, which was just as much a surprise to Pulis as it was to everyone. However, Sparky overreaches himself again, this time replacing unavailable Ireland with...yes, Wilson Palacios! Realising his mistake, he rushes on Charlie as Willy's replacement, but by then Stoke are overrun. Palacios never plays for Stoke again...but still hangs around for another whole season! Young Mohamed Salah thwacks in on the half-hour, before being floored in the box by sub Wilko on the hour. Begovic breaks the habit of a lifetime by actually saving Lampard's penalty...but putting it straight back for Lampard to tap in the rebound. Has Sorensen taught him nothing?! Finally, Willian curls one for 3-0. Only good news is that Demba Ba stays on the bench.

12/04/2014 Stoke (1) 1 Newcastle 0 – The wheels are beginning to fall off Alan Pardew's Newcastle, but somehow Stoke fail to yank them off completely, and thus leave the Toon vehicle mounted on bricks. Without Remy, they've only scored 1 in 11 games ("A problem Stoke once had whenever Kitson was injured," wits Spinky dryly.) Arnie, though, is on fire, but Crouchy is in one of his I-might-need-several-goes-at-this moods, and unbelievably misses all of Marko's assists. More understandably, Erik "the Viking" Pieters messes up a cross so much that it soars straight into the top of the goal before the break. 1-0, but it should have been 4-0.

19/04/2014 Cardiff (0) 1 Stoke (1) 1 – Odemwingie returns to his old club, and the fans aren't too pleased to see him, surprisingly. They apparently blame him for dumping mis-firing Kenwyne Jones on them (rather than grinning dopey manager Ole Gunnar Solskjaer). Peter also earns a penalty on half-time for Arnie to bash home for 1-0. Kenwyne meanwhile only gets 10 minutes at the end, by which time Cardiff have done just enough to climb off the bottom of the league on goal-difference. Nzonzi concedes the 2nd half penalty for 1-1, but Cardiff are surely doomed as Stoke scupper their chance of getting 40 points. Well, their next home game is against Chelsea, and it's wrong to have false hope; Stoke probably did them a favour.

26/04/2014 Stoke 0 Spurs (1) 1 – So, why do Stoke fans hate Danny Rose? For rolling around just after the break to ensure our Ryan gets a second yellow. Then when Cameron scythes him into touch, he leaps up and shoves him, somehow avoiding a straight red. Oh, and scoring on the half-hour. Referee Marriner is the other baddie. A few weeks ago he sent off the wrong Arsenal player (Gibbs instead of Oxlade-Chamberlain) at Chelsea, and is remembered by Stokies for NOT sending off Gary Neville in a clear 2nd yellow lunge a year or two ago. Actually, the third baddie is Adebayor who gives Ryan an elbow in the jaw before taking out Charlie. But the odd thing is Adam isn't actually on the pitch - he is just jogging along the touchline warming up when he gets hit! Meanwhile, making only his 4th start for Spurs is a young Harry Kane. He's scored in his previous 3, but here he is quelled. It won't always be like this.

Harry Kane plots a future hat-trick at The Brit

03/05/2014 Stoke (1) 4 Fulham (0) 1 – The obsession is which Welsh manager will finish higher: Hughes's Stoke or Crystal Pulis? Well, despite Palace getting their astonishing 3-3 with Liverpool, it's this Fulham game that decides the issue. Fulham are stuffed anyway, and sure for the drop, and here they get stuffed again: Odemwingie, Arnie, Assaidi and sub Walters pile on the breakaway goals. In what should be his last game for Stoke, Assaidi is on fire, which'll make him too expensive for the likes of Stoke. He's replaced late-on by Etherington, who gets a chance to say goodbye after 5 great years. Everyone's happy (well, obviously not Fulham), and the final game is at West Brom, which'll be a giggle surely. Stoke guaranteed a top-half finish, but it's Pulis who wins Manager of the Year, so everyone's got something to grumble about.

11/05/2014 West Brom (0) 1 Stoke (1) 2 – Odemwingie returns to his old club, and the fans aren't too pleased to see him, surprisingly. Hang on, we've done this one before as well! But never mind him, it's Nzonzi and Arnie who trick McAuley into an own-goal on 22. Although Albion equalise just before the hour, it's really just a matter of time before Stoke pull off their unlikely win, as they always seem to do against The Baggies. C'mon, who's it to be? Yes, it's Charlie Adam, who comes on as sub for the last 10 minutes, and hits the winner from the edge of the box with 3 minutes left! Oh, it's just too funny for words. Player of the season Asmir Begovic misses out on the fun with a sore toe, but all the other usual suspects get in on the act. The win takes them to 50 points! And 9th spot rather than 10th thanks to good-old-Charlie! Their highest finish for 39 years! And Stoke finish the highest Midlands team for the first time EVER! Everyone's happy; Sparky has arrived, and has his feet firmly under the table.

	Team	P	Wh	Dh	Lh	GFh	GAh	Wa	Da	La	GFa	GAa	W	D	L	GF	GA	GD	Pts
1	Manchester City	38	17	1	1	63	13	10	4	5	39	24	27	5	6	102	37	+65	**86**
2	Liverpool	38	16	1	2	53	18	10	5	4	48	32	26	6	6	101	50	+51	**84**
3	Chelsea	38	15	3	1	43	11	10	4	5	28	16	25	7	6	71	27	+44	**82**
4	Arsenal	38	13	5	1	36	11	11	2	6	32	30	24	7	7	68	41	+27	**79**
5	Everton	38	13	3	3	38	19	8	6	5	23	20	21	9	8	61	39	+22	**72**
6	Tottenham	38	11	3	5	30	23	10	3	6	25	28	21	6	11	55	51	+4	**69**
7	Manchester Utd	38	9	3	7	29	21	10	4	5	35	22	19	7	12	64	43	+21	**64**
8	Southampton	38	8	6	5	32	23	7	5	7	22	23	15	11	12	54	46	+8	**56**
9	Stoke City	38	10	6	3	27	17	3	5	11	18	35	13	11	14	45	52	-7	**50**
10	Newcastle Utd	38	8	3	8	23	28	7	1	11	20	31	15	4	19	43	59	-16	**49**
11	Crystal Palace	38	8	3	8	18	23	5	3	11	15	25	13	6	19	33	48	-15	**45**
12	Swansea City	38	6	5	8	33	26	5	4	10	21	28	11	9	18	54	54	0	**42**
13	West Ham Utd	38	7	3	9	25	26	4	4	11	15	25	11	7	20	40	51	-11	**40**
14	Sunderland	38	5	3	11	21	27	5	5	9	20	33	10	8	20	41	60	-19	**38**
15	Aston Villa	38	6	3	10	22	29	4	5	10	17	32	10	8	20	39	61	-22	**38**
16	Hull City	38	7	4	8	20	21	3	3	13	18	32	10	7	21	38	53	-15	**37**
17	West Bromwich	38	4	9	6	24	27	3	6	10	19	32	7	15	16	43	59	-16	**36**
18	Norwich City	38	6	6	7	17	18	2	3	14	11	44	8	9	21	28	62	-34	**33**
19	Fulham	38	5	3	11	24	38	4	2	13	16	47	9	5	24	40	85	-45	**32**
20	Cardiff City	38	5	5	9	20	35	2	4	13	12	39	7	9	22	32	74	-42	**30**

2014-15 - Not where u start, it's where u finish

16/08/2014 Stoke 0 Aston Villa (0) 1 - "Seldom in my Stoke City supporting life can I recall such a level of expectation & excitement as that which has been evident during the summer months," gush The Oatcake so eloquently. And how are they & a vibrant & expectant full house Brit rewarded? With this dogs-dinner of a game, worthy only of a "5/10" from The Sentinel (worst grade of the season/century/etc). New boys Bojan, Bardsley & Diouf look "ok" (albeit confused as to what the hell's going on), but Marc Wilson is the one too limp-wristed for Villa's lucky scrappy 50th minute winner. Mark Hughes almost has a "barney" with Paul Lambert's genteel assistant Roy Keane when a sub dawdles going off, but Sparky denies it. Afterall, Lambert would be a doddle, but Keane? "I'm not that daft!" admits Hughes. 37 games later, Villa stay up by the skin of their teeth, which makes this game all sound far worse than it was. And it was bad.

Adjusting Sparky's microphone was a delicate operation

24/08/2014 Hull (1) 1 Stoke (0) 1 - And this wasn't much better, and this was against 10 men! After a quarter-hour, Hull are caught - what's the technical way of explaining this - "messing around with the ball" (The Sentinel), so Whelan robs them, and the last defender James Chester is red-carded for chopping him down. Then the moment Glenn is replaced (41 mins) by Bojan, Hull take the lead. Stoke only finally get in gear after beefy Charlie replaces newbie Steve Sidwell, with the defenders snatching a late equaliser - Bardsley combining with Shawcross, with the help of goal-line technology. But the players then amble around Pulis-style, ie. content with a draw against 10 men. Despite currently still playing in the Europa League (Hull?! Really?!), a very sorry Hull are later relegated. Dross.

27/08/2014 Stoke (1) 3 Portsmouth 0 - (Capital One) - 3-0 sounds good, but this should have been 7-0 against now sorrowful lower-league Pompey. Gross-offenders are Walters - who may have scored on 16 and 47 minutes, but missed a pile more & his hat-trick - AND Crouch - who finally headed Stoke's 3rd in injury-time, but missed a pile more AND his hat-trick too! Spinksy seems happy to give this one-sided affair 8/10, but it's best remembered for the arrival of Victor Moses on loan (from

Chelsea), Ollie Shenton (debut sub aged only 16), and the return of Sparky's least favourite defender...The Huth!

30/08/2014 Man City 0 Stoke (0) 1 – OMG!! As Stoke haven't scored at The Etihad in their last 6 league visits, Sparky recalls Crouch & Walters, and hurls new boys Moses & Diouf at them at the expense of Arnie. How's that going to work? Well, apparently Hughes had a thing called a "game plan", and amazingly it worked. But no one can quite understand why Diouf sets off on an 80m run on the hour, and somehow slips the ball through Joe Hart. Mind you, he had a stonewall penalty turned down in the first half & should also have reached Odemwingie's late cross. Blimey, could have been 3-1. The "1" is the penalty Yaya Toure could so easily have won for the home side in the 87th, but instead the ref rightly yellows him for simulation. Nice try, mate. So, ok, sure it's a memorable victory & revenge against Pellegrini's 2nd placed Citeh, but with only 27% possession? Hell, we're not proud.

13/09/2014 Stoke 0 Leicester (0) 1 - This is more like it! 60% possession, 24 shots to Leicester's 8, a full house at The Brit, and... a 0-1 defeat to a side slowly sliding down to bottom place. In fact, it is ironic that Leicester do to Stoke what Stoke did to Citeh the week before. Leicester score on the hour mark, but Stoke could huff-&-puff all day, and never get near. However, although Leicester are hopelessly bottom by Xmas, they do manage to beat Man Utd 5-3 in their very next game.

20/09/2014 QPR (1) 2 Stoke (1) 2 - More relegation fodder. This time it's QPR, who spend almost the entire season in the relegation zone, before finally obliging everyone and finishing bottom. But here, a last-minute equaliser from an unnecessary free-kick (Sidwell!! Detention!!) is crushing for Stoke. What was the point of Crouch crawling all over Rio Ferdinand to set up Diouf on 11 minutes for 1-0? Or Crouch slicing his lunging clearance into his own net for 1-1 on 42? Or Crouch slipping past hapless Ferdinand (again) on 51 minutes to make it 2-1? To cap it all, big Pete is referred to as "The Old Man" in the Sentinel. I ask you!

23/09/2014 Sunderland (1) 1 Stoke (1) 2 (Capitol One) - The Marc Muniesa legend stems from these two cracking goals to overturn The Black Cats. He combines with Assaidi (who's strangely still hanging around at Stoke) on the half-hour to equalise for 1-1. He then scores the winner too in the 71st from "an impossible angle", before going on the hunt for his hat-trick! Cocky or what? Huth makes a rare appearance (after being ignored by Hughes, he'll soon be off to save Leicester & win the League). This game is also remembered for Nzonzi grabbing Rodwell round the throat. Steady on, Steven!

29/09/2014 Stoke (1) 1 Newcastle 0 - Starting the season with 2 home defeats is risky business for Sparky. So, along comes bottom club, Pardew's winless Newcastle, to really stick the knife in; but despite the Toons huffing & puffing (dominating possession, shots, corners, cards, glove-wearing), they get nowhere. Neil Baldwin (paraded pre-match after TV success in "Marvellous") is beaten off by

Muniesa to replace Erik at left back. But it's Moses who's the hero on the left, crossing for Crouch's 15 min winner. 5 mins later Diouf walks off coz he's not given a clear penalty (well, & his hamstring's gone), & later Crouch finds himself nose-to-chest with keeper Krul after Tim objects to Pete's spot-kick claim. Drama! Not really, the most interesting thing is that this defeat actually moves United off the bottom. Work that one out.

04/10/2014 Sunderland (2) 3 Stoke (1) 1 - Sparky spent a LONG time in the away dressing room after this one against a winless side begging to be ripped apart by the likes of Nzonzi, Muniesa, Arnie, Moses, Assaidi, & even late-on Bojan. But Stoke concede early, equalise quickly (Charlie), lose Moses, & then concede again. It's all over after only 23 minutes. Steven Fletcher makes it 3-1 at the end, which makes it a typical Hughes-start-of-season-game: ie. not worth the long trip.

19/10/2014 Stoke (1) 2 Swansea (1) 1 - Oh boy! Garry Monk calls Victor Moses a cheat!! On half-time Vic goes down in the box, & Monk is convinced he's diving. ("Disgraceful...blatant... punish...cheating...ashamed!!!" he rants.) Only later do the replays show Angel Rangel sneakily pulling Moses' shirt to unbalance him, proving volatile Monk wrong, but the Swansea donkey refuses to apologise. (How does that work, Garry?) Particularly as 15 minutes earlier Shawcross is penalised similarly, and a penalty conceded. Nobody's calling Bony a cheat. The real hero though is hitherto overlooked Jonny Walters, who caps off a fantastic week of helping Ireland get a 1-1 draw in Germany (in the Euros), by coming on on-the-hour & heading the winner.

25/10/2014 Southampton (1) 1 Stoke 0 - High-flying high-spending Saints make Stoke look like car-booters with their bargain-basement signings (Diouf, Muniesa, etc). They pen back Stoke and pound Begovic's woodwork mercilessly! (Sooth to say, Asmir is not amused.) But the free-kick for the only goal is a farce: the ref plays advantage after Charlie's foul, only for Southampton to push into the box & lose the ball. But hang on, the ref calls it back and the free-kick results in Sadio "tres-expensive" Mane slotting home. Sparky has his normal fit etc etc, when really he should be thankful not to lose by 4 or more. Thank god we don't have to play these guys every week.

29/10/2014 Stoke (0) 2 Southampton (2) 3 (Capital One) - Bloody hell, do we have to play these guys every week? We just played them 4 days ago! 16,340 get their money's worth, if by "money's worth" we mean inept first half ("hopeless!" say The Oatcake), comeback in the 2nd half, late red-card & capitulation. Nzonzi's 49th min goal is speculative, but the 82nd minute equaliser - Adam's corner flicked on by excellent Walters & headed home by Diouf - is splendid. But the star of the show is Crouchy. He comes on in the 73rd minute, he sparks confusion in the penalty area for Diouf's goal, then he gets harshly booked in the 86th. Yet, 90 seconds later he hacks into Davis, studs raised, and earns a 2nd yellow. (In truth it could have just been a straight red.) Then to rub salt into the wound, Pelle scores from the free kick. Sparky has his normal fit etc etc... He just doesn't like Southampton, and swears not to have anything to do with them ever again. Probably.

01/11/2014 Stoke (1) 2 West Ham (0) 2 - ...and there was much gnashing of teeth! The crowd fall for Bojan in a big way, plus Walters, Geoff, and even Steve Sidwell (no, really!) are brilliant. But West Ham have ref Chris Foy as their 12th man (despite Big Sam's blustering on the subject); oh, and Stewart Downing, who masterminds a comeback after Stoke go 2-0 up. Moses on the half-hour & Diouf's header on the hour should have put this to bed, but The Hammers have 2 shots on target after the hour-mark, and that's all they need. No one cares that it was a "Superb advert for Premier League football" because it could - no, SHOULD - have been 5-2. Only Diouf can explain why he didn't get a hat-trick. When asked he just said: "Gnash gnash gnash!!!" (It's those gnashing teeth.)

Still Haven't Found What I'm Looking For... many fans still searching for U2 at The Brit

09/11/2014 Spurs (0) 1 Stoke (2) 2 - And now the THIRD victory at White Hart Lane in 100 odd years. Here Bojan ambles forward, does a wall-pass, & let's fly...in just the 6th minute for 1-0 (with Walters heading in on the half-hour for 2-0). Pochettino quietly does his nut on the touchline as Spurs' performance is succinctly described in The Oatcake: "Terrible!!" (Their star-studded team will go on to finish 5th.) The Hotspur's consolation goal is an impressive volley from an impossible angle. It "defied geometry", claims Martin Spinks, but that's Londoners for you; bending space on the quiet. It's Bojan's first goal. It's 40% possession (compared to 34% with Pulis' victory). Oh, and Spurs have a player sent off late for a near biblical killing of Moses. There'll be a plague of locusts, mark my words. The Oatcake's Martin Smith claims it made him "purr" whilst watching & rewatching it on MotD. But The Oatcake claim this comes in SECOND to the Citeh win! Really?! That had 27% percentage & only 2 shots on goal! What is the matter with you?!?

22/11/2014 Stoke (1) 1 Burnley (2) 2 - A great away win, an international break, then this stinker of a game comes along. Fans wanting to watch a Stoke team with loads of possession (yes, 73%! Happy now?) also have to sit through City self-destruct in the 13th minute, conceding TWO goals in quick succession. The second is from a cross from a discarded Michael Kightly. Walters heads one back on the half-hour, but it's too-little-too-late - yes, you heard me right: a whole hour of pressure was never going to get Stoke back in this game. 25 chances later, and the

worst set of crosses you've ever seen (& no, Erik wasn't even playing!), prove that this Stoke side (Arnie, Bojan, Muni, Moses, Nzonzi, Bego, Ryan, SJW) sometimes just looks better on paper.

29/11/2014 Liverpool (0) 1 Stoke 0 - Bizarrely, Stoke are one place above Liverpool (11th & 12th), and Brendan Rodgers is under pressure. But it's the same old story, leaving fan AndyK in philosophical mood: "I think we're just going to have to face up to the fact that we are all going to die before Stoke win a game at Anfield." But fear not, Andy, Mark Hughes has a plan: As Glen Johnson heads the 85th minute winner, Sparky googles the right-back's phone-number. "All I need is GlenJ," he thinks. Hm, we'll see how that turns out. Sub Steven Gerrard looks on smugly as he thinks this is the last time he'll ever have to face Stoke. How wrong is he.

02/12/2014 Man Utd (1) 2 Stoke (1) 1 - Stoke may not have won at Anfield since Wolves last won the League, but they haven't even had a draw at Old Trafford since New Order released a decent single (controversial). But with the squad so threadbare, Assaidi makes his only league start of the season, Ireland is recalled from obscurity, and...and...good god, that's Palacios on the bench! Even fellow-sub Oliver Shenton is surprised to see him. As for the match, Fellaini is allowed to head a goal, fake an injury, and generally move around like a loo-brush on a unicycle. Another really nice guy, Robin Van Persie (previously seen red carded for attacking Sorensen) steps on Erik's leg and gets away with it, in an incident that Charlie would NOT have been so lucky with. Nzonzi equalises on 39 mins with a cool shot, but United win it from a free-kick on the hour, despite Arnie & Diouf almost levelling it late on. Sentinel sum it up nicely by mis-printing Stoke's possession as "6%". No, it wasn't that bad. Was it?

06/12/2014 Stoke (3) 3 Arsenal (0) 2 - DON'T GET ME STARTED! Like a perfect midnight dream, it's 3-0 to Stoke and Bojan is on fire. Then on 65 minutes, he swerves in from the left, and thwacks one in that the keeper can't keep out. It's 4-0, and....hang on, the ref (Anthony Taylor) reckons Diouf is offside and SOMEHOW interfering with play by being on the pitch somewhere vaguely near the goalkeeper. Lunacy. It's not just me, it's the watching world who are dumbfounded, particularly after Rooney's controversial goal last week which really should have been disallowed for a more obvious offside/interfering incident. The pundits go crazy. Worse still, 4 minutes later & it's 3-2 (a penalty & Aaron Ramsey), and Stoke are hanging on for dear life. It's wrong wrong wrong. Particularly after Crouch taps in on 19 SECONDS, Bojan side-foots on 35 minutes, and Walters crashes in his 100th career goal for 3-0 on the stroke of half time. But best of all, Arsene Wenger becomes welded to his seat in the dug-out, refusing to be drawn out to the touchline. "They love me so much here," he says afterwards. To be honest, we do. Probably more than his own supporters. Long may he reign.

13/12/2014 Crystal Palace (1) 1 Stoke (1) 1 – This battle of the lower-mid-table isn't worth the admission money. A lucky header beats otherwise brilliant Begovic on 10 minutes, but 90 seconds later & Crouch gets another tap-in for 1-1. Now a point at Warnock's Palace is not to be sniffed at, unless you're Neil Warnock who is sacked 14 days later. Well, they should have kept Pulis.

22/12/2014 Stoke 0 Chelsea (1) 2 - The secret is, if you're playing the champions (& now champions-elect), don't give away an early goal. So, it's really all over when Terry heads home a 90th second corner. Without the likes of Moses, Stoke look pedestrian, even with recalled Arnie and Muniesa, the latter doing his best alongside big Ryan. Fabregas slots home in 78 minutes, and Jose Mourinho goes home happy, smiling and doing a little jig. Well, possibly. Not. But Chelsea look like they're in a different league, even with mad-dog Diego Costa. Maybe it's the Justice League.

26/12/2014 Everton 0 Stoke (1) 1 - With Diouf's shooting so wayward, Bojan decides to take his 38th minute penalty himself, and thankfully just beats Tim Howard for 1-0, despite a laser pen being pointed at his eye during his run-up. But Krkic and Walters are lucky to still be on the pitch in this rain-sodden Boxing Day fest after early over-enthusiastic fouls. A third away win leaves Everton fans "chuntering" (A good Sentinel word). Thankfully the inclement weather forbids the inclusion of Palacios, who's watching from the bench. Too much wind.

28/12/2014 Stoke (0) 2 West Brom 0 - "We always beat West Brom," merrily sing the fans, and here is yet another example as we send yet another of their managers to the scrap-heap – this time it's Alan Irvine who's sacked THE FOLLOWING DAY. Two 2nd half Diouf goals do for him - one miraculously from a Pieters cross, believe it or not – and this finishes off a lively Albion, tormented by on-form Bojan. Stoke fans go home happy in the knowledge that it's now only 2 defeats in 34 games against West Brom. None of them - and I mean none of them - notice the dark clouds on the horizon heading towards this fixture. And so it came to pass that 4 days later Tony Pulis is appointed Albion manager. "Never in a million years did we see that coming!" exclaim The Oatcake.

01/01/2015 Stoke (1) 1 Man Utd (1) 1 - Stoke fans (& TV pundits) can't believe that Stoke don't beat Van Gaal's 3rd placed United. It's Crouch's header hitting Smalling's waving arm in the 2nd half that is the bone of contention. (I think it's the Humerus.) Up till then, it's Shawcross volleying home against his old team in just 106 seconds, and Falcao's 25th minute equaliser (both goals from corners) that are the bullet points. But, oh sure, Michael Oliver's OK giving penalties against Stoke for grappling (see Swansea game), but blatant hand-ball against United? Nah, it was never going to happen. Even if it was the Radius.

04/01/2015 Stoke (0) 3 Wrexham (0) 1 (FA Cup) - Mark Hughes' home-side comes to town and it's nearly an almighty cock-up. 7 changes bring in Butland, Sidwell & Assaidi, plus the much overlooked Huth, Adam, Wilson & Bardsley. But despite having Arnie, Geoff, Ryan & Diouf on the pitch, the whole team feel like Sparky's neglected zombies. Meanwhile, the green-shirted Wrexham wait patiently till the 73rd minute before heading themselves 1-0 up. For Stoke this is a perfect time to panic, but 7 minutes later the Welsh side start to be bulldozed over by Stoke subs Crouch and Ireland. Arnie finishes off a deflect-fest from the Crouch/Ireland pairing, Ireland scores from a Crouchy nod-down in the 87th, and Stevie-boy makes it three in time-added from a sharp angle. Yes, Ireland beats the Welsh! Er, yes, harsh on Wrexham, but then probably harsh on everybody watching for the first hour.

10/01/2015 Arsenal (2) 3 Stoke 0 - We came, we saw, we went away again. And that's now 12 defeats in a row at Arsenal. Enter Philipp Wollscheid for his baptism of fire, but all he gets is a yellow card. He's preferred over out-of-position Wilson & Muniesa, but also remaindered Huth (who's struggling to even make the bench). Meanwhile, the team are already "on the plane" to Dubai as Arsenal tear them apart (Koscielny's unopposed header on 6 minutes, and two by Sanchez either side of half-time), and it could easily have been 5-0. Best remembered for Arnie shoving Debuchy into the advertising boards, dislocating Mat's shoulder. Naughty boy. I hope he said sorry.

How could we fail under the watchful eye of Hairy Potter

17/01/2015 Leicester 0 Stoke (0) 1 - Bojan is just unplayable. This is his golden era. Supported by Moses, Arnie and Walters, he barges through on the hour to hit the only goal. If he stays fit, he'll be a Stoke icon. It's now 4 away wins by mid-January and 3 clean sheets in 5 games. So, Mark Hughes says they can fly out tonight. But then this is bottom club Leicester, surely - SURELY - heading for relegation. Huth watches from the bench as Muniesa gets the nod standing in for Shawcross, and Wilson even gets a game at Left-back. Rob looks over at Leicester and wonders if he can do a job for them. Off he goes (initially on loan) with just a black bin-bag of old clothes, and the rest is history. He rescues them from certain relegation, scores in a 3-2 win at Pulis' West Brom, and goes on to win the league. Really, Sparky? Really? Thank goodness Stoke have got Wollscheid...

26/01/2015 Rochdale (0) 1 Stoke (1) 4 (FA Cup) - Bojan is just unplayable...hang on, haven't we just done the unplayable thing? No, he really is unplayable after half an hour as his knee gives way as he stumbles in the box putting him out for the season. His truly wondrous volley on 4 minutes winds up the locals, but his ungentlemanly yellow card just before his injury makes him a target for the miserable Rochdale fans who label him a "cheat" as he hobbles off. So, after an even first half Ireland, Moses and Walters put the Dale to the sword after the break. Typically, ref Martin Atkinson gifts them the consolation.

31/01/15 Stoke (2) 3 QPR (1) 1 - Oddly, Sparky leaves Diouf and Crouch on the bench, and makes Johnny Walters centre forward. He's not the only one to be amazed when SJW not only scores a perfect hat-trick, but gets a 9/10 from Spinksy in The Sentinel! In his 200th game for Stoke, John does a right and a left foot goal before half-time, and nods in a header in time-added. Not bad for a guy labelled "only a Championship player" by fans when he arrived. Sparky's former club make it 2-1 just before the break to add a bit of tension, but Redknapp's side are sooo going down.

07/02/15 Newcastle (0) 1 Stoke (0) 1 - "A draw that feels like a win," proclaim The Oatcake. Well, as Newcastle have Friends in high places (ie ref Kevin Friend), it's an uphill struggle against 12 men. Not as bad as last year's 2 red cards for Stoke, but instead Colback should walk for a clear 2nd yellow after slicing up Moses. Would you believe it, not THREE minutes later he converts a Cisse cross in the 74th. Typical. But, to the away fans' delight, in the last minute Cameron's deep cross is superbly headed home by Crouch. Coolest dude of the day? Super Johnny Walters (SJW) who, whilst congratulating Crouch on scoring, stops to pick up and read a programme that's been thrown on to the pitch. Fans describe him as "indefatigable", but I don't know what that means.

11/02/15 Stoke (1) 1 Man City (1) 4 - Hard to believe, but this game could easily have gone 4-1 the other way! And that doesn't even include Milner handling on the line in the opening few minutes, which he gets away (so he's bound to score later on). Aguerooo scores his 20th goal of the season on the half-hour, with Crouch equalising from an Arnie cross. But with chances and disallowed goals, Stoke could've been 3-1 up against a possible 10-man Citeh by half-time. But instead, the second-half allows Milner (somehow still on the pitch - sorry to keep on about it) to head in for 2-1, followed by an Aguerooo penalty and a Nasri dribble to make it 4-1 against a resigned Stoke side. Ollie Shenton comes on for a 2 minute debut. Palacios and Teixeira aren't so lucky. Citeh go on to finish 2nd.

14/02/15 Blackburn (2) 4 Stoke (1) 1 (FA Cup) - An easy ride into the Quarter Finals of the FA Cup turns into a utter disaster. Enter a Championship mid-table side, who make EIGHT changes to play Stoke including unknown Norwegian Josh King. Stoke make only ONE change, Jack Butland in for Begovic, and even go 1-0 up on 10 minutes thanks to Crouch belting home. But then Stoke take their foot off the pedal, King equalises, and suddenly it's 1-2 with Cameron red carded for a penalty foul on King. After the break, King quickly gets his hat-trick, and the humiliation is complete. Surely. No, not yet. Nzonzi, who'd left Rovers under a cloud, is embarrassingly reduced to playing in the back-4 as Sparky runs out of defenders. By the end it could be 5 or 6-1. Get this, though: King is subsequently dropped again by Blackburn for the next few games, but later becomes a star at Bournemouth. Rovers lose a replay to Liverpool in the next round. Captain Whelan has a rant at his lacklustre colleagues. But the Sparky honeymoon is over. As Martin Spinks points out: "Stoke have conceded 4 goals in successive matches for the first time since 1994". Stoke fans can't imagine that happening again for decades.

21/02/15 Aston Villa (1) 1 Stoke (1) 2 - Poor old Villa. No longer the top Midlands side, stuck in a relegation battle, and now Tim Sherwood has turned up to finish them off, replacing luckless Paul Lambert. In Timmy's first game in charge, little Scott Sinclair inexcusably beats Stoke's tall but makeshift defence to glance home on 20 minutes, and Villa are clearly on the new-manager bounce. But Villa are no Blackburn (something you thought you'd never hear), and Diouf heads in Ireland's cross from the right on half-time. Whilst Stoke's defence goes extreme-makeshift (debutant Teixeira has to come on late for Erik), Moses somehow wins a penalty in time-added with Villa's captain Ron Vlaar red carded for "lunge-ing". Walters decides not to argue with Victor, and lets Moses send the keeper the wrong way. Yes, Blackburn is forgotten & forgiven. Ha! You think?! No, not really.

Watching Pulis & Hughes was often more interesting than watching their teams competing

28/02/15 Stoke (0) 1 Hull (0) 0 - Steve Bruce's Hull are doing ok...until they play Stoke. Then they career off the road finishing the season with only 2 wins in 12 games, and go down with 35 points. Who can Steve blame? Well, firstly Stevie Ireland for bleeding all over the pitch after Figueroa's studs ripped his leg apart. Ugh! Then there's forgotten Charlie Adam, for replacing Ireland at half-time with a stonking performance and supplying the cross for Stoke's goal. Or what about Crouch for coming on in the 70th minute, & heading the winner only seconds after coming on! Or the linesman for not giving Crouchy offside (although it's too tight to mention really, but that doesn't stop Bruce). No, what the Hull manager should have focussed in on was that Stoke had 17 goal attempts whilst Hull had just one, and even that was wide of the mark. 10th place Stoke hit 39 points, & it's still February.

04/03/15 Stoke (1) 2 Everton 0 - Finally, Stoke do the double over Everton for the first time since before Gordon Banks joined the club. And with a makeshift team, Wollscheid joins Shawcross in the treatment room after only 15 minutes. But a gritty performance by the "W"s (Whelan, Wilson & Walters) inspires Moses to head home a cracker on 32 mins for 1-0, & Diouf to put in an Arnie rebound off the post on 84. Martinez pays the price for concentrating on the Europa League. It's only Dynamo Kiev, Roberto; they're a pushover.

14/03/15 West Brom (1) 1 Stoke 0 - It's almost quaint to watch Stoke players freeze against their old boss Tony Pulis, although frankly it's the same old story: Pulis wants it more than Hughes, Albion get the goal (Ideye header after 20 mins) to hang on to, Stoke have the possession (nearly 60% away from home), Albion have the chances (14-9), but then with Berahino none of them were likely to go in. It's actually a Sparky player, Bardsley, that misses the clearance for the goal, but the rest of Stoke's players (including the returning Shawcross) are awful today...apart from Wilson, who's the only one to put in a decent shift (first half at centre-back, 2nd half as left-back). Hm, maybe Marc's thinking he might need a job from TP sometime in the future?

Peter Crouch's tries every trick in the book to beat Albion's keeper Myhill

21/03/15 Stoke (1) 1 Crystal Palace (2) 2 - Another "how did we lose this one?" game, pivoted on spot-kick decisions. Diouf stabs home on the quarter-hour, but weirdly Andre Marriner gives Palace a penalty on 40 mins when Bolasie charges foot-first into Begovic. How is that a penalty?! Nemesis Glenn Murray converts, before Zaha nips in to make it 1-2 minutes later. Then on the hour, Ward clearly handles Diouf's shot in the box with both hands...and the ref gives nothing. How does that work? Well, new manager Alan Pardew's riding his luck, & Sparky's run out of honeymoon credit.

04/04/15 Chelsea (1) 2 Stoke (1) 1 - Yes, it's Charlie Adam from a whole 65 yards away! Yes, that one! Five minutes after Chelsea's penalty lead, Charlie picks up the ball in his own half, whilst Chelsea players are distracted from claiming a foul. This gives Charlie the split-second of freedom to reach the edge of the centre-circle before letting fly his bullet of a shot over retreating keeper Courtois, who makes the faintest of touches. Sadly, it's Begovic's poor throw-out in the 2nd half that gifts Remy the winner, which leaves historians to wonder why Chelsea would rather buy Asmir over Charlie. Might it have been Adam's robotic-goal-celebration for the benefit of Crouch, scorer of Stoke's previous wonder goal?

11/04/15 West Ham (1) 1 Stoke (0) 1 - Oh yes. The game Arnie scores a hat-trick, but almost comes away with nothing. With two goals (66th & 92nd minutes) disallowed for offside, he waits until the game is over (well, nearly, in fact the 95th minute!) to battle through the throng and unleash a shot into the far corner. Yeah, away-fan-mental time. West Ham go mental too, as they'd been leading since a 7th minute free-kick that deceives Begovic. All this clearly ages Big Sam Allardyce, but Hammers' executives make a secret note of Arnie's name for the future.

18/04/15 Stoke (0) 2 Southampton (1) 1 - These were the days when Charlie really was our darling. This time he only has to shoot from 10 yards (not 65), but who cares. A late winner is a late winner, particularly in a duff game against stingy Saints & their 1st half lead. Goal of the day though is on 47 mins when Nzonzi nonchalantly lobs the ball high & goal-ward. The fans groan as it looks like it's wastefully going over the bar, but then the gusty wind pulls it back, it comes down & off the bar to Diouf who half-volleys it home. No one can quite believe it.

25/04/15 Stoke (1) 1 Sunderland (1) 1 - Not Charlie again?! After fumbling Begovic gifts Sunderland the lead on only 57 seconds, Charlie comes to the rescue on the half-hour with a rocket of a shot to a loose ball with his supposedly weaker right foot. (Who's he fooling?!). What a guy! Pity the rest of the team couldn't deal with that wind or finish off this struggling side, who just manage to stay up.

02/05/15 Swansea (0) 2 Stoke 0 - Begovic - clearly on his way out the door to Chelsea - is dropped for Butland to try out as the new "Glovenor" (as Martin Spinks handily puts it). Asmir's not even on the bench - something he'll have to get used to at Chelsea. But even Jack can't stop Swansea's late strikes, as Stoke finally cave in. Mind you, nor can Marc Wilson stop them, as he earns Stoke their first red-card of the whole season, 2nd-yellowed for a professional foul trying to keep the score at 0-1. Not worth it, mate.

09/05/15 Stoke (2) 3 Spurs 0 - Bloomin' 'eck! Never mind Stoke's first ever double over Spurs, their highest ever victory over Spurs, most number of Premier wins (14 so far), and 50 points in the bag. No, bloomin' 'eck, Charlie has scored again, his 4th in 6 games! And it's with a header! Of sorts! Nzonzi makes it 2-0 on the half-hour, and Diouf finishes off Arnie's coup-de-grace in the last 5 mins, but it's Charlie that fans think might be coaxed away by a top club. I know! Who'd have thought?! Spurs even go down to 10 men when Vlad is second-yellowed just after the break, but nobody notices. However, Martin Spinks is caught lamenting: "What a pity this wasn't the last game of the season". Hm, I think he's worried about that forthcoming Liverpool game...Yeah, that could end in tears.

16/05/15 Burnley 0 Stoke 0 - Sure, this draw takes Stoke to a record 51 points, but for a side so close to Europa League qualification playing a side already relegated, it is a bit timid. Begovic returns to the bench to ensure he's still in the shop window, whilst soon-to-be England manager Gareth Southgate casts his eye over Butland. It's the future being made here.

24/05/15 Stoke (5) 6 Liverpool (0) 1 - Steven Gerrard's last game! All Liverpool fans remember where they were for Steven Gerrard's last game. The unlucky ones are at The Brit having their side viciously ripped apart in their worst league defeat for over 50 years! Diouf starts the ball rolling on 22 mins after keeper Mignolet spills; he then cracks in for 2-0 on 26; Walters takes 2 attempts for 3-0 on 30; Adam robs Lucas to make it 4-0 on 41; and even Nzonzi unleashes a cracker to make it 5-0 by half-time. As Liverpool replace their full-backs (who are never heard of again), it becomes trickier in the 2nd half. So, Sparky sends on Crouch late on to score a record-breaking 47th Premier League header. It's hard to say which goal is celebrated with most relish, but Gerrard's lame 70th minute consolation goal gets a genuine standing ovation, despite Steven's truly humiliating jog back to his own half. Despite having just scored he looks like he wants the ground to open up and swallow him. Meanwhile, Martin Spinks gives the game 10/10, and all Stoke's players a 9! Bloody hell! Yes, even Pieters, Diouf and Cameron. Brendan Rodgers's side hasn't won a trophy for 3 years (a 50 year record, supposedly), and after losing today actually fall below Spurs to finish 6th. But somehow Bren holds on to his job. Stoke finish a rampant 9th, 7 points off Europe, which is a real blast. However, Mark Hughes has set the bar high, and he could struggle to get near it again. Just glad that Spurs wasn't the last game of the season.

	Team	P	Wh	Dh	Lh	GFh	GAh	Wa	Da	La	GFa	GAa	W	D	L	GF	GA	GD	Pts
1	Chelsea	38	15	4	0	36	9	11	5	3	37	23	26	9	3	73	32	+41	**87**
2	Manchester City	38	14	3	2	44	14	10	4	5	39	24	24	7	7	83	38	+45	**79**
3	Arsenal	38	12	5	2	41	14	10	4	5	30	22	22	9	7	71	36	+35	**75**
4	Manchester Utd	38	14	2	3	41	15	6	8	5	21	22	20	10	8	62	37	+25	**70**
5	Tottenham	38	10	3	6	31	24	9	4	6	27	29	19	7	12	58	53	+5	**64**
6	Liverpool	38	10	5	4	30	20	8	3	8	22	28	18	8	12	52	48	+4	**62**
7	Southampton	38	11	4	4	37	13	7	2	10	17	20	18	6	14	54	33	+21	**60**
8	Swansea City	38	9	5	5	27	22	7	3	9	19	27	16	8	14	46	49	-3	**56**
9	Stoke City	38	10	3	6	32	22	5	6	8	16	23	15	9	14	48	45	+3	**54**
10	Crystal Palace	38	6	3	10	21	27	7	6	6	26	24	13	9	16	47	51	-4	**48**
11	Everton	38	7	7	5	27	21	5	4	10	21	29	12	11	15	48	50	-2	**47**
12	West Ham Utd	38	9	4	6	25	18	3	7	9	19	29	12	11	15	44	47	-3	**47**
13	West Bromwich	38	7	4	8	24	26	4	7	8	14	25	11	11	16	38	51	-13	**44**
14	Leicester City	38	7	5	7	28	22	4	3	12	18	33	11	8	19	46	55	-9	**41**
15	Newcastle Utd	38	7	5	7	26	27	3	4	12	14	36	10	9	19	40	63	-23	**39**
16	Sunderland	38	4	8	7	16	27	3	9	7	15	26	7	17	14	31	53	-22	**38**
17	Aston Villa	38	5	6	8	18	25	5	2	12	13	32	10	8	20	31	57	-26	**38**
18	Hull City	38	5	5	9	19	24	3	6	10	14	27	8	11	19	33	51	-18	**35**
19	Burnley	38	4	7	8	14	21	3	5	11	14	32	7	12	19	28	53	-25	**33**
20	QP Rangers	38	6	5	8	23	24	2	1	16	19	49	8	6	24	42	73	-31	**30**

2015-16 - The Tide Turns

09/08/15 Stoke 0 Liverpool (0) 1 - Bloody hell, not Liverpool again. Back-to-back home games with the multi-spending scousers, but a lot has changed over the summer. Stoke seem happy to lose Huth to Leicester for £3m, resolved to lose Begovic to Chelsea for £8m, and reluctant to lose Nzonzi to Sevilla for £7m (after signing him for £3m 3 years before). In come Ibrahim Afellay (free from Barcelona), Marc Van Ginkel (loan from Chelsea), Glen Johnson (free from Liverpool), plus £5.5m Joselu (on the bench). Frankly, it's a mixed bunch, and without Shawcross (back surgery till Holloween), the heart seems to have been knocked out of the side that tore The Reds apart just a few weeks before. In the end, it's a cracker from Coutinho, who's just about to be subbed, that steals it. But it can never make up for their 6-1 drumming last season, so "Tough luck!". As for the new signings, question marks are raised over all of them. They all look to be bargain basements or remainders. In contrast, of the 3 leaving the club, 2 go on to win major silverware (Huth the Premier League, Nzonzi the Europa League) less than 9 months later, and there is the bizarre situation of these two later facing each other in the last-16 of the Champions League! A sobering thought indeed. Of course, by this time Begovic is welded to the Chelsea bench (although he does win a Premier League medal the following season despite only playing TWO games), and by this time all of Stoke's new signings are drifting into obscurity. (Oh, and Steven Nzonzi wins the World Cup with France in 2018.) Meanwhile up in the stand is a guy called Xherdan Shaqiri, who will be Stoke's £12m record signing. Just what we need: a player whose name begins with "X".

15/08/15 Spurs (2) 2 Stoke (0) 2 - What's Shaqiri still doing in the stand? Apparently (and worryingly) serving out an old suspension from his Inter days. Meanwhile, Spurs go 2-0 up via Dyer and Chadli, and stats say that Spurs ALWAYS win when they go 2-0 up. But Joselu steps off the bench, and tumbles over in the far corner of the penalty area. Reborn Arnie Arnautovic obliges with the penalty, before super-sub Ireland's cross from the left goes straight in for 2-2. What? Diouf reckons his head makes the faintest of touches for the equaliser? Really? I don't think so, Mame, but somehow he gets credited with it. Would you credit it? Not in a million years. But a credible result against a side that later finish 3rd.

22/08/15 Norwich (1) 1 Stoke (1) 1 - Up against Cameron Jerome again now Norwich are back, but Butland is more than a match for him and the rest. Shaqiri FINALLY gets to play, and his 11th minute free kick is headed home by Diouf for 1-0. Norwich equalise on the half-hour, with Russell Martin nutmegging Jack, but this is mundane stuff against a side who'll surely not last the season.

25/08/2015 Luton (0) 1 Stoke (0) 1 (Capital One) (Stoke win 8-7 on penalties) - Oh, this is far worse than in looks. With 72% possession, this much-changed Stoke side couldn't punch their way out of a paper-bag. On paper the likes of Arnie, Crouchy, returning Bojan, Walters, Ireland, Erik, Bardsley etc look formidable, but for most it's their first game since Newcastle Town. And League 2 Luton aren't any better (half of them are reserve players, postmen, OAPs, etc). So, everyone watching on TV prays that Walters' lobbed goal on 66 mins will settle it, but no. The pain is prolonged by Luton's under-21 substitute (he probably works at McDonalds by day) firing home an innocent-looking cross in time-added. Everyone's clearly been practicing their penalties, except Griffiths who hits the bar, leaving Stoke sub Geoff Cameron to finish this debacle by 8-7. "An epic encounter," reckons Nigel Johnson, clearly trying to be kind. However, Stoke's performance is described on social media as "poor" (hardly), "the worst under Hughes" (getting there), and even "disgraceful" (oh, you wait!).

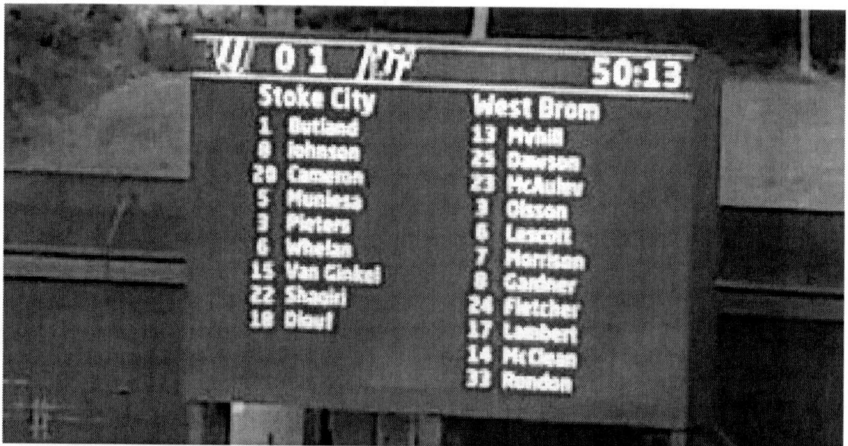

To even things up, Stoke decided to play against Pulis' Albion with only 9 men

29/08/2015 Stoke 0 West Brom (1) 1 - Ding Dong, and Tony Pulis is back at The Brit for the first time in over 2 years (a miserable home defeat to Spurs, if I remember rightly), and it's a complete farce. On 25 minutes, Afellay slaps Gardner in the face and walks. Then ONLY SIX MINUTES LATER, Charlie Adam (picked out of the blue to intimidate Pulis & Albion) nonchalantly treads on Dawson's leg, and he's off too. In fairness, Charlie just looks off-balance (when doesn't he?), and Ibrahim slaps like "a dandy challenging a ruffian to a duel". Meanwhile, Ricky Lambert crosses for Salomon Rondon to head home on the stroke of half-time [both players TP had targeted for Stoke], and then Pulis does what he does best: hang on for the 3 points. Oh, what a jolly jape! Stoke fans commend the remaining 9 players for trying to make a game of it, lash West Brom for not crucifying a hopeless Stoke side, and are quick to blame it all on Charlie. But frankly Hughes & co just seem at a loss as to how to cope with Pulis. Apart from the "pistols at dawn" moment, this was predictable.

12/09/2015 Arsenal (1) 2 Stoke 0 - Stoke fans are having to be very tolerant of Sparky's lacklustre starts to seasons. This year's team looks particularly flakey: The sight of Van Ginkel trying to emulate the departed Nzonzi in the middle is curious, Cameron & Muniesa standing in for recuperating Shawcross at the back is eqully unconvincing, but Jack Butland is clearly the star in the making, keeping this from being a 0-6 disaster. How much better is he? Well, The Oatcake give him 9 out of 10, and the rest 5 or 6. Eventually, Walcott gets through on the half-hour, and Giroud heads the 2nd late on. But thank goodness we've got Jack. He's even been called up by Roy Hodgson to play for England! Meanwhile, Stoke sink to the bottom of the league.

Due to incredibly poor eyesight, it was amazing if Pulis & Hughes ever shook hands at all

19/09/2015 Stoke (2) 2 Leicester (0) 2 - 2nd place Leicester arrive full of bluster. Here Stoke fall for the same trick, with first half goals from Bojan & Walters, although the latter is a treat as he beats off Huth to score. In the 2nd half Arnie gives away an early penalty, and Vardy does what he does best to make it 2-2. A point to high-flying Leicester is progress - it keeps them above bottom clubs Newcastle & Sunderland - but blowing a 2-0 lead to Leicester mustn't become a habit...just saying.

22/09/2015 Fulham 0 Stoke (1) 1 (Capital One) - The Sentinel are billing this as Stoke's first win of the season (excluding the Luton penalty shootout). And what a pile of pants it is. If Stoke's first team aren't much to write home about, then this reserve team (featuring Given, Sidwell, Pieters, Cameron, Afellay & returning Odemwingie) is in a right state. Thankfully (or "luckily" as The Oatcake put it), Crouch grabs a goal on the half-hour from an Odemwingie through-ball, but Stoke have to hang on desperately as Fulham's reserves miss an open goal, despite Arnie & Shaq coming on to stop things completely falling apart. A sobering look behind the scenes of the Hughes/Bowen/Niedzwiecki empire. However The Oatcake are direct & philosophical: "A win is a win & a clean sheet is a clean sheet". Well, I'm glad we've cleared that up.

26/09/2015 Stoke (1) 2 Bournemouth (0) 1 - Stoke are found guilty of starting to look cool with Shaq & Arnie skilfully combining to set up a Walters tap in on the half-hour. But a minute after Van Ginkel comes on in the 75th minute (I'm just saying) Gosling grabs an equaliser (coincidence? I think not). But just as it seems that Stoke will never win again in the Prem (yes, it's getting that worrying), Whelan takes a quick free kick on the half-way line (despite the ball still moving, tut tut) which results in Diouf stooping to head the winner in the 83rd min from a lazy bouncing Johnson cross. Phew. The Oatcake reckon, "A win is a win" (er, right), mainly because they can't say "a clean sheet is a clean sheet". However, bad-decision-of-the-month goes to Eddie Howe & crew for allowing injured Callum Wilson to play on when his knee is clearly about to blow. A few seconds after receiving treatment, he twists and collapses in a heap in agony with a ruptured anterior cruciate ligament, and is out for 6 months. Cruel and avoidable.

03/10/2015 Aston Villa 0 Stoke (0) 1 - Finally we get to play a team lower than us. Yes, it's Tim Sherwood's sagging Villa. (Paul Lambert is long-since gone, ousted in February), and Villa Park is a happy hunting ground for us scavengers. So, cocky Charlie tries to lob the keeper from well inside his own half (he only just misses). But it takes Arnie to put them out of their misery, finishing neatly from a through ball on 55 mins from Johnson (yes, him again. Surprise!). Two weeks later Sherwood is history, and Villa go on to finish bottom with only 17 points. Yep, it's all Stoke's fault.

19/10/2015 Swansea 0 Stoke (1) 1 - Headline: Butland survives his England debut without mishap. But then he comes to The Liberty and goes crazy, rushing out to do a feet-first tackle after he scuffs a pass. The things they teach these kids at St George's. But this game's really about Bojan's 3rd minute mazy run that results in a soft penalty that he converts himself. 90 minutes later (& some of those minutes are a bit tense), and Stoke have a rare win at Swansea. Shout out to Joselu, Bojan and Arnie up front (I know, it sounds unlikely), and Cameron, Whelan and Johnson at the back (which sounds even more unlikely). Stoke rocket to mid-table obscurity.

24/10/2015 Stoke 0 Watford (1) 2 - Some people may say I'm often a bit too cutting about Stoke. And so to balance things out, this is what The Oatcake said about this game: "Best we don't dwell too long on this game. The fact is that Stoke were abysmal. Utterly, utterly dreadful...We were genuinely shocking. A serious contender for our worst game at home since promotion to the Premier League. We started brightly enough for 20 minutes, but then it all went to pot and we just fell apart really." In comparison, The Sentinel's headline reads "below-par", but even they note that Sparky ("enjoying" his 100th game in charge) and his team are booed off by the few remaining supporters (& after two 9th place finishes. Who'd have thought?). Deeney is given too much room before the break for 0-1, and sub Marc Wilson is unusually caught messing about with the ball in the 69th minute for 0-2. Stoke now haven't scored against Watford since Pulis' 1-0 binary-season away win (so long ago that Sean Dyche was Watford's captain!). And THAT game was 10 times better than this. Now that's what you call a "cutting" remark.

Eden Hazard could dance all he liked, but he couldn't beat Jack Butland from 12 yards

27/10/2015 Stoke (0) 1 Chelsea (0) 1 (Capital One) (Stoke win 5-4 on penalties) - Stoke always beat Chelsea in the League Cup, and so it's no surprise when Walters beats returning Asmir Begovic (making a rare first-team appearance) just before the hour with a shot in off the bar. But Remy equalises in injury time, despite all of tireless Diouf's defensive efforts. Then Mame turns right-back when Bardsley is 2nd-yellowed 3 minutes into stoppage time, but after extra time, Butland brilliantly saves from Eden Hazard in the penalty shoot out. A young Kurt Zouma makes a rare appearance for The Blues alongside John Terry, putting his penalty down the middle to make it 4-4. Costa goes to hospital with cracked ribs ("I think he punched himself," says unsympathetic Jose Mourinho, who's heading for the door at Chelsea). And Ryan Shawcross is back, although probably knackered after this experience.

31/10/2015 Newcastle 0 Stoke 0 - For those who made the horrendous 6 hour coach trip to St James' Park (or whatever it's called this week), a point (courtesy of the God-they-call-Butland) was their only real reward. Jack is on fire, whereas the rest of the team look like they're having a tepid smoulder. After the several hours that it took to beat Chelsea, Shawcross seems right-as-rain, but Diouf looks like he's taking a well-deserved snooze on the bench.

07/11/2015 Stoke (0) 1 Chelsea 0 - With 37% possession and only one corner, Stoke put a stop to the idea of a Chelsea league revival (they're now down to

16th!). And so (& live in front of the cameras) it came to pass that on 53 minutes Shaq puts a through ball to the impressive Glen Johnson, who crosses for Walters to lay on Arnie to acrobatically volley past Begovic. Make no mistake this is a decent Chelsea side held up by the likes of Whelan and Wollscheid. A month later, with the shame of 2 defeats to Stoke in only 11 days (oh, and 9 league defeats out of 16), Mourinho is squeezed out. I blame Asmir. Sparky is seen smirking about that deal on the touchline, and doesn't even shake hands with Jose...mainly because Jose isn't there as a result of a stadium ban. Stoke starting to look - dare I say it - formidable (which means "inspiring fear or respect through being powerful, horrifying, disturbing, spooky, stiff..." Yeah, and that's just Marko Arnautovic).

21/11/2015 Southampton 0 Stoke (1) 1 - Stoke haven't won in Southampton since the Titanic set sail from there in...er, 1980. Exaggeration? Well, Martin Spinks is comparing this run of 4 away games without conceding to the Binary Season of 2005. But this is Koeman's tough 7th place Southampton, and surely they won't put up with any unbelievable nonsense? But unbelievably, one of Erik Pieters' crosses comes up trumps, sort of, as Bojan nips in for a 10th minute goal. For the rest of the game Wollscheid hacks away at Saints players (particularly poor Pelle) as if determined to give away a penalty, but he could hack all day as ref Lee Mason refuses to give any. So, The Oatcake make him Man Of The Match. That's Wollscheid, not Mason (although arguably Mason deserves it more).

28/11/2015 Sunderland (0) 2 Stoke 0 - Famous for three strange events: Just after the break, Shawcross is off after the softest of 2nd yellows (Ryan even got the ball!). What's strange? Well, it's the sight of (of all people) Charlie Adam standing beside the ref scratching his head at the decision that's surreal. It's like he can't understand why it's not him being sent off. More surreal is the Enterprise Car rental advert which springs up on the advertising boards just as Van Aanholt hits a drive from distance in the 82nd minute. The ad is the exact same black & green as Stoke's strip, & it must have looked like an army of defenders were charging at him (which they were actually). In a panic he just lets fly, and miraculously puts Alladyce's struggling Sunderland 1-0 up. Two minutes later it's 2-0, but more importantly, what was keeper Pantilimon doing grabbing the ball from outside the area, and pulling it back in?? Doesn't he realise that's against the rules? But what you don't remember is that Mike Dean is refereeing. (Hence Ryan's red card.) But if I'd told you that at the start, you'd never have read this story.

01/12/2015 Stoke (1) 2 Sheffield Wed 0 (Capital One) - Without his normal strikers - well, Joselu appears out of nowhere to replace Crouch after only 12 minutes - Sparky's Stoke could end up going to penalties yet again. But Afellay's classy volley (set up by Joselu) on the half-hour and sub Bardsley's 75th minute free-kick see off Wednesday on a Tuesday.

05/12/2015 Stoke (2) 2 Man City 0 - One of those iconic games where people remember where they were etc etc. Top of the table, title favourites, & multimillionaires Man City get unexpectedly hammered by a side featuring Wollscheid, Afellay, Cameron & Johnson (yes, really!). OK, so it's the bold move of playing Arnie, Shaq AND Bojan that dumps Citeh on their arse, despite the fact that the cold wind is in danger of knocking poor little Krkic over. Before anyone's even noticed that Kompany and Agueroooo aren't playing, Arnie fires home from a Shaq cross, before making it 2-0 from a Shaq through ball. And that's all in the first 15 minutes. The Shaq/Arnie/Bojan show powers on, but somehow it never gets to 4 or 5-0. Arnie misses a hat-trick several times over, hitting the post so hard it almost breaks, and then Shaq misses a tap-in from Arnie. Citeh are shell-shocked. This defeat knocks them off the top of the league overtaken by Leicester, who storm through to win the Premier League. Citeh are later relegated and go out of business...no, maybe that's going a bit far. Stoke move from formidable to invincible!...just how long will that last?

12/12/2015 West Ham 0 Stoke 0 - After last week's win, a 0-0 draw at a 7th place club is seen as a disappointment. But scoring only 13 goals (the joint-lowest in the Premier, equal with bottom club Villa) is a worry. To solve this Stoke have Van Ginkel again trying to prove he's no Shaqiri as he steps in for Xherdan...well, until he's subbed early for Diouf. A satisfactory last trip to Upton Park.

19/12/2015 Stoke (0) 1 Crystal Palace (1) 2 - The game with that last minute wonder strike from Chung-Yong Lee (a distant cousin I rarely talk about). Up until then it's just the tale of two penalties: Whelan up-ends Zaha just before half-time for 0-1, but a 2nd half penalty equaliser for a soft handball is converted by Bojan on 75 minutes. Wayne Hennessey (like Jack, he's a Pulis signing) performs miracles in Palace's goal to keep it 1-1. But in the last minute, sub Chung-Yong Lee (who's off my Xmas Card list) only on for a few minutes, latches on to a loose ball after Stoke fail to fully clear a corner. It's a 30 yard screamer, one worthy to win any game, and Chung-Yong Lee is suddenly Alan Pardew's hero. He'll never hit another one like that, reassures Mark Hughes. Me, I'm off to re-write my will.

26/12/2015 Stoke (2) 2 Man Utd 0 - When things are going well, you can achieve anything. Two first-half goals see off Louis Van Gaal's under-whelming United, currently 5th. Bojan converts Johnson's cross on 20 minutes, and Arnie beats De Gea with a Christmas cracker 5 minutes later. This is what they call a great team effort, which probably explains why The Oatcake's league table of player's performances has all the defenders and goalkeeper at the top, with the likes of Shaq and Bojan towards the bottom. Hm. What we really need is goals.

28/12/2015 Everton (1) 3 Stoke (2) 4 - Ah, this is what we need, goals!! (although perhaps a few too many here). One of the greatest games of Stoke's 10 year tenure in the Premier League. Shaqiri finally gets a goal on 15 minutes, but Stoke are soon pegged back by Lukaku for 1-1. Then on the stroke of half-time, Bojan sends a long-ball through to the flying Shaqiri, who half-volleys in one of the great Stoke goals of all time to make it 2-1. Some sad pundits claim it was a fluke, that Shaq didn't mean to shoot, that he was passing to - I dunno - Harvey The Invisible Rabbit. Uh?! Anyway, rampant Lukaku levels again, before Everton deservedly go 2-3 up. But with the added firepower of subs Walters and Joselu, it's soon 3-3, with Joselu even getting his first goal on 80 minutes, latching on to a loose ball after Arnie's cross causes panic in the Everton goalmouth. Finally, Arnie is tumbled in the box by John Stones in injury time (Joselu famously embraces ref Clattenburg as a touchingly-weird thank you) and the Austrian converts the penalty for 4-3. Now, THIS is the best Christmas present ever. And a rare win at Everton. After a poor start, this is turning into a sensational season! Let's just hope we don't have to face Tony Pulis next.

Mame Diouf, the only known striker looking for the chance to play at right-back

02/01/2016 West Brom (0) 2 Stoke (0) 1 - Damn, we have to face Tony Pulis next. Even I knew what was coming, tweeting: "Pulis' West Brom don't play like that against everybody, but they do play that way against US! And we fall for it every time." Martin Spinks bizarrely compares it to Claudia Schiffer vs Hilda Ogden, but he has to admit that Hilda (a) "scrubs up pretty well", (b) is well prepared (which Stoke are not), and (c) takes the lead on the hour - although it's not Hilda, it is in fact Sessegnon who slips through to beat Butland. For once Hughes doesn't actually freeze up against Pulis, and throws on strikers Joselu and Walters, who combine on 81 minutes for Walters to equalise with a bullet-like header. SJW respectfully doesn't celebrate madly, like when he scores against Liverpool, but then can't conjure up a winner. Cameron is then sent off 2 minutes later when Yacob over-acts from Geoff's petulant shove. (Naughty Yacob can be seen peaking to see if he's got away with it.) This leaves just enough time for Pulis to steal the points: Darren Fletcher wins a corner in the last minute, and Jonny Evans stabs in from the subsequent chaos. Characteristically, Pulis' Albion reach 39 points in early March, and then don't bother winning any of their last 9 games. God, how annoying must that be.

05/01/2016 Stoke 0 Liverpool (1) 1 (Capital One Semi Final 1st leg) - Poor, even against a makeshift Liverpool side, who come out the stocks firing on all cylinders thanks to new manager Jurgen Klopp. Sub Jordon Ibe scores in the first half, and Stoke chase shadows for the rest of the game. 64% possession can't buy Stoke a goal, even with Shaq, Arnie, Bojan, Joselu, Crouch & Walters (although not all at the same time). The second leg looks impossible now.

09/01/2016 Doncaster (1) 1 Stoke (1) 2 (FA Cup) - Joselu paying back some of that transfer money by crossing for Crouch to flick home for 1-0. Rovers grab an equaliser from a Haugaard parry. But with the likes of Diouf and Crouch back in the team to show us how to miss unmissable chances, it's left to Super Johnny Walters (SJW or Long John Silver, as Spinksy reckons his beard makes him look like a pirate) to rocket a winner. Impressive for a side featuring Haugaard, Wilson, Van Ginkel, Charlie and sub-Sidwell, who've hardly had a run all season.

13/01/2016 Stoke (0) 3 Norwich (0) 1 - Sometimes weird "stuff" just happens. Gary O'Neil decides out-of-the-blue to slide tackle Afellay from behind on a whim (the ball's practically out of play), and Norwich are down to 10 men for the last hour (and we may never know why). In the 2nd half, Stoke wake up a bit, and Walters slots in from an awesome Arnie cross for 1-0. Howson soon equalises with a cracker strike, before Joselu slips in a long-range shot for 2-1, & the game is settled when an Afellay free kick deflects in for 3-1. Thank you, Gary O'Neil, Man Of Mystery!

17/01/2016 Stoke 0 Arsenal 0 - Stoke don't need to beat Arsenal, they just have to suitably humiliate them. They bring multi-million pound players to The Brit, and they're given the run around. That well known strike force of Walters and Joselu (yes, how has that come about) supported by Stokelona trio Afellay, Bojan and Arnie have The Gunners clearing off the line in desperation. But Stoke are 7th, above Chelsea, Liverpool, Everton and Villa (actually, Villa are rock-bottom), and there's a good possibility of a place in Europe, judging from the remaining fixtures. However, writer Rob Doolan has spotted a change in the wind at Stoke since the Everton 4-3 win. Fatigue? Lack of depth? Whatever it is, there's something wrong in paradise. "Begs the question of whether we've gone from a manager who spent too much time worrying about the opposition to one who doesn't worry enough."

23/01/2016 Leicester (1) 3 Stoke 0 - Effectively annihilated by champions-elect Leicester, with the smuggest-German defender in the world. Yes, Sparky is already learning to regret letting Huth go, particularly when Shawcross goes off injured on the half-hour. With the returning Shaqiri, but no Arnie, Stoke look ropey enough for The Foxes to pick them off like chickens. Drinkwater's strike makes it 1-0 before the break, Vardy rounds keeper Butland for 2-0 after the hour, and sub Ulloa taps in late on for 3-0. Mark Hughes' worst game in charge, shouts everyone.

26/01/2016 Liverpool 0 Stoke (1) 1 (Capital One Semi-final) (6-5 on penalties) - 4,500 Stoke fans cheer on Stoke in the impossible task of overturning the 0-1 defeat in the first leg, and winning at Anfield for the first time since 1959 (literally!). But somehow Arnie gets on the end of a Bojan cross on the stroke of half-time, and it's all-square. Sure it's marginally offside, but that just makes it funnier. Van Ginkel hits the post, but it ends with penalties. Walters, Whelan, Afellay, Shaqiri, and Van Ginkel score, Crouch and Muniesa are saved. For Liverpool, a guy called "Can" proves he "can't" take penalties, but then a guy called Joe Allen (who'd only come on as a late Liverpool sub) scores the winning spot-kick to send The Reds to Wembley. A great Stoke performance, an actual win at Anfield over 90 minutes (well, and 120 minutes too), but for Sparky and Stoke City, it's like the bible reference Job 38:11 in the DaVinci Code: 'This far you may come, and no further'. Revealingly, Sparky's Stoke have peaked.

30/01/2016 Crystal Palace (1) 1 Stoke 0 (FA Cup) - Whilst Stoke's transfer-acquisition-committee ponder over the bank-busting choice of Giannelli Imbula or Saido Berahino (oh joy!), The Sentinel tellingly report: "A wretched week capped off a pretty wretched month as Stoke find themselves dumped out of both cup competitions and taking just 4 points from 12 in the Premier League." Here, a team led by Odemwingie, Haugaard, Van Ginkel, Ireland and Joselu unsurprisingly never really get going, and Zaha slips through to grab the early goal. Most worryingly is Marc Wilson's awful knee injury at the very end, which could be career-changing. With Ryan also out, Stoke should concentrate on signing a defender, to try and stop the mounting number of goals going in.

02/02/2016 Man Utd (2) 3 Stoke 0 - Oh sure, 53% possession away at Old Trafford is something Stoke fans used to long for, but this damp squid of a performance is something to forget, and quick. Highlight? Walters puts the ball in the net after Crouch has crawled all over Smalling. However, minutes later, Lingard and Martial make it 0-2, and Rooney (as always) finishes off a decent move after the break. Feeble performance, personified by Bojan, who is scored only 5/10 by Spinksy! I didn't think he had that number on his typewriter.

06/02/2016 Stoke 0 Everton (3) 3 - A third consecutive 0-3 defeat, and alarm bells are starting to ring. 66% Stoke possession this time (some even report it as high as 70%), but literally nothing to show for it. Butland tears out to concede an early penalty for Lukaku, unmarked Seamus "tiny" Coleman heads in for 0-2, and Wollscheid passes the ball to Lennon to make it 3 by halftime. Debutant Giannelli Imbula (£18.3m) looks assured and impressive, but he must wonder why the stonking Stoke of December 2015 has changed into the whithered Stoke of February 2016.

13/02/2016 Bournemouth (0) 1 Stoke (1) 3 - The false-dawn of Imbula, whose passing and movement are sublime. Stoke, playing in a bespoke all-white strip due to Bournemouth's obnoxious black and red togs, overrun the struggling Cherries, with Imbula volleying the first, Afellay the second, and (even more unlikely) Joselu the third. Bournemouth are below par, and sub Matt Ritchie's consolation is barely deserved. But this is the game the Legend Of Diouf As Right Back is born, as Muniesa is added to the injured-defenders list (replaced by Dionatan Teixeira) & then Glen Johnson too. Unfortunately, Hughes (who failed to sign a defender in the January-window) continues to play Mame up-front to little avail.

27/02/2016 Stoke (0) 2 Aston Villa (0) 1 - Guess who's just got back from Dubai? And boy, do they look it. The Dubai trips seem to do little to improve the Stoke squad, and fans question whether the players are deserving. Afterall, this game is against Aston Villa, adrift at the bottom by 6 points, and yet neither side has a single shot on target in the first half. In fact, at halftime an evacuation message is wrongly broadcast, and fans look more than happy to make a run for it, things are that poor. Thankfully, Arnie then sinks a penalty, before breezing in a few minutes later to head in for 2-0. "Hopeless" Villa (yes, it's agreed they have no hope of survival in The Prem) manage a consolation, but a Stoke win is a Stoke win. Cracks, paper...well, you get the idea. Just hope Stoke don't ever lose the plot like Villa are doing.

Shaqiri's popularity soars as he effectively sends Newcastle down with a 25 yarder

02/03/2016 Stoke (0) 1 Newcastle 0 - Steve McClaren's sinking Newcastle are sunk by an 80th minute strike from Shaqiri, who everyone had forgotten about after Arnie's goal revival and Imbula's expensive arrival. Diouf diligently wins the ball to set up Shaq's 25-yarder that even the keeper doesn't even bother going for (well, this is a star-less Newcastle who are going down in 8 weeks time). This flash of genius is a bit of a surprise in this mundane fixture, although Arnie casually volleys against the bar as the ref blows the final whistle. And, of course, Bardsley is typically added to the injury list, leaving a City defence held together with sticky-backed plastic. Yet, despite all this, suddenly Stoke (7th, 4 points behind West Ham) are dreaming of Europe!

05/03/2016 Chelsea (1) 1 Stoke (0) 1 - ...but if you're serious about Europe, you've got to get past clubs like Chelsea, where Stoke lose regularly. So, imagine everyone's surprise when, after Traore hits a first-half "screamer" for Blues to lead 1-0, Mame Diouf equalises 5 minutes from time. The sublimer-than-normal Imbula wins the ball, Bojan sets up Shaqiri, who crosses from the right, enabling hapless keeper Courtois to flip it up for Diouf to head in for 1-1. Nobody can believe it, mainly because Mame hasn't scored for 6 months (although it was the winner at The Etihad, so we'll let him off). Finally, a point at The Bridge!

12/03/2016 Stoke (0) 1 Southampton (2) 2 - The high-flying Saints of Ronald Koeman have a guy called Pelle to slice up Stoke like a kipper in the first half-hour. Even Arnie's 52nd minute goal (from an Afellay cross) is nothing more than a consolation against a side showing Stoke how it should be done in the upper-middle of the Premier League. The ref tries to help with the curious (& later rescinded) red card for Sadio Mane in the last minute for being naughty with Erik, but frankly this is just garnish. A record crowd at The Brit (27,833), but if any mid-table Prem club beginning with the letter "S" is going to the Europa League, it's The Saints.

Jack Butland fondles his lucky towel before going off to play for England vs Germany...

19/03/2016 Watford (0) 1 Stoke (1) 2 - Six away wins in a Premier League season? "Isn't it SEVEN?" asks Mark Hughes, after the match. Nope, mate, remember Job 38:11. Sparky must be thinking of the 4 away wins in the cups. At Vicarage Road, Phil Bardsley is the star, crossing hard for Walters for 1-0 on 18 mins, with Joselu making it 2-0, exploiting a poor Gomes clearance. Deeney gets a consolation, but Watford are too busy thinking about their forthcoming FA Cup semi. 6 away wins is now Stoke's record in the Prem. It must be the cool black-with-green-stripe shirts (although, after saying that, they're not needed today).

02/04/2016 Stoke (1) 2 Swansea (0) 2 - Yeah, it's OK winning away from home, but throwing away a 2-0 lead at home is a serious NO-NO! To make matters worse, Jack Butland has just broken his ankle playing for England against Germany, and could be out for seemingly an eternity. Haugaard does his best, but when the dynamic isn't there, it isn't there. It was going OK when Afellay heads in for 1-0, and in the 2nd half Bojan runs at The Swans, who scatter as he shoots for 2-0. Two deflections later, and the crowd are grumbling about Sparky's choice of subbing tired Whelan & Bojan. There's trouble at the mill, but when Stoke are 8th, just above Chelsea and Liverpool, no one dare say anything.

10/04/2016 Liverpool (2) 4 Stoke (1) 1 - Oh, NOW some are wondering if everything is as it seems at Stoke. A severely weakened Liverpool (resting for Europa action) romp over Stoke in this game, & the table. Bojan manages a headed equaliser on 22 mins from Shaqiri, but despite Shawcross' return (albeit clearly unfit), Stoke's defence (Bardsley, Wollscheid, Pieters, Cameron...the usual suspects) are a shambles. But Haugaard is the one clearly out of his depth. It's like boys against men. No, old men vs. young boys. Whatever it is, most of it is unprintable. Embarrassing.

18/04/2016 Stoke 0 Spurs (1) 4 - Hm, let's see if Shay Given can do any better? Nope, didn't think so. Harry Kane reaches 30 goals for the season, and Dele Alli adds the other two. Stoke have over an hour (from the 9th minute to the 71st) to come back from Kane's early wonder-strike, but are no match for a Spurs side who seriously think they can catch Leicester (yeah, right). And with Kevin Wimmer on their bench. As The Oatcake put it: "The difference between the two sides was staggering, & it's hard to believe that we held them to a 2-2 draw at White Hart Lane earlier in the season". Hm, probably best to pretend this never happened, which in the case of Stoke's Directors, is probably what will happen.

24/04/2016 Man City (2) 4 Stoke 0 - The Potters are now a house built on sand without the likes of Butland and Johnson etc. The worst of the three 4-goal defeats, and against a side resting themselves for The Champions League against Real Madrid. How bad are Stoke? "You miserable bunch", "truly embarrassing", "woeful", "nightmare", and that's just The Sentinel! Sparky is so desperate that he's thinking of recalling Charlie Adam! Highlights? Shay Given strains his groin on half-time trying to save an Aguero penalty (replaced by Haugaard), and Wilfried Bony comes off the bench to set up Iheanacho to round the keeper. Oh god, it really was that bad.

30/04/2016 Stoke (0) 1 Sunderland (0) 1 - Somehow Sunderland are staying up. No idea how. AND they send rivals Newcastle down. Well, that's Big Sam for you. Meanwhile, Sparky recalls (yes, you guessed it) Charlie Adam, and he rocks the boat so much that Arnie even scores a goal from an Adam cross (& a Crouch swivel). Imbula is put through & misses, and is never the same again. After conceding so readily, it's a surprise to see Stoke almost keep a clean sheet...almost....until Cameron makes too much contact with Jermaine Defoe, and 4 minutes into time-added, The Black Cats steal a point from the spot. A good result? We'd have taken a point at the start of the game? Really? Not in a million years.

07/05/2016 Crystal Palace (0) 2 Stoke (1) 1 - If you're not convinced that Sparky's third season is deteriorating into a farce, here are some quotes about this game: "It's a toss up whether it's the players or their fans who want the season to end quickest", "lacking fitness, focus, desire", "a season going nowhere...with white flags flying". And that's just The Sentinel again; the fans' comments are unprintable! This game features Imbula, Shaqiri, Arnie, Bojan etc, but the star player by a mile? Charlie Adam. Yes, none of the Stoke players are a match for Charlie. He even scores a goal on 26 mins, whilst Crouch & Shaq miss scorable chances. But Palace, who find it so easy to beat Stoke these days, hit back with two goals by Dwight Gayle, the winner a curling free-kick round a poorly-positioned wall. Unsurprisingly, Haugaard isn't at his best, & Stoke are down to Daniel Bachmann as substitute-keeper in waiting. It's slim-pickings.

15/05/2016 Stoke (0) 2 West Ham (1) 1 - An unexpected finale. Most Stoke fans had written off a Top-10 finish, particularly when up against a West Ham side wanting to secure their automatic Europa League place. So, when Antonio has time to control the ball on his chest from a corner in the 23rd minute, spin round, file his nails, write a thesis on Einstein's theories, oh & boot the ball past recalled Shay Given, home supporters fear the worst. By half-time, Stoke are lucky to be alive at all. But after Hughes explains some basic facts to his side (in no doubt brutal fashion), the second half is a different game, and even Imbula is up there equalising. The Hammers suddenly realise that their Europa League spot might be at risk, with Liverpool looking like they might sneak a winner at West Brom, and it's end to end stuff. Whelan somehow clears off the line, and sub Charlie almost scores from his own half. But it's the other sub, Mame Diouf, who heads home a Charlie corner two minutes from time that brings the house down. Stoke go back above Chelsea to finish 9th with 51 points, top of the middle clubs, and just below Liverpool. And amusingly, West Ham now have to go through qualification rounds for the Europa League (sadly, they didn't make it through, getting knocked out early). However, Stoke supporters aren't convinced by all this - a late Leicester equaliser at Chelsea is really what secures Stoke that 9th spot - and there's more talk about decorating (papering over the cracks) and rebuilding (hiring a skip for certain players). Interestingly, the club hierarchy see this as a third 9th place finish, and nothing to be concerned about. It remains to be seen if this really is a house built on sand, and how fine that sand is.

	Team	P	Wh	Dh	Lh	GFh	GAh	Wa	Da	La	GFa	GAa	W	D	L	GF	GA	GD	Pts
1	Leicester City	38	12	6	1	35	18	11	6	2	33	18	23	12	3	68	36	+32	**81**
2	Arsenal	38	12	4	3	31	11	8	7	4	34	25	20	11	7	65	36	+29	**71**
3	Tottenham	38	10	6	3	35	15	9	7	3	34	20	19	13	6	69	35	+34	**70**
4	Manchester City	38	12	2	5	47	21	7	7	5	24	20	19	9	10	71	41	+30	**66**
5	Manchester Utd	38	12	5	2	27	9	7	4	8	22	26	19	9	10	49	35	+14	**66**
6	Southampton	38	11	3	5	39	22	7	6	6	20	19	18	9	11	59	41	+18	**63**
7	West Ham Utd	38	9	7	3	34	26	7	7	5	31	25	16	14	8	65	51	+14	**62**
8	Liverpool	38	8	8	3	33	22	8	4	7	30	28	16	12	10	63	50	+13	**60**
9	Stoke City	38	8	4	7	22	24	6	5	8	19	31	14	9	15	41	55	-14	**51**
10	Chelsea	38	5	9	5	32	30	7	5	7	27	23	12	14	12	59	53	+6	**50**
11	Everton	38	6	5	8	35	30	5	9	5	24	25	11	14	13	59	55	+4	**47**
12	Swansea City	38	8	6	5	20	20	4	5	10	22	32	12	11	15	42	52	-10	**47**
13	Watford	38	6	6	7	20	19	6	3	10	20	31	12	9	17	40	50	-10	**45**
14	West Bromwich	38	6	5	8	20	26	4	8	7	14	22	10	13	15	34	48	-14	**43**
15	Crystal Palace	38	6	3	10	19	23	5	6	8	20	28	11	9	18	39	51	-12	**42**
16	Bournemouth	38	5	5	9	23	34	6	4	9	22	33	11	9	18	45	67	-22	**42**
17	Sunderland	38	6	6	7	23	20	3	6	10	25	42	9	12	17	48	62	-14	**39**
18	Newcastle Utd	38	7	7	5	32	24	2	3	14	12	41	9	10	19	44	65	-21	**37**
19	Norwich City	38	6	5	8	26	30	3	2	14	13	37	9	7	22	39	67	-28	**34**
20	Aston Villa	38	2	5	12	14	35	1	3	15	13	41	3	8	27	27	76	-49	**17**

2016-17 - 41 Shades Of Grey

13/08/2016 Middlesbrough (1) 1 Stoke (0) 1 - Sparky is now famous for his slow starts to seasons. This time it's not helped by Jack Butland not being fully recovered from injury, replaced initially & ominously by Shay Given. But a brilliant curling free-kick equaliser by Xherdan Shaqiri on 67 minutes makes everything alright as Stoke typically start sluggishly against newly promoted Boro, who'd taken an early lead. It's Stoke's first free-kick goal in the Prem since October 2013! Joe Allen (£13m) comes on late to make his debut. A 1-1 draw: Yes, it's Stoke's best ever start to a season under Mark Hughes!
(Premier League position: 8th=, Order on ***Match Of The Day*** (MotD): 6th out of 7 matches). (Gary Lineker appears in underwear)

20/08/2016 Stoke (0) 1 Man City (2) 4 - Is it a bird? Is it a plane?! Well, it certainly isn't a penalty, but that's ref Mike Dean for you. He's clearly been told to stop Stoke "grappling" in the box, so Stoke are 0-2 down by half-time. After missing a stonewall penalty on Joe Allen, Dean then gives Stoke the softest penalty ever to make amends, converted by Bojan Krkic in the 49th minute. But with Agueroooo & Nolito...well, it's downhill from there...
(League position: 17th, MotD: 2nd of 8)

23/08/2016 Stevenage (0) 0 Stoke (2) 4 (EFL Cup) - Peter Crouch scores a hat-trick with two headers and a dangerous looking overhead scissor-kick. But full-back Phil Bardsley steals the show on the half-hour with a left-footed rocket from several streets away. As Marc Espley tweeted: "Bardsley hit that harder than he hit Wayne Rooney!" Harmless EFL fun in the sun.

27/08/2016 Everton (0) 1 Stoke (0) 0 - England manager, Sam Allardyce, looks on in disbelief as Shay Given saves an extremely-dodgy-looking penalty, only for the ball to hit the post, bounce off the back of his head and into the goal. You Could'ner Make It Up! Big Sam lasts another 31 days, Shay only 22.
(League position: 20th, MotD: 6th of 8)

10/09/2016 Stoke (0) 0 Spurs (1) 4 - Oh dear. Stoke lose to Spurs by 4 goals...again...and again! Sparky gets sent to the stands (for tip-toeing inches out of his technical area), then struggles to get a phone signal up there - much like everyone else. Arnie's early goal is disallowed, then it just goes downhill from there...again. Spurs fans merrily sing "It's happening again...!" First-starts for new loanees Wilfried Bony and Bruno Martins Indi who must be wondering what they've signed up for! "Bringing in Bony," says Hughes sagely, "is a no brainier. Let's just enjoy him." Er, what?
(League position: 20th, MotD: 4th of 8)

18/09/2016 Crystal Palace (2) 4 Stoke (0) 1 - Stoke's worst start to a season just gets worse. The first 12 minutes are appalling, with Stoke going 0-2 down, and then it just goes downhill...well, you get the idea of that. Arnie scores in time-added, and not only that, it's from open-play! But the knives are out for a manager who can't stop his side falling apart at the back. After seemingly criticising Stoke's defensive training methods ("it would help if we ever did any defensive training - which we don't"), Marc Wilson leaves to join Bournemouth then later WBA. "He's entitled to his opinion," grunts Mark Bowen, not realising that this grunt would come back to haunt him. Likewise, Wollscheid is also pushed out of the nest, and never heard of again. As Shay Given concedes his 26th goal in 10 Premier games for Stoke, his replacement watches from the sideline. (League position: 20th, MotD: 2nd of 4)

Pochettino: "Same time next week?!"

21/09/2016 Stoke (1) 1 Hull (1) 2 (EFL Cup) - More like it for Stoke...but their first-team still lose easily at home to a seriously-understrength Hull. Arnie hits a cracker to make it 1-0, Hull equalise on half-time, and win it in the 91st minute. First starts for the brilliant teenager Ramadan Sobhi and credible new emergency-loan goalie Lee Grant are overshadowed by the fact that Stoke just aren't, well, any good.

24/09/2016 Stoke (0) 1 West Brom (0) 1 - Strangely, this is the turning point. Pulis was never going to lose this one; he's beaten Stoke every time since he left, so a draw is a major breakthrough! Joe Allen scores on 73, but it's typical heartbreak as Rondon heads home Albion's equaliser from an unnecessary corner in injury time. (League position: 19th, MotD: 8th of 8)

02/10/2016 Man Utd (0) 1 Stoke (0) 1 - Finally, Stoke get a result at Old Trafford for the first time in 36 years...well, it might as well be a century. Sub Anthony Martial looks like he's won it for United on 69 mins, before Joe Allen pokes home the equaliser in the 82nd to take Stoke off the bottom of the League. Mourinho is not amused. Well, he never is. (League position: 19th, MotD: 2nd of 4)

15/10/2016 Stoke (2) 2 Sunderland (0) 0 - "Two first half goals for Stoke" is a phrase that hasn't been heard for a long time at Stoke, but Joe Allen obliges with a brace in this must-win-October-bottom-of-the-league-clash. Shaq & Arnie combine for Joe's early header, and Shaq's corner sets Joe up for 2-0 on half-time.

Puzzlingly, Joe has hardly scored in his career, but now Stoke can't stop him. The question is, if David Moyes can't win here, where can he win?? Bless. Sunderland go on to be relegated. (League position: 18th, MotD: 6th of 7)

22/10/2016 Hull (0) 0 Stoke (1) 2 - Stoke's 100th Premier League victory. And another two goals, these ones by Shaqiri! The first is a typical Shaq gold-plated 25 yarder, the second a free-kick "dinked" over the wall. But like last week's opponents, this is a very poor side, much poorer than Stoke and Sunderland! Interestingly, this full-strength Hull side at home isn't as good as the part-timers who beat Stoke away a couple of weeks ago, which is why they also go on to be relegated.
(League position: 16th, MotD: 4th of 8)

Hughes in danger as Stoke loses its identity

Potters have lost five of six as they slip down standings into relegation territory

ROB HARRIS
THE ASSOCIATED PRESS

LONDON—Wherever Mark Hughes turns, it's hard for the Stoke manager to escape the rebellion growing among fans.

When the floundering squad was spotted at the city's rail station disembarking from another recent miserable away trip, gesticulating sup-

Paris Saint-Germain after failing to settle for a season on loan in the modest Staffordshire surroundings.

There was early promise: A debut goal to clinch a 1-0 victory over Arsenal in August. But Jese has failed to score since then. He lost a place in the starting lineup in October and has made only two substitute appearances since then. He has not played since being disciplined for leaving the substitutes' bench early and returning to the dressing room during a game.

"He's still very much in my plans."

Sparky under pressure, even from this Canadian newspaper

31/10/2016 Stoke (1) 3 Swansea (1) 1 - THREE goals! For Stoke! In front of the Sky cameras! Yes, another poor side is seen off by Stoke, whilst Stoke go from strength to strength. Ex-Swans Joe Allen and Bony tear their old club apart, with Wilfried slotting in from Joe after only 3 minutes. Routledge (all 5ft 6in of him) somehow heads home the equaliser 5 minutes later. Yes, explain that, Bruno-Ryan-Bards. Ramadan's strike is diverted in after the break, before Joe does all the work for Bony to head in for 3-1. A good day's work, but poor Wilfried, a striker finally on the score sheet: he never scores for Stoke again. (League position: 12th, MotD: N/A)

05/11/2016 West Ham (0) 1 Stoke (0) 1 - Stoke now proving hard to beat, particularly with the remarkable Lee Grant in goal – where has he been hiding? However, even Grant can't stop Glenn Whelan's headed own goal on 65 minutes. 7 minutes later and Hughes makes the bizarre substitution of Bojan for Whelan (and thankfully Crouch for limp Bony). Suddenly, everything is put right in the 75th with a Bardsley-Walters move that is finished off by Bojan. Sparky's Stoke is fast becoming a right bogey side for The Hammers, unbeaten in 7. But Stoke fans aren't impressed with the new stadium, reckoning they're nearer to Harrods than they are to Joe Allen.
(League position: 12th, MotD: 5th of 5)

19/11/2016 Stoke (0) 0 Bournemouth (1) 1 - A litmus-test game for Stoke against a side they did the double over the previous season. There are just too many well-organised mid-table sides and "Boscombe" are but one. However, for "well-organised", read "rolling around on floor and time wasting" – yes, Bournemouth are that shabby. A 26th min goal from a free header by Ake when he's surrounded by 11 Stoke players speaks volumes, but then Bojan blazing a 2nd half penalty off towards the Michelin factory mutters away several more! (League position: 13th, MotD: 7th of 8)

27/11/2016 Watford (0) 0 Stoke (1) 1 - Hard to say who was more surprised by Stoke coming fast out of the blocks at Watford: Stoke fans? Sparky? Or shell-shocked Watford players? Charlie Adam creates mayhem in the box, heading against the post on the half-hour, only for the rebound to bounce in off hapless goalie Gomes. As everything's going Stoke's way, the resentful Watford fans chant: "1-0 to the referee". All this shock and mayhem is capped by Imbula returning from isolation and having a decent game! Yes, really! It won't last. (League position: 11th, MotD: 4th of 4)

03/12/2016 Stoke (2) 2 Burnley (0) 0 - Two amazing first-half goals against a side who are traditionally rubbish away from home. Walters cracks one over the keeper and in off the far post, but the second is even better. Marc Muniesa starts the move from his own penalty area, beats 2 men, feeds it to Imbula-then-Shaqiri-then-Arnie who crosses into the penalty area for...hang on, what's Muniesa doing there! One brilliant finish later, and it's 2-0. He then almost concedes a penalty and a red card for a professional foul on Andre Gray, but just about gets away it. However, it's really keeper Lee Grant who is saving Stoke's bacon. Right, that's the end of a run of games against bottom-half sides; so, how will Stoke fare against Top 10 sides?
(League position: 9th, MotD: 7th of 7)

10/12/2016 Arsenal (1) 3 Stoke (1) 1 - No surprises here. Stoke lose at The Emirates again. It's their 15th consecutive defeat at Arsenal since The Jam broke up (1982, OK?). Oh sure, other mediocre sides can get results here, and Adam even puts Stoke 1-0 on the half-hour. Joe Allen is poleaxed in the box, and as Charlie is made captain today (yes, this really happened), he gets to take the spot-kick. But with goals from Walcott, Ozil, & Iwobi, it's downhill all the way...
(League position: 11th, MotD: 2nd of 6)

14/12/2016 Stoke 0 Southampton 0 - Arnie is red carded for a daft tackle on 26 minutes, and it's all hands to the pumps for the rest of the game. So, it's just as well that Shawcross & Whelan are back from injury, aided by returning Jon Walters. Hey, the old band are back together! Not much else to say about this home draw. (League position: 12th, MotD: 8th of 8)

17/12/2016 Stoke (2) 2 Leicester (0) 2 - But THIS home draw has a LOT to say about it, and will be talked about for years, but all for the wrong reasons. By half time Stoke are 2-0 up, and Leicester are down to 10 men with most of the rest (6 including Huth!) on yellow cards. Vardy is red carded after two-footing Diouf on the half-hour, and even his manager Ranieri (thinking it a tad harsh) has a dicky-fit and has to be restrained. On 40 minutes, Bojan gets a clear penalty for handball, and Leicester & Ranieri get even more in a tizzy. Then 5 minutes after Bojan sends Schmeichel the wrong way, Joe Allen taps in for 2-0, with Leicester in total disarray.

That's a long way for Stoke to come downhill from, but somehow they completely cock this up, and a dreadful...no, a disastrous...no, a pathetic second half almost sees Stoke tumble all the way to the bottom of a deep pit of oblivion. Stoke come out for an afternoon stroll, whilst Leicester come out meaning business. Then Ranieri makes a double substitution on 72 minutes, and the new boys conjure a goal back in just 2 minutes. Of course, Leicester inevitably equalise with 2 minutes left. "Mark Hughes' worst day as Stoke manager," claim The Oatcake. "A panicking manager chucking away two points." He later claims the team were tired after Wednesday's Southampton game, which doesn't go down well with hard-working Stoke fans. Hope it doesn't prove costly at the end of the season. It's going to be a cold cold Christmas after this debacle (League position: 11th, MotD: 2nd of 6)

As Bojan scores from the spot, one fan points out his brother stewarding the Seddon Stand

27/12/2016 Liverpool (2) 4 Stoke (1) 1 - Stoke start up front with ex-Liverpooler Crouch and staunch Everton fan Walters, and sparkle for 30 minutes. Walters even heads home a Pieters cross on 11 minutes, putting an away side ahead for the first time at Anfield since Chelsea's visit last May! But it's all downhill from there. Glen Johnson has a nightmare, Imbula glances in an own-goal, and Ryan does the backpass from hell. Oh knickers. (League position: 13th, MotD: (N/A)

31/12/2016 Chelsea (1) 4 Stoke (0) 2 - Stoke keep on conceding 4 goals. They've now lost 8 games conceding 4+ goals in a calendar year (2016) for the first time since 1952, and the first time it's EVER happened in the Premier League. Well, a New Year's Eve game against league-leaders Chelsea, who've won their previous 12 Premier games, was always going to end badly. On the plus side? Chelsea have only conceded 4 goals at home all season, so Stoke's two goals looks quite impressive...er, doesn't it...? Well, Martins Indi's equaliser just after the break certainly was a surprise. And Crouchy's on 64 minutes was too. But with a defence described as "catastrophic" by Hughes, the result should be no surprise.
(League position: 14th, MotD: 1st of 8)

03/01/2017 Stoke (1) 2 Watford (0) 0 - Stoke complete their first double of the season, faster than any other club in the Prem (er, well, apart from Man City), and it's only January 3rd! Scruffy goals either side of half-time...well, they all count. Ryan scores then cups his hand to his ear in the direction of the fans. Odd, even for him. But Crouch's goal famine is definitely over with his 2nd in 3 days. Nothing to write home about, but then we're about to go on a cup run, aren't we? Aren't we?! (League position: 11th, MotD: N/A)

07/01/2017 Stoke (0) 0 Wolves (1) 2 (FA Cup) - Stoke's first-team lose easily at home in the cup to a seriously-understrength gold-shirted brace-scoring side ...hang on, haven't we had this one already this season?! No, that was the annoying Hull City cup defeat; this is the annoying Wolves cup defeat. It's the highlight of manager Paul Lambert's ropey Molineux season as he tries to steer Wolves away from relegation. (Although in fairness they do go on to win at Anfeld in the next round.) But for Mark Hughes, he's "a man clearly feeling somewhat betrayed by his highly-paid flair players". Martin Spinks says this because Sparky starts with Arnie, Shaq, Bojan, Imbula, and Afellay, for all the good it does him. And the defence is even worse, a "shambles" and an "embarrassment". "The season now feels over to all intents & purposes," reveals Spinks, rather shockingly. The only argument amongst Stoke fans surely is whether this is worse than the Leicester debacle?

14/01/2017 Sunderland (1) 1 Stoke (3) 3 - These doubles are turning up thick and fast as David Moyes' flaky Black Cats are swept aside in the first half-hour by Shaqiri & Arnie. With 2 goals in 7 minutes, Arnie is on fire, particularly his second which is a passing-fest goal-of-the-season, with one-twos with Shaq & Crouchy. On 34 minutes Crouch heads in his 99th Premier League goal – oh, the excitement! – and practically-relegated Sunderland are overwhelmed. Defoe pulls one back before half-time, but no one really cares. (League position: 9th, MotD: 6th of 8)

21/01/2017 Stoke (1) 1 Man Utd (0) 1 - The late-late-late-late equaliser for Wayne Rooney, as he breaks United's scoring record, is all anyone wants to hear about in the media. He hits a free-kick from the side in the 94th minute which finds the top corner, when nobody can understand why the game hasn't finished – where does Clattenburg get 5 minutes from?? Stoke had been leading since the 19th minute thanks to a Mata own-goal from (would you believe it) an Erik Pieters cross. So, Rooney's intervention is doubly cruel, and thus nobody wants to know about Stoke being unbeaten by United in a season & their heartbreak at the end of this game. All together: It's not fair!! (League position: 9th, MotD: 3rd of 7)

01/02/2017 Stoke (1) 1 Everton (1) 1 - Crouch does The Robot goal-celebration after scoring his 100th Premier goal on 7 minutes from an Arnie cross! Worth the admission price alone. But in one of the most surreal moments in modern football, the ref goes against all guidelines in the 39th minute and unwisely overrules the linesman's offside flag, after being savagely mobbed by Everton players (who somehow all get off being punished scott-free!), and awards them a goal! Despite the final touch from intercepting Shawcross, Lukaku is clearly already offside and interfering with our little Ryan! Everyone rushes over to get their rule book out. As a distraction, Hughes introduces new £12m signing Saido Berahino, who looks keen enough for his 20 minutes, but despite trying to lob the keeper, he's never really going to score, now is he? (League position: 9th, MotD: N/A)

Saido Berahino knew all he had to do to revive his career was to sign for Mark Hughes...

04/02/2017 West Brom (1) 1 Stoke (0) 0 - As predictable as the seasons, Tony Pulis beats his former club again with a 6th minute goal from James Morrison and then clings on to the lead for 84 minutes. In return Sparky thinks this is great time to bring on Berahino, coming on as sub on the hour against his old side to a really hostile reaction. Hughes even gives 20 minutes to Julien Ngoy to no avail. Typically, Pulis and Sparky fail to shake hands, and each rightly blames the other. Might it have something to do with a leaked story about Saido and a failed drug test? Ah, pantomime at its very best! (League position: 11th, MotD: 8th of 8)

11/02/2017 Stoke (0) 1 Crystal Palace (0) 0 - At last, Palace are tamed after a run of 5 humiliating defeats to them...yes, but that's enough of that. Big Sam Allardyce returns to the bet365, but for some reason he's no longer manager of England. Brilliant young Egyptian Ramadan Sobhi finally makes his first home start, only to find Arnie wants to play on the left wing too. Embarrassing! So, they take it in turns, and between them they combine to create the only goal for Joe Allen on 67 minutes. If only all matters can be solved so easily. (League position: 9th, MotD: 6th of 7)

26/02/2017 Spurs (4) 4 Stoke (0) 0 - In yet ANOTHER 0-4 tonking by Spurs, at least Stoke don't have a disallowed goal & Sparky sent to the stands in search of Wi-Fi signal. What luck! Nope, instead Stoke concede a Harry Kane hat-trick in a horrific 23 minutes spell...and it's downhill all the way etc...well, to half time anyway. As it's now 0-4, Mark Hughes allegedly gives them a piece of his mind in the form of a "hair-dryer", and they put on an adequate 2nd half showing. It does not go unnoticed that Stoke players have just had their Dubai break, whereas Spurs stayed home and squeezed in some extra matches in the British cold climate. And who looked the fitter?

Maybe if Crouch had equalised early in the game...er, actually, would it really have made any difference? (League position: 10th, MotD: 2nd of 3)

04/03/2017 Stoke (2) 2 Middlesbrough (0) 0 - It's really hotting up in the competition between Ramadan & Arnie. Arnie scores the goals, but Ramadan wows the crowd. The Austrian and the Egyptian; the odd couple. Arnie loses 2 defenders to make it 1-0 on the half-hour, and volleys in from a corner on 42 to make it 2-0. Injured Shaqiri is probably wondering if he'll make the team on his return, whereas Saido gets just 12 minutes, which is never going to be enough. Interestingly, Sparky has now been at Stoke for 3 years & 9 months, longer than he's managed any club; "I've another 2 yrs & I'd like to think I will get to the end of that." Who's with him on that? (League position: 9th, MotD: 7th of 8)

Despite losing, cheerful Hughes & Bowen deliberately avoid Pulis (seen here shaking Eddie Niedzwiecki's hand) before claiming it was Pulis who avoided them! Kids, eh?

08/03/2017 Man City 0 Stoke 0 - Nope, dunno what happened here. Third place Man City manage just ONE attempt on goal, AND - even more strangely - Stoke fail to fall apart & go downhill faster than an out-of-control gazelle. Their "David-Icke-level insane starting line-up," as Rob Doolan puts it, somehow does the business, much to everyone's surprise, probably even Sparky. It's just so random: Berahino gets his first start, and back come Walters & Diouf. But Stoke become the first team to keep a clean sheet at The Etihad this season; that's Aguerooo, De Bruyne, Silva, Toure, Sane, and all ports in-between. A great achievement against Pep Guardiola's side...but nobody remembers it. (League position: 9th, MotD: N/A)

18/03/2017 Stoke (1) 1 Chelsea (1) 2 - The Champions-to-be are held up impressively...well, apart from Lee Grant misjudging an early Willian free-kick at his near post (0-1) and Pieters misjudging at the death, gifting Cahill (1-2)...oh and Bardsley being 2nd yellowed in time-added. So, maybe not so impressive. Walters' 38th minute penalty is Stoke's only shot on target, but Chelsea celebrate at the end like they've won the league (which, for all intents & purposes, they have).
(League position: 9th, MotD: 2nd of 7)

01/04/2017 Leicester (1) 2 Stoke City (0) 0 - Bloody Foxes! Bloody Robert Huth! Not the right time to play Leicester as they are suddenly back on the rails, but the two super-strikes by The Foxes (Ndidi from 25 yards and a Vardy volley) are the only real difference between these two Cities.
(League position: 9th, MotD: 5th of 8)

Haunted! Mark Hughes felt that his every move was being watched...

04/04/2017 Burnley (0) 1 Stoke (0) 0 - Stoke have now played TWENTY mid-week Premier League away games...and lost 15 of them, winning only ONE (Fulham back in 1846 or summat). Burnley, usually so good at home, are poor, but Stoke just seem clueless to take advantage, particularly after the Clarets take the lead on the hour. But the game is more famous for Charlie Adam tripping over whilst taking a corner. You can't buy fame like that. (League position: 12th, MotD: 10th of 10)

08/04/2017 Stoke (1) 1 Liverpool (0) 2 - The "Substitution" game. With Stoke leading from a first half Walters header (from Shaqiri's cross), the managers decide to make their just-after-the-hour substitutions. Sparky strangely swaps Walters, who just loves scoring against Liverpool, with...Glenn Whelan? Meanwhile, wily Klopp brings on Firmino and Courtinho. Five minutes later and it's 1-2 to Liverpool, and 4 defeats in a row for Stoke. And guess who scores? Yes, Firmino, whose goal even wins MotD's Goal Of The Month. But surely this could have been avoided? (League position: 13th, MotD: 3rd of 7)

15/04/2017 Stoke (1) 3 Hull (0) 1 - Heavy weather and great goals. Arnie actually gets a brilliant early goal that ISN'T ruled out for a change. But after Hull equalise after the break, Mark Hughes makes another one of those crazy substitutions, taking off Adam and Berahino (logical) and bringing on the old guard of Crouch and Walters (seemingly illogical). This time it works, as they combine to make it 2-1.

Shaqiri then scores a goal of the season screamer from 30 yards. But you can't please everyone. (League position: 11th, MotD: 3rd of 7)

22/04/2017 Swansea (1) 2 Stoke (0) 0 - Swansea couldn't buy a win, as they approached this game after 6 defeats and a 0-0 home draw with hopeless Middlesbrough. Enter Stoke "Generous-to-a-fault" City. And just to help them out, Arnie blasts a penalty off towards the Bristol Channel. Swansea score their second 60 seconds later. However, unexpectedly, Jack Butland is back in goal! Well, somebody's happy then. (League position: 12th, MotD: 2nd of 4)

29/04/2017 Stoke 0 West Ham 0 - Sometimes it's hard to believe that the former United maverick and ***prolific goal-scorer*** Mark Hughes is Stoke's manager. Why can't he get his players to score goals? Instead, Jack Butland wins today's Man-Of-The-Match; and even The Oatcake announce in disbelief that their Player Of The Season is defender Bruno Martins-Indi, who at the 11th hour overtakes Joe Allen who's led the table all season! Where are the strikers? Go on, guess. Nowhere near the goal, that's for sure. (League position: 12th, MotD: 5th of 5)

Even at Bournemouth Peter Coates had surreptitiously sewn up all the advertising

06/05/2017 Bournemouth (0) 2 Stoke (1) 2 - After 10.5 hours, Stoke finally score away from home. Ok, it's an own-goal from a corner on the half-hour, but a goal is a goal. It all starts with Harry Arter's appalling "2-footed" diving challenge on Joe Allen, for which he amazingly only gets a yellow. The sickening slow-motion replays show that he should have been locked up and the key thrown away. It spurs Stoke into action, but Bournemouth keep equalising; first on 62 minutes, then after Diouf pokes home on 73 for 2-1, Shawcross deflects in to square it again. Both clubs are now mathematically safe (41 pts). (League position: 13th, MotD: 7th of 7)

13/05/2017 Stoke (0) 1 Arsenal (1) 4 - Stoke have now only beaten teams below them, all of them in fact, and failed to beat any of the teams above them! This is reinforced as Arsenal make mincemeat of them in front of their own fans and the Sky cameras. Crouch scores brilliantly from a scorcher cross by Arnie, but slo-mo shows that it hit his hand not his head. But after a vote on social-media, the goal is still seen as brilliant coz it's against Arsenal. Gooners want Arsene Wenger to go, but Stoke fans wind them up, telling him they want him to stay! However, the lap of honour...I mean the lap of appreciation...is a little subdued. Change is clearly needed, but the Board are clearly not watching. (League position: 14th, MotD: 4th of 7)

21/05/2017 Southampton (0) 0 Stoke (0) 1 - Unbelievably, Stoke get a win in the last game of the season thanks to a Crouch goal on the hour, putting them, as Mark Hughes observes, just 2 points off 8th spot. (Is it those two points you "chucked away" in the Leicester game, Mark?) (And it's actually THREE points thanks to Stoke poor goal-difference, Mark.) But a-miss-is-as-good-as-a-mile, and Stoke actually finish 13th! Whereas Southampton get the coveted 8th spot, and are crowned "champions of middle-Premier"...they are promptly booed off by their own supporters and sack their manager! Blimey, there's no pleasing some folk. It's Sparky 150th league win as a manager, Crouch's 50th Premier League headed goal (a record), a Stoke goalscorer has finally reached double figures, and it's Stoke's shortest season – only 41 games played in all – since 1906. But it doesn't go unnoticed that former manager Tony Pulis not only finishes above Stoke, but that his Albion snatch the kings-of-the-midlands trophy. Still, after being ignored by Match Of The Day for the whole season, at least now the BBC will give Stoke the coverage it deserves...er, no, hang on...back to the drawing board. (League position 13th, MotD: 10th of 10).

	Team	P	Wh	Dh	Lh	GFh	GAh	Wa	Da	La	GFa	GAa	W	D	L	GF	GA	GD	Pts
1	Chelsea	38	17	0	2	55	17	13	3	3	30	16	30	3	5	85	33	+52	**93**
2	Tottenham	38	17	2	0	47	9	9	6	4	39	17	26	8	4	86	26	+60	**86**
3	Manchester City	38	11	7	1	37	17	12	2	5	43	22	23	9	6	80	39	+41	**78**
4	Liverpool	38	12	5	2	45	18	10	5	4	33	24	22	10	6	78	42	+36	**76**
5	Arsenal	38	14	3	2	39	16	9	3	7	38	28	23	6	9	77	44	+33	**75**
6	Manchester Utd	38	8	10	1	26	12	10	5	4	28	17	18	15	5	54	29	+25	**69**
7	Everton	38	13	4	2	42	16	4	6	9	20	28	17	10	11	62	44	+18	**61**
8	Southampton	38	6	6	7	17	21	6	4	9	24	27	12	10	16	41	48	-7	**46**
9	Bournemouth	38	9	4	6	35	29	3	6	10	20	38	12	10	16	55	67	-12	**46**
10	West Bromwich	38	9	2	8	27	22	3	7	9	16	29	12	9	17	43	51	-8	**45**
11	West Ham Utd	38	7	4	8	19	31	5	5	9	28	33	12	9	17	47	64	-17	**45**
12	Leicester City	38	10	4	5	31	25	2	4	13	17	38	12	8	18	48	63	-15	**44**
13	Stoke City	38	7	6	6	24	24	4	5	10	17	32	11	11	16	41	56	-15	**44**
14	Crystal Palace	38	6	2	11	24	25	6	3	10	26	38	12	5	21	50	63	-13	**41**
15	Swansea City	38	8	3	8	27	34	4	2	13	18	36	12	5	21	45	70	-25	**41**
16	Burnley	38	10	3	6	26	20	1	4	14	13	35	11	7	20	39	55	-16	**40**
17	Watford	38	8	4	7	25	29	3	3	13	15	39	11	7	20	40	68	-28	**40**
18	Hull City	38	8	4	7	28	35	1	3	15	9	45	9	7	22	37	80	-43	**34**
19	Middlesbrough	38	4	6	9	17	23	1	7	11	10	30	5	13	20	27	53	-26	**28**
20	Sunderland	38	3	5	11	16	34	3	1	15	13	35	6	6	26	29	69	-40	**24**

2017-18 - From The Sublime To The Bloody Ridiculous

12/08/17 Everton (1) 1 Stoke (0) 0 – Somehow it doesn't seem quite right starting a season without Jon Waters (sold to Burnley), Glenn Whelan (sold to Villa) or even Marko Arnautovic (who wanted to play for a top club, but joined West Ham instead for £25m). Everton, though, have some guy called Wayne Rooney returning from a footballing career. Meanwhile, Butland punches Calvert-Lewin & somehow gets away with it. Kurt Zouma (Stoke's big new cool loanee defender from Chelsea) then makes a last ditch tackle to save Butland having to punch anyone else. Bojan is here, but he gets blown over by the wind. Unbelievably, Rooney (clearly the tallest player on the pitch)(uh?!) heads home the only goal from way out (well, near the penalty spot). Stoke fans are impressed that the team don't capitulate like they did so often last season, but less impressed by the lack of an equaliser. Apart from that, Martina is booked for pulling new-boy Choupo-Moting's shirt; he obviously can't believe Stoke have managed to fit that number of letters on Eric's back.

19/08/17 Stoke (0) 1 Arsenal 0 – Arsene appears on the touchline, and 25,000 fans DO THE WENGER! Yea! This is what we pay our money for. Stoke playing 5-4-1, but as the "1" is Berahino, who's on early for injured Shaqiri, it might as well be 5-4-0. This time Butland punches Shawcross! Then nearly punches Ramsey!! What is his beef?! But then suddenly just after the break Jesé Rodriguez (on loan from Paris St Germain) exchanges passes with Berahino, and beats Cech for 1-0!! Yes, this really did happen! Subsequently, Choupo is chopped, and Lacazette scores...but his foot is offside, which doesn't please the Arsenal fans much. Re-signed Martins Indi replaces battle-worn Pieters, or at least what's left of him after a 2-footed tackle. The crowd are adamant that Wenger "Didn't see that".

23/08/17 Stoke (3) 4 Rochdale 0 (Carabao Cup) – Bojan is treading carefully, remembering that last time he played Rochdale he couldn't walk for 6 months. But it's Captain-for-the-day Joe Allen who steals the glory, starting with a flying header on 15 minutes from a right-footed cross by Erik! Poignantly, Pieters points frantically at his right leg during the goal celebration with the glee normally reserved for successful leg transplants. After Crouch taps in for 2-0 on the half-hour, Sparky is out in his box seemingly juggling with invisible giant marshmallows – no one has a clue what he is on about. Pieters then crosses from the right with his left foot for Allen to make it 3-0, and later Ramadan rounds the keeper for 4. Baby Josh Tymon (from Hull) makes a reasonable debut, and Verlinden and 6ft 6in Harry Souttar come on as subs, but why the hell doesn't Hughes give desperately-short-of-match-fitness Berahino a run? Pretty dumb, unless Sparky is saving him for the Albion game.

27/08/17 West Brom (0) 1 Stoke (0) 1 – Nope, Berahino not picked for this one either, although that's probably just as well as it's against his former boss TP. Meanwhile, Zouma is having a brainwave: after watching the Rochdale video, Kurt slings pass after pass to Pieters on the left, in the misjudged belief that Erik The Viking can now cross the ball. Not happening. Sky TV executives begin to doubt that this Hughes vs Pulis game was such a good choice for live TV, despite Albion being on the cusp of leading the Premier League. Jay Rodriguez, who's hardly done a thing all day apart from put on the right shirt, heads home from close range on the hour, but after a comical mix up between keeper Foster and defender Hegazi, Crouch heads into an empty net for 1-1. Funniest moment: Butland boots a back-pass from Martins Indi back out again narrowly missing Bruno. The full-back turns & gives Jack the dirtiest of looks as if to say, "WTF was that??"

09/09/17 Stoke (1) 2 Man Utd (1) 2 – United have an 100% start to the season, and Stoke have Eric Maxim Choupo-Moting, a free-transfer from Schalke, and a debut from £18m defender Kevin Wimmer. No one can see this ending well. But Shaqiri keeps testing the keeper De Gea, who unhelpfully keeps diving full length to catch the ball. Then, against the script, on 43 minutes, Choupo heads home from a Diouf cross!!! although Rashford heads an equaliser from Pogba 2 minutes later. Lukaku makes it 1-2 on the hour, only for Choupo to head in a Shaq corner on 63. 2-2! And he even does his little dance with Zouma. BT Sports executives break out the sherry & ice-creams! The game is a box office hit, being watched by literally dozens of BT customers. Jose won't shake hands with Sparky, as he's fed up of being kicked out of Mark's technical area. "Your question is a bad question," Jose says afterwards. "It makes it look like it's my fault." If it's anything to do with a handshake, it's ALWAYS Sparky's fault. Get a grip.

16/09/17 Newcastle (1) 2 Stoke (0) 1 – Joselu looks 10 times the player he wasn't at Stoke, but note, he is still unable to score, although this is partially thanks to super Jack Butland. Somehow it's only 0-1 at halftime - Atsu sneaks around Stoke's now famous back-5 to score. Although Shaqiri curls in a bouncy equaliser on the hour ("fantastic finish" claim the BBC), Rafa's newly-promoted Magpies are always going to win this, & Stoke concede from a corner 10 minutes later. In truth it could be 1-5, as although Zouma is excellent, Wimmer & Indi struggle even to cope with Joselu. Everybody blames zonal marking, despite the fact that most people don't know what it means, in particular the Stoke players. Now in 4th place, Benitez says the fans are thinking about Europe; yes, they're all thinking, why the hell did we vote for Brexit.

19/09/17 Bristol City (0) 2 Stoke 0 (Carabao Cup) - Stoke fans struggle hard traversing the closed M5 motorway for this game; far harder than their team do on the pitch, & they've got 9 internationals. Conversely, Bristol fans are heartily entertained by Charlie & Glen Johnson alarmingly giving the ball away & blasting the ball over the bar towards Cornwall. The rest (apart from Grant in goal) also need singling out for their ineptness; so Sparky switches from 5 at the back to 4-4-2 at half-time, & Stoke are soon 2 goals down. Berahino (naturally) misses a late open goal - you can't buy entertainment like this. Well, Stoke did make 6 changes for this game. Mind you, Bristol made NINE changes! How cocky can you get? Can you imagine the score if they'd played their first team? Or changed ALL 11 players? Spinksy describes it as a "Cupset", but it's far worse than that.

23/09/17 Stoke City 0 Chelsea (2) 4 – The prediction was 0-3, but who could predict Sparky suddenly bringing on Afellay & going 4-4-2. Morata (£60m from Real Madrid) has already scored on just 2 minutes, with Pedro making it 0-2 on the half-hour. But after Sparky's changes, Morata completes his hat-trick with 2 goals in 5 minutes. Defence cuts means Mark Hughes is scraping the barrel to find anyone willing to play alongside Martins Indi in a dodgy back-3. Up first are Glen Johnson and Erik Pieters (oh dear), with forwards playing as full-backs (yes, Diouf & Ramadan). Playing players out of their positions?? As early as September?? Who'd have thought that would ever happen at Stoke. Clearly, the transfer-window has been a farce. Even Crouchy has to come on for Jesé, resulting in Cahill amusingly looking over to the bench with a "I didn't sign up for this" look. Easy to get out of the carpark today - half the Stoke fans leave early. All Sparky can say is: "It flattered them." Well, Chelsea did only have 4 shots on target.

Mark Hughes peruses the Etihad carnage & Mark Bowen starts looking round for a new job

30/09/17 Stoke (1) 2 Southampton (0) 1 – Yes, it's serious comedy time: Saido Berahino, who hasn't scored for 2 1/2 YEARS, gets a penalty...and it's SAVED by Forster, diving gently to his left. Yes, this really did happen. Whereas it only takes 15 minutes for Peter Crouch to come off the bench & score the winner in the 85th. Well, it's against one of his many ex-clubs, so no surprise there. Not bad for only 29% possession (Is Sparky Pulis-in-disguise?). Great defending tackles & clearances by Choupo – he should be careful, Sparky will have him in the back-5 before you have a chance to say 'Glen Johnson'.

14/10/17 Man City (3) 7 Stoke (1) 2 – Hughes puts his "bits" on the line by starting rookie right-back Thomas Edwards & central-defender Wimmer away at The Etihad, but at 0-3 after only 27 minutes Sparky's career looks like it's slowly slipping away. Jesus, Sterling & Silva do the damage, assisted by the brilliant De Bruyne, making Stoke look 3rd Division. But then suddenly, it's 2-3! What the hell is going on?! Well, it's all Diouf deflection: a deflected Diouf shot on 44 minutes & then

Diouf's poor header deflected in off Walker & the post just after the break!! Suddenly Sparky is back in business...well, until Stoke are soon steamrollered back to 2-7. Fernandinho's rocket & Sane's nutmeg of Jack are the highlights. Sparky is DEFINITELY back on the menu.

21/10/17 Stoke (0) 1 Bournemouth (2) 2 – "Scruffy" Shawcross ("the world's scruffiest man" as he's described in Shay Given's "lad" book) is back. Unfortunately, he clumsily concedes an early penalty, and Stoke are 0-2 down after less than 20 minutes. Back also (hopefully not out of desperation) is Glen Johnson, but he doesn't look the same player at all. And now Begovic is back at Stoke for the first time since a Chelsea cup defeat when things were rosier for Stoke. Although Diouf pulls one back in the 2nd half, the biggest cheer of the day is when Johnson is going off. Things are so array that Shawcross thinks he's a centre forward, and he's even bossing Begovic around. Stoke lose their must-win defining game, with Crouch making his teammates look very ordinary. "We've got to get back on the horse," says Sparky. Er, what game is HE playing?

28/10/17 Watford 0 Stoke (1) 1 – Stoke's blue away shirts are proving a disaster of style & practicality. So much so that Stoke create a new white away shirt. Suddenly, Stoke have 3 away points. Darren Fletcher hits a cool volleyed goal on the quarter-hour from Shaq's corner, and this proves that they do practice something during training, but it's obviously not the goal celebration (Fletch eventually heads towards the dug-out). However, this is the game that Deeney is seen fingering Joe Allen's face looking alarmingly like that horror scene from Blade Runner! It's quite disgusting to watch. Tired Charlie tries a long-shot on an open goal after Gomes stupidly comes up for a late corner, but it hits the post in an almost sarcastic manner, as if to say "It's just not your season, mate".

04/11/17 Stoke (1) 2 Leicester (1) 2 – Winter is coming and EIGHT players are wearing gloves today. Leicester have an incomprehensible new manager, and so take the lead twice. But they are pegged back by Shaqiri curling one in before the break, and sub Crouch powering home one of his best ever headed goals from Shaq's corner on 73 minutes. (The replay comically shows two defenders arguing over who should have stopped the big guy.) The ref has to swap with the 4th official as he's pulled something; Leicester fans sing "You're not fit to referee" and for once they're right. A game where the gloves didn't come off. "You should celebrate every time you get a Premier League point," reckons Mark Hughes. Celebrations go on long into the...early-evening.

20/11/17 Brighton (1) 2 Stoke (2) 2 – Stoke fans are suitably annoyed that this tasty fixture is moved to Monday night for TV purposes. And it's a shame as it's quite reasonable fare, with Choupo converting from Shaqiri, and then Zouma heading in a loose ball on the stroke of half-time, just after Albion had equalised. Brighton equalise again on the hour, but the main controversy is when Glenn Murray is pulled down by Shawcross for a certain penalty. Murray though is denied by the ref, and soon after escapes a red-card himself. At 2-2, given Stoke's form, Brighton & the media seem bewilderingly excited that they manage a home draw with Stoke. These are either really simple folk, or Brighton really are chronically poor. The media even get excited that Crouchy holds the all-time record for Premier League substitute appearances (143, one ahead of Shola Ameobi!). It's like they haven't even noticed Stoke've scored 2 goals away from home? Last time that happened it was at The Etihad. Er, yes, The Etihad...

25/11/17 Crystal Palace (0) 2 Stoke (0) 1 – Roy Hodgson, the manager of the League's bottom side, reckons Palace don't deserve to go 1-0 behind just after the break, even to a super-strike from Shaqiri. What?! Are we sure Roy doesn't just work in the local chippy?! Loftus-Cheek cuts an equaliser just 3 minutes later through Stoke's weedy defence. But cries of "Sakho" sound more & more like "SackHughes", particularly with Sakho poking home an injury-time winner in a goalmouth scramble.

29/11/17 Stoke 0 Liverpool (1) 3 – Yes, another adventure in time and space with ref Martin Atkinson. He seems happy to let The Reds play in bright orange, the same colour as the stewards. This is an offside-confusion-involving-the-linesman-&-a-steward waiting to happen! Instead the linesman gives the ball out every time it goes near Diouf; and to rub salt in the wound on the quarter hour, Liverpool take the ball OUT of play on the by-line, dragging it back for Mane to make it 0-1, and get away with it! Sparky later suggests that the home side usually gets "the call" on these decisions. But not today, obviously. So, just before the break when Diouf is hacked down by Mignolet, somehow the keeper isn't red-carded. Any other player, any other day, on any other part of the pitch, and that would be red, says all & sundry, particularly (as the crowd point out) if it'd been a Stoke player. Mo Salah comes on as a sub, and scores an awesome volley on 77 minutes, and another on 83. But his genius cannot paper-over a game ruined by officialdom.

03/12/17 Stoke (2) 2 Swansea (1) 1 – Yes, both managers have been told this is a must-win game; a six-pointer against (in Swansea's case) a relegation side. So, Sparky has risked everything on broken-finger-boy, Jack Butland. Back-with-Swansea Wilfried Bony sweeps in and scores a REAL EASY GOAL in the 3rd minute for 0-1. He didn't even look like he was trying...just like he wasn't at Stoke!! It's Wilf's first goal since scoring for Stoke against Swansea! Laughter can be heard from here to Timbuktu. So, Jack's first action after returning from injury is picking the ball out of the back of the net. But on 35 mins Shaqiri squeezes through the middle on to Joe Allen's pass, and slips it past Fabianski. 4 minutes later Diouf controls from a head-on from Crouch, and rips it home for 2-1. Who'd have thought? Best action in 2nd half is

Shawcross' header, which looks like a certain goal before the goalie makes an amazing save. Unfortunately, the keeper in question is Butland. Welcome back, Jack.

Sparky finally takes Stoke City to Wembley

09/12/17 Spurs (1) 5 Stoke (0) 1 – Sparky finally takes Stoke to Wembley, and brings them home by train. As such, Hughes reckons it's time for another start for defender Tommy Edwards, who nervously gives away a corner with the startled look of The Alarm singing "68 Guns". But it's Shawcross who diverts in Spurs' first goal after 20 minutes. With a defence like this, Sparky is in disbelief at half-time that it's not already 0-4; yeah, you & me both. But after the break 2 goals in a minute bring back balance to the universe. Of course, Harry Kane finally puts away a couple of goals, which is just as well as people were starting to think he was rubbish. Ryan thankfully heads in at the right end for 1-5. Really though it's Heung-Min Son who does a good job of making Stoke look like a League One side. Stoke fans agree, & vent their anger on Hughes & his players when they all get off the train together at Stoke station later that evening. But deep down Stoke fans know that City are very very lucky: it could so easily have been 1-8.

12/12/17 Burnley (0) 1 Stoke 0 – It just isn't going to go unnoticed if you take star-player Shaqiri off for Choupo in the 84th minute, and then Stoke concede the only goal 4 minutes later. Crouch hits the post, but Stoke have got a real problem if they can't score or defend against an average side like this. After this freezing cold sleet-blustery fruitless performance, I'm sure the players will enjoy arriving back to the peace and quiet of Stoke Station after another bad day at the office.

16/12/17 Stoke 0 West Ham (1) 3 – The ref is listed on the team-sheet as Geoff Scott, whom no one's ever heard of. It turns out to be Graham Scott, whom no one's ever heard of. Well, Sparky reckons the 17th minute penalty for 0-1 is a dive, that Zabaleta goes on to deliberately handle the ball, that Diouf is dragged back by the neck by Agbonna, & Antonio trips himself up and wins a free kick! What is going on?? Maybe this really is hitherto unknown "Geoff" Scott refereeing, and he's not actually a real ref! He does however spot Crouch being molested later in the game. But it doesn't matter as soon the "serpent" (as fans dub Arnie for ditching Stoke) makes it 0-2 in the 75th minute & Sakho then makes it 0-3, as Wimmer looks every bit the £800k player he isn't. As Hammers fans sing "Sacked in the morning", many Stoke fans can't help but lustily join in.

Even the loving Hammers fans couldn't convince Arnie that he'd joined a big club

23/12/17 Stoke (2) 3 West Brom (0) 1 – They're pulling down beards on all the Santas at the bet365 in case Tony Pulis is hiding behind one. Why? Because there are 14 Pulis signings on the pitch at the same time, and 5 are playing for Stoke. However, it's now Alan Pardew on the touchline for WBA, desperate to work out what system Stoke have lumbered themselves with this week. As it's a vital 6-pointer (17th vs 19th), Sparky throws on Tom Edwards for his home debut in a devil-may-care move. But (minus Pulis) it's business as usual when it comes to The Baggies, with Albion trying to be Brazil and Stoke 2-0 up by the break – Joe Allen poking home on 19 mins, and Choupo (who's having one of his rare decent games) dribbling in on the stroke of half time. Rondon turns it into a thriller after the break, beating tardy Ryan to make it 2-1, and we have to wait till 4 minutes into injury-time before Choupo runs the length of the pitch to gift Ramadan a goal. Sobhi rips his shirt off, but puts it back on when he realises they're still full-price in the club-shop. Hell, he doesn't earn ***that*** much.

26/12/17 Huddersfield (1) 1 Stoke (0) 1 – Choupo-Moting is now getting cocky, as he produces a spectacular overhead kick on the half-hour. But this stupid goal-technology denies him a goal by a couple of millimetres as it's clawed back by the goalie. Meanwhile Joe Allen has to explain what the BBC describes as "the worst back-pass of the century". (Butland saves his bacon, only conceding a corner.) The goals aren't as good as these moments (Ince on 10 minutes, and Ramadan converting Allen's cross on the hour), but a point on Boxing Day is not to be sniffed at, particularly when you're up to 13th with a nosebleed. [To be fair, the BBC said Allen's back-pass was the worst of the "season" not the "century", but who's counting.]

30/12/17 Chelsea (3) 5 Stoke 0 - The infamous save-the-players-for-the-Newcastle-game incident. With Zouma ineligible, and 4 defenders out injured (including Shawcross), in come teenager Josh Tymon beside Tom Edwards, plus (OMG) Afellay and (OMG again) Berahino. Not surprisingly, it's 0-2 after only 9 minutes, and 0-3 after 23, so by now there seems little point in bringing on Joe or Shaq etc. Saido gets Stoke's ONLY shot of the day, and it's a weedy one. Hughes explains it's OK for Chelsea as they've got 4 days to prepare for their next game, whereas he has only 2. What he can't explain is that he brings on Julien Ngoy in the 71st minute, and 2 minutes later it's 0-4. Everyone reckons that this is all very well, but Sparky had better get a win on Monday. Yes, ***really***.

Hughes somewhat perplexed as ZappaCosta makes it 0-5 to Chelsea. Zappacosta?! Who?!

01/01/18 Stoke 0 Newcastle (0) 1 - Two days later, and everyone is watching to see Sparky with his eggs in one basket. Should be easy this. After all, you wait for a winnable home game against a side below Stoke, then THREE come along in a row. This one's sponsored by Potteries Waste, which is poignant as £18million-man Kevin Wimmer, worth 20p and box of sticks, blasts the ball into the stand when there's no one challenging him at all! The crowd (an alarmingly low 28,471) stare on in disbelief. Just to make things really weird, Hughes replaces Erik for Saido on 71 minutes. With nobody immediately in place to play at left back, Newcastle hurtle down that side and score 82 seconds after the substitution! Well, what do you think they are, stupid or something? United had been pounding down Stoke's left all day. Could it be any worse? Yes, Joselu coud have scored it, but he's left on the bench. "What would you have done?!" strops Sparky to one journo, before questioning another who doubts his future, "Who else is going to do the job?" Stoke 16th with a bullet. But it's the relief of the FA Cup next. Yea!

06/01/18 Coventry (1) 2 Stoke (0) 1 – If you're going to have an appalling day at the office, always make sure ref Martin Atkinson is there to truly stick the boot in. But Stoke don't need him when they have Mark Hughes. Sparky finally appears on the touchline in the 23rd minute, and 33 seconds later (not making this up) Coventry head home a corner for 0-1. By half-time it could be 0-3! But after the break, Ramadan is pulled down, and Charlie puts away a penalty like he could do it all day long. As if. Order is restored with a guy appropriately called Grimmer blasting Coventry 1-2 up, and Stoke are out with a whimper. "Sacked in the morning!" rings out for the manager after his 200th game in charge. They're all wrong: Sparky is in fact sacked 3 hours later. So, Mr Chairman, "who else ***IS*** going to do the job"?

15/01/18 Man Utd (2) 3 Stoke (0) 0 – Oh, joy. A Monday night trip to Old Trafford in front of the cameras. And sitting in the stand is Stoke's new manager. After courting several possibilities (Martin O'Neil and Quique Flores both turn it down), the only one wanting the job it seems is out-of-work Paul Lambert, who (in the subliminal style of Mike Bassett) is clearly amazed to be offered it. Over the weekend, Stoke have dropped into the relegation zone, and this game was never going to help that. But new right back Moritz "Jack" Bauer is impressive, and...well, that's it really. Coach Eddie Niedzwiecki picks Tymon (whom he amusingly replaces at half-time with Wimmer) and Ireland for his first start in 3 years. But with Paul Pogba running wild, it's all over after 9 minutes (Valencia), then 23 minutes (Martial), and 72 minutes (Lukaku). Jose Mourinho is so sweet about hapless Stoke: "They created problems for us in the first half," he says, generously. The only problem he could be referring to is "understanding Eddie's team-choices". Humiliating.

20/01/18 Stoke (0) 2 Huddersfield (0) 0 – Stoke have a another tracksuited manager roaming the Technical Area, and it's not Tony Pulis. (Where's the bloke in the suit?? White hair, you must remember him.) It's Paul Lambert, and he gets a huge deafening "Lambo" welcome. Stoke show evidence of having actually done some preparatory training; defending corners, staying till the end of the game, etc. In this lively atmosphere, Joe Allen converts Choupo-Moting's cross in the 53rd minute, and the place goes MAD! Diouf then makes it 2-0 on the 69th after a Shaqiri back-heal puts him through. Shaq goes on to blow loads of chances, but this is surely a false-dawn-of-a-game making everyone very happy, particularly as Stoke briefly crawl out of the relegation zone.

31/01/2018 Stoke 0 Watford 0 – In the second of four "winnable" games, Lambert's side immediately seize-up. Sure, Paul focuses on the positives: back-to-back clean-sheets, 4 points from 2 games when previously it was 4 from 8, and Stoke move out of relegation up to 16th. But it's a lousy game where nearly everyone gets booked, and Joe Allen keeps clear of Deeney's grubby little fingers just in case they get near his eyes. Shaq fires point blank at the keeper, but Diouf gets the best chance & guess what, he heads it wide. So, late-on Lambert throws on his saviour Saido Berahino...well, you can guess the rest. But this really was a must-win game for Lambert, and The Oatcake pulls no punches: "A dreadful game of football. The 1st half was as bad as anything we've seen from Stoke this season." But this is a game Stoke would have lost under Hughes, so Lambo is upbeat: "4 points out of 6 & two clean sheets is a good start for me personally and for the team." Really? Wait till you see March & April's fixtures.

Dunk takes out Charlie for (a) a penalty (b) a red-card (c) a corner or (d) none of the above?

03/02/2018 Bournemouth (0) 2 Stoke (1) 1 – No kidding, The Sentinel lead with "Four points from the last three games is a worrying return". It takes only FOUR days for "a good start" to turn into "a worrying return". But Stoke had this one, and threw it away. Ok, so it's a minor miracle that Shaqiri scores in the first 5 minutes...from a header! He's 5ft 6in!! He leaps millimetres into the air beating the giant defenders from a left wing cross by ex-Galatasaray midfielder Badou Ndiaye (£14m). But this is Bournemouth, fresh from a 3-0 win at Chelsea, who wait until the 71st minute for desperate defending results in Joe Allen & Zouma colliding and Josh King bowling through to equalise. Eight minutes later, and Stoke's defence disappear as a free kick drifts in, and it's 1-2. Even new signing Kostas Stafylidis is here, but (like Stoke's defence) isn't really. Lambert starts bemoaning his lack of "luck" and the need for a bit of "lady-luck". Goals & wins might be a better objective.

10/02/18 Stoke (0) 1 Brighton (1) 1 – The one with Jesé, Charlie & the late penalty. Yes, the last of the 4 "winnable" games turns into a nightmare. Paul

Lambert is taken on by Peter Coates because of his knowledge of the Stoke squad. However, this knowledge doesn't stretch to the strikers. He genuinely believes he has a plethora of forwards all waiting to score. So, today he starts with Choupo-Moting & Diouf, though deep down he knows if anyone is going to score it's going to be Shaqiri. But these three only touch the ball (in total) 6 times in Brighton's box! So, Lambo throws on his soulmates, the supposedly reborn Berahino & Jesé. By now, of course, Stoke are 0-1 down to a superb passing movement goal, before Shaq curls one into the corner on the hour for 1-1. But the real drama is when Jesé goes to ground after a soppy flappy-hand push, and then wants to take the penalty himself. But late-sub Charlie Adam has the ball (well, he's never missed a spot-kick for Stoke), and the idiotic Jesé has to be subdued. Predictably in these circumstances, Charlie's penalty is good but saved, with the ball rebounding nicely for him to score, only for him to be hacked from behind by Lewis Dunk, who not only should be red carded for the foul on Adam (& another penalty given), but he was encroaching as well! The replay even has him hand-balling the ball out for a corner!! (He admits all this after the game!) But somehow Brighton get away with it, and Chris butter-wouldn't-melt Hughton even has the gall to say that he sees it as two points dropped! Unbelievable. Luck? Don't talk about luck.

"How did that get there?!" The mystery of Jack Butland's goal at Leicester ranked higher than the Mary Celeste, Loch Ness & Jamie Ness

24/02/2018 Leicester (0) 1 Stoke (1) 1 – The one where Jack drops the ball into his own goal. A nightmare that just won't go away. As the "tricky" games in Stoke's run-in start stacking up, City look like they might actually win this one! Just before half-time Joe wins the ball & slips it to Shaqiri. Shaq can't believe how much space he's got, so strolls forward and hits it in the corner like it's the easiest thing in the world. But nobody can explain how Albrighton's 70th minute low cross bounces off Butland's chest in an easy grab and into the goal. Jack makes a brilliant save minutes later, and Leicester hit the post late-on, but everyone will always remember the surprised look on Jack's face. And everyone else's, for that matter. Surprise turns to bewilderment as junior giant Tyrese Campbell comes on for his debut & hops around like a rabbit in the headlights. Is there a plan here? It seems to be how-many-academy-players-can-be-sneaked-on-without-anyone-noticing.

Against Everton it was a toss-up whether to play football or go sledging

03/03/2018 Southampton 0 Stoke 0 – "A few months ago we'd have lost this fixture," says Paul Lambert. "Look at the table & 3 points takes you to 13th. Momentum is with us." Yes, credit where credit is due, this is the only point obtained by Stoke so far in their 2nd strip of blue, which hasn't even witnessed a single goal. So, a point at sinking Southampton is a miracle. Diouf dislocates his shoulder after 20 minutes, so Lambo throws on that well-known striker, er, Erik Pieters. Some time later he's joined by Jesé & Crouch, but Butland is the one that really earns the point. Already out of favour with Paul Lambert are Berahino (can't turn up on time), Wimmer (can't turn up), Afellay (not even allowed to turn up - some "disagreement" with boss behind the scenes), and Jesé is next (neither here nor there when it comes to turning up, taking compassionate leave & wearing an ill-fitting Batman cap). However, floundering Southampton do something really strange: 10 days after this game (& with a near-impossible run-in of fixtures) they appoint Mark Hughes, who promptly loses 3 league games in a row.

12/03/2018 Stoke 0 Man City (1) 2 – That momentum that Lambert was talking about certainly isn't visible here, but then Citeh are 3 wins from winning the league. David Silva pokes in a Sterling cross on 10 mins, and a second on 50, and frankly there's not much else to tell. Lambo remains chipper, but did he really mention that this was improvement on the 2-7 defeat earlier in the season?

17/03/2018 Stoke (0) 1 Everton (0) 2 – It's mid-March, so of course it's going to snow. And of course Lambo is going to start Charlie Adam. And of course after 30 minutes of near-blizzard conditions something stupid is going to happen. So, as if to oblige, Charlie lunges in on Wayne Rooney in "a 50/50 ball" (say the media, charitably), and Stoke are down to 10. Ref Martin Atkinson waves the red card at Shaqiri to begin with - well, visibility is at a minimum here, Martin! - but eventually Charlie walks off for a lovely hot bath, whilst we nearly all catch pneumonia. But although Lambert gives the ref the benefit of the doubt over Charlie, he is incensed by Everton's first goal on 69 mins as it's offside, & nobody spotted it. (Look, it's bloody snowing, Paul!) Sub Choupo-Moting equalises 8 minutes later, injuring himself stretching for Allen's brilliant free-kick (Was he properly warmed up, or was he dreaming of Charlie's hot-bath?) The sickener is the Everton winner a few minutes after that. Everybody has a rant, apart from Big Sam, who reckons he's doing a great job at Everton. Oh, he's a wag! But what would Stoke have done if they'd secured his services earlier in the season. Lambert just reckons he needs a bit of luck. What he doesn't need is to be playing Arsenal next.

Paul Lambert watching his career disappearing in the Everton blizzard

01/04/2018 Arsenal (0) 3 Stoke 0 – Despite 10 defeats out of 10 Emirates visits, Arsenal are kind on Stoke: they haven't won by more than 3 goals against The Potters since 1984. Well, it's good to look on the bright side occasionally. But despite battling hard (Shaqiri hits the bar), Stoke come unstuck thanks to a poor referee decision, giving a penalty on 74 minutes as Ozil reckons he's been fouled by Martins Indi. Nobody seems to agree with the ref, but soon it's 0-2, and then 0-3 with another penalty, care of despondent Ndiaye. Looks worse than it is, because it is worse.

07/04/2018 Stoke (0) 1 Spurs (0) 2 – There's an old saying in football. It goes: "Diouf could play all day and never score. The only way he could perhaps score is if he's concussed in a collision with the goalkeeper, and then whilst totally dazed he taps home the stray ball." And so it comes to pass [er, I'm not actually sure how real that old saying is] that after Mame misses 2 golden chances and Stoke put up a decent stoic performance, Christian Eriksen puts Spurs 0-1 up in the 52nd minute. It's clearly not going to be Diouf's day...until the 57th minute when he thunders forward chasing a Shaq ball, colliding with blundering keeper Hugo Lloris who clearly doesn't know what he's doing. (If he did, he would have just let the Stoke forward have the ball to typically blast over.) Diouf sticks out his leg, it pokes the ball, and suddenly it's 1-1. Unfortunately, Diouf is so out of it that he thinks he's in Pepperland. Of course, Spurs win it 6 minutes later with an Eriksen free kick that either goes straight in (with interfering Harry Kane offside) or (as Kane tells it) the ball brushes off Harry's shoulder (there, told you he was interfering! and offside!) for 1-2. But forget all that. This game is the one where, with 10 minutes left, Stoke break with FOUR strikers against ONE defender, but the striker with the ball passes it straight to the only defender. Go on, guess who did that? Well, he's so concussed, he's still away with the Blue Meanies. But to cap it all, Diouf is named Man Of The Match. You Could'ner Make It Up.

After scoring at West Ham, Crouch foolishly set off on a marathon towards the Stoke fans

14/04/2018 West Ham (0) 1 Stoke (0) 1 – All we had to do, & I mean ALL we had to do, was hang on for 10+ minutes. That's all. After battling away for a draw, Stoke somehow take the lead through substitute Peter Crouch (his first goal since Guy Fawkes) in the 80th minute as Joe Hart spills. The long-suffering City away fans go stark-raving mad, and it's all Crouch can do to stop himself from jumping in with them. But as they're two miles away in Kent (due to poor stadium design) he decides to stop short and save himself a booking. But you know it's going to end in tears as the other tall sub, Andy Carroll, volleys the ball rather hopefully from the edge of the box in the LAST MINUTE. It somehow finds the corner of the net past otherwise resolute Butland for 1-1. Pantomime villain Arnautovic wants the evening to be about him - he heads home a goal on the hour, disallowed for offside - but Stoke don't need him around for it to feel like a 0-5 defeat. Heartbreaking.

21/04/2018 Stoke (1) 1 Burnley (0) 1 – This was seen as an end-of-season winnable game a few months ago. Now, it's a must-win game against a Top-7 Europa League Qualifier, which is what Stoke aspired to under Mark Hughes...what went wrong?! Well, after some appalling early-season signings - Wimmer has disappeared and Jesé has been removed from Stoke's books - Stoke are propping things up with perky new signings like Badou Ndiaye and Moritz Bauer. Ndiaye (a master passer) scores from the edge of the box in the 11th minute as if passing into the corner of the goal (it actually takes a slight deflection, but let's gloss over that). Bauer, meanwhile, has been turfed out of right back by adequate Glen Johnson so Moritz can play "out-of-position" at left wing. He used to play on the wing in his youth, claims Lambert, but this does not pacify fans still smarting from Bauer being dropped for the Everton game. But the defining moment of the game is just before the break when perky new-signing Bauer tears down the right, crosses gloriously for Diouf alone in front of goal...only for Mame to mis-kick the ball completely. Diouf's miserable season is now complete. It just can't get any worse for him. Of course, Barnes blunders in an equaliser on the hour, and of course Lambert brings on Ireland for Bauer (and Campbell for Diouf). But with 3 games left, and 2 or 3 wins needed, Ndiaye and Bauer must be wondering what they're doing here. The idea is to enjoy them while they are.

The Three Amigos wash up at Southampton, & seem very pleased with themselves

28/04/2018 Liverpool 0 Stoke 0 – Yes, this really did happen. This game had been written off by Stoke fans since August, so to walk away with a point and a clean sheet in front of the cameras is astonishing. It shouldn't be so much of a surprise really as Lambert's record at Anfield is an incredible Played 5, Won 3 Drawn 2! It has to be said that most of Stoke's recent games have been live on TV, as voyeurs tune in to see a side clearly going down & getting pulverised. Instead the voyeurs witness a side "going down fighting" (The Oatcake), with "spirit, discipline, organisation, will-to-succeed, and pride" (The Sentinel), although maybe that's going a bit far. The fact that they manage to quell goal-scoring machine Mo Salah is the most astonishing, with Ryan, Erik & Bruno standing firm in the centre and Kurt Zouma having his turn at right-back (Bauer has wandered off down the wing somewhere). But a draw at Anfield, however good that is, is never going to be enough (except for Lambert, for whom it's now 3 wins and 3 draws at Anfield). However, the big question is: When will Stoke next play in front of 50,000+? However long that is, Shaqiri can't wait, and has a good look round Anfield before he goes. Well, he does think he's Ronaldinho.

05/05/2018 Stoke (1) 1 Crystal Palace (0) 2

– 10 years & a day since promotion on May 4th 2008, Stoke are finally relegated. Paul Lambert can drag it out no longer, with an unlikely string of 7 draws & only ONE win in 14 games. Any Stoke fan could have predicted this game – Stoke take the lead with a Shaqiri free kick then Palace catch them out with 2 breakaway goals – so why the players look so shell-shocked at the end is anyone's guess. They didn't really think that after 1 win in 17 that they were going to beat Roy's on-form Palace? Butland and Shawcross are in tears, but Shaq just stands there in the centre-circle like a statue busking for coins from passers-by. It's a defiant performance by Stoke, & Shaq's goal on half-time is a peach, so many supporters stay behind to show their appreciation. But they are left scratching their heads as to how Palace score "breakaway" goals. If ever there was a game in the last 10 years where it's necessary to park-the-bus, then this is it. Obviously, the bus-station's been closed down by CEO Tony Scholes. Well, more fool him. There's little point mentioning the chances Diouf misses, or the unlucky interception/pass-back by Ryan that leads to the winner. What is worth a mention is that the much-maligned Chris Kamara was in charge 20 years ago the last time Stoke were relegated, and he also only won 1 in 14 games, and was therefore sacked. The difference here is that people are suggesting Lambert stays on with the same record. At least Kamara had the forethought to sign a striker...although it was Kyle Lightbourne.

It was always going to end in tears

13/05/2018 Swansea (1) 1 Stoke (2) 2

– Somehow Mark Hughes has effectively rescued Southampton from relegation after only being in charge for 7 games, tricky games at that. He even condemns Swansea by beating them 1-0 at The Liberty earlier in the week. Stoke fans are now livid. So, they've worked out that if Stoke lose by several goals (& Saints lose at Citeh) then Sparky goes down with Stoke (as he would have done if he'd stayed). Now, that would have been bizarre. Lambert is urged to recall Haugaard, Wimmer, Tymon, Johnson, Edwards, Afellay, Charlie, Jesé, Saido, Campbell, Diouf, & Choupo-Moting. What a game that would have been! In fact, Diouf actually does play, putting in a decent shift, but Choupo-Moting is too busy taking selfies (much to visiting pundit Liam Lawrence's annoyance). Instead, Lambert starts rookie Lasse Sorensen in midfield, & he's actually quite good. However, for the first half-hour the Stoke team are truly awful, and the Sky reporter threatens to go home & leave them to it. Swansea even take the lead on the quarter-hour, and there are clear indications that this could indeed turn into an avalanche. To help out, Stoke fans launch into songs about heroic older players. Suddenly, on 31 minutes, Shaqiri plays in Ndiaye who, thinking he's the real Saido Berahino, lobs the keeper for 1-1. 10 minutes later, Sorensen, who thinks he's the real Ibrahim Afellay, puts a perfect free kick in from the left, and Crouch heads home for 2-1. But no one in the world (betting firms included) believe Stoke can hang on to this lead, and so when Shaq takes a penalty just before the hour, everyone knows it's not going in. ("Weak", "unconvincing", & "tepid" are just 3 adjectives Martin Spinks' pen spits out, & even then he's just being kind.) Fans are perplexed by Shaq high-fiving the keeper after he's saved it, but are equally amazed that Stoke have scored at all; up until this game Stoke haven't scored a single goal this season wearing their blue away strip (with its "My-printer-has-run-out-of-red-ink" design). Astonishingly, Stoke hang on, and 2000 away fans celebrate in the sun. "I would have paid to watch them sing Delilah at the end," exclaims Paul Lambert. But as Bob Dylan once wrote, "It's all over now, Baby Blue". Stoke finish 19th, above West Bromwich Albion, and wave goodbye to the Premier League that has been their home for 10 great years. Five days later Stoke split with Paul Lambert, and prepare for a season with 48+ games under ex-Derby boss Gary Rowett. Here's to the next 10 years!

	Team	P	Wh	Dh	Lh	GFh	GAh	Wa	Da	La	GFa	GAa	W	D	L	GF	GA	GD	Pts
1	Manchester City	38	16	2	1	61	14	16	2	1	45	13	32	4	2	106	27	+79	**100**
2	Manchester Utd	38	15	2	2	38	9	10	4	5	30	19	25	6	7	68	28	+40	**81**
3	Tottenham	38	13	4	2	40	16	10	4	5	34	20	23	8	7	74	36	+38	**77**
4	Liverpool	38	12	7	0	45	10	9	5	5	39	28	21	12	5	84	38	+46	**75**
5	Chelsea	38	11	4	4	30	16	10	3	6	32	22	21	7	10	62	38	+24	**70**
6	Arsenal	38	15	2	2	54	20	4	4	11	20	31	19	6	13	74	51	+23	**63**
7	Burnley	38	7	5	7	16	17	7	7	5	20	22	14	12	12	36	39	-3	**54**
8	Everton	38	10	4	5	28	22	3	6	10	16	36	13	10	15	44	58	-14	**49**
9	Leicester City	38	7	6	6	25	22	5	5	9	31	38	12	11	15	56	60	-4	**47**
10	Newcastle Utd	38	8	4	7	21	17	4	4	11	18	30	12	8	18	39	47	-8	**44**
11	Crystal Palace	38	7	5	7	29	27	4	6	9	16	28	11	11	16	45	55	-10	**44**
12	Bournemouth	38	7	5	7	26	30	4	6	9	19	31	11	11	16	45	61	-16	**44**
13	West Ham Utd	38	7	6	6	24	26	3	6	10	24	42	10	12	16	48	68	-20	**42**
14	Watford	38	7	6	6	27	31	4	2	13	17	33	11	8	19	44	64	-20	**41**
15	Brighton & Hove	38	7	8	4	24	25	2	5	12	10	29	9	13	16	34	54	-20	**40**
16	Huddersfield	38	6	5	8	16	25	3	5	11	12	33	9	10	19	28	58	-30	**37**
17	Southampton	38	4	7	8	20	26	3	8	8	17	30	7	15	16	37	56	-19	**36**
18	Swansea City	38	6	3	10	17	24	2	6	11	11	32	8	9	21	28	56	-28	**33**
19	Stoke City	38	5	5	9	20	30	2	7	10	15	38	7	12	19	35	68	-33	**33**
20	West Bromwich	38	3	9	7	21	29	3	4	12	10	27	6	13	19	31	56	-25	**31**

Club	2008/09 H/A	2009/10 H/A	2010/11 H/A	2011/12 H/A	2012/13 H/A
Arsenal	W 2-1, L 1-4	L 1-3, L 0-2	W 3-1, L 0-1	D 1-1, L 1-3	D 0-0, L 0-1
Aston Villa	W 3-2, D 2-2	D 0-0, L 0-1	W 2-1, D 1-1	D 0-0, D 1-1	L 1-3, D 0-0
Bournemouth					
Birmingham		L 0-1, D 0-0	W 3-2, L 0-1		
Blackburn	W 1-0, L 0-3	W 3-0, D 0-0	W 1-0, W 2-0	W 3-1, W 2-1	
Blackpool			L 0-1, D 0-0		
Bolton W	W 2-0, L 1-3	L 1-2, D 1-1	W 2-0, L 1-2	D 2-2, L 0-5	
Brighton					
Burnley		W 2-0, D 1-1			
Cardiff					
Chelsea	L 0-2, L 1-2	L 1-2, L 0-7	D 1-1, L 0-2	D 0-0, L 0-1	L 0-4, L 0-1
Crystal Pal					
Everton	L 2-3, L 1-3	D 0-0, D 1-1	W 2-0, L 0-1	D 1-1, W 1-0	D 1-1, L 0-1
Fulham	D 0-0, L 0-1	W 3-2, W 1-0	L 0-2, L 0-2	W 2-0, L 1-2	W 1-0, L 0-1
Huddersfield					
Hull City	D 1-1, W 2-1	W 2-0, L 1-2			
Leicester					
Liverpool	D 0-0, D 0-0	D 1-1, L 0-4	W 2-0, L 0-2	W 1-0, D 0-0	W 3-1, D 0-0
Man City	W 1-0, L 0-3	D 1-1, L 0-2	D 1-1, L 0-3	D 1-1, L 0-3	D 1-1, L 0-3
Man Utd	L 0-1, L 0-5	L 0-2, L 0-4	L 1-2, L 1-2	D 1-1, L 0-2	L 0-2, L 2-4
Middlesboro	W 1-0, L 1-2				
Newcastle	D 1-1, D 2-2		W 4-0, W 2-1	L 1-3, L 0-3	W 2-1, L 1-2
Norwich				W 1-0, D 1-1	W 1-0, L 0-1
Portsmouth	D 2-2, L 1-2	W 1-0, W 2-1			
QPR				L 2-3, L 0-1	W 1-0, W 2-
Reading					W 2-1, D 1-1
Southampton					D 3-3, D 1-1
Sunderland	W 1-0, L 0-2	W 1-0, D 0-0	W 3-2, L 0-2	L 0-1, L 0-4	D 0-0, D 1-1
Swansea				W 2-0, L 0-2	W 2-0, L 1-3
Tottenham	W 2-1, L 1-3	L 1-2, W 1-0	L 1-2, L 2-3	W 2-1, D 1-1	L 1-2, D 0-0
Watford					
WBA	W 1-0, W 2-0		D 1-1, W 3-0	L 1-2, W 1-0	D 0-0, W 1-0
West Ham	L 0-1, L 1-2	W 2-1, W 1-0	D 1-1, L 0-3		L 0-1, D 1-1
Wigan	W 2-0, D 0-0	D 2-2, D 1-1	L 0-1, D 2-2	D 2-2, L 0-2	D 2-2, D 2-2
Wolves		D 2-2, D 0-0	W 3-0, L 1-2	W 2-1, W 2-1	

2013/14 H/A	2014/15 H/A	2015/16 H/A	2016/17 H/A	2017/18 H/A	W	D	L
W 1-0, L 1-3	W 3-2, L 0-3	D 0-0, L 0-2	L 1-4, L 1-3	W 1-0, L 0-3	5	3	12
W 2-1, W 4-1	L 0-1, W 2-1	W 2-1, W 1-0			7	6	3
		W 2-1, W 3-1	L 0-1, D 2-2	L 1-2, L 1-2	2	1	3
					1	1	2
					6	1	1
						1	1
					2	2	4
				D 1-1, D 2-2		2	
	L 1-2, D 0-0		W 2-0, L 0-1	D 1-1, L 0-1	2	3	3
D 0-0, D 1-1						2	
W 3-2, L 0-3	L 0-2, L 1-2	W 1-0, D 1-1	L 1-2, L 2-4	L 0-4, L 0-5	2	3	15
W 2-1, L 0-1	L 1-2, D 1-1	L 1-2, L 1-2	W 1-0, L 1-4	L 1-2, L 1-2	2	1	7
D 1-1, L 0-4	W 2-0, W 1-0	L 0-3, W 4-3	D 1-1, L 0-1	L 1-2, L 0-1	5	6	9
W 4-1, L 0-1					5	1	6
				W 2-0, D 1-1	1	1	
W 1-0, D 0-0	W 1-0, D 1-1		W 3-1, W 2-0		6	3	1
	L 0-1, W 1-0	D 2-2, L 0-3	D 2-2, L 0-2	D 2-2, D 1-1	1	4	3
L 3-5, L 0-1	W 6-1, L 0-1	L 0-1, L 1-4	L 1-2, L 1-4	L 0-3, D 0-0	4	6	10
D 0-0, L 0-1	L 1-4, W 1-0	W 2-0, L 0-4	L 1-4, D 0-0	L 0-2, L 2-7	3	6	11
W 2-1, L 2-3	D 1-1, L 1-2	W 2-0, L 0-3	D 1-1, D 1-1	D 2-2, L 0-3	2	5	13
			W 2-0, D 1-1		2	1	1
W 1-0, L 1-5	W 1-0, D 1-1	W 1-0, D 0-0		L 0-1, L 1-2	6	4	6
L 0-1, D 1-1		W 3-1, D 1-1			3	3	2
					2	1	1
	W 3-1, D 2-2				3	1	2
					1	1	
D 1-1, D 2-2	W 2-1, L 0-1	L 1-2, W 1-0	D 0-0, W 1-0	W 2-1, D 0-0	4	6	2
W 2-0, L 0-1	D 1-1, L 1-3	D 1-1, L 0-2	W 2-0, W 3-1		6	5	7
D 1-1, D 3-3	W 2-1, L 0-2	D 2-2, W 1-0	W 3-1, L 0-2	W 2-1, W 2-1	7	3	4
L 0-1, L 0-3	W 3-0, W 2-1	L 0-4, D 2-2	L 0-4, L 0-4	L 1-2, L 1-5	5	3	12
		L 0-2, W 2-1	W 2-0, W 1-0	D 0-0, W 1-0	4	1	1
D 0-0, W 2-1	W 2-0, L 0-1	L 0-1, L 1-2	D 1-1, L 0-1	W 3-1, D 1-1	8	5	5
W 3-1, W 1-0	D 2-2, D 1-1	W 2-1, D 0-0	D 0-0, D 1-1	L 0-3, D 1-1	5	8	5
					1	7	2
					3	2	1

INDEX